The Frontiers of Europe: A Transatlantic Problem?

Brookings-SSPA Series on Public Administration

Published in conjunction with the Scuola Superiore della Pubblica Amministrazione, Rome, this series is devoted to the study of international issues of public administration and public management.

Federiga Bindi, *Italy and the European Union* (2011)

Federiga Bindi and Irina Angelescu, editors, *The Frontiers of Europe: A Transatlantic Problem?* (2011)

The Frontiers of Europe: A Transatlantic Problem?

FEDERIGA BINDI
IRINA ANGELESCU
Editors

SCUOLA SUPERIORE DELLA PUBBLICA AMMINISTRAZIONE (SSPA)
Rome

BROOKINGS INSTITUTION PRESS
Washington, D.C.

ABOUT BROOKINGS

The Brookings Institution is a private nonprofit organization devoted to research, education, and publication on important issues of domestic and foreign policy. Its principal purpose is to bring the highest quality independent research and analysis to bear on current and emerging policy problems. Interpretations or conclusions in Brookings publications should be understood to be solely those of the authors.

Library of Congress Cataloging-in-Publication data
The Frontiers of Europe : a transatlantic problem? / Federiga Bindi and Irina Angelescu, editors.
p. cm. — (Brookings-SSPA series on public administration)
Includes bibliographical references and index.
Summary: "Investigates the ramifications of enlarging the size of the European Union, including the effects on policies relating to energy, immigration, security, democracy and the rule of law, and economic development, and how a larger EU would affect NATO and relations with China, Latin America, Russia, and the United States"—Provided by publisher.
ISBN 978-0-8157-0545-1 (pbk. : alk. paper)
1. European Union—Membership. 2. European Union countries—Politics and government—21st century. 3. European Union countries—Foreign relations—21st century. I. Bindi, Federiga M. II. Angelescu, Irina.
JN30.F78 2011
341.242'2—dc23 2011023062

9 8 7 6 5 4 3 2 1

Printed on acid-free paper

Typeset in Minion

Composition by R. Lynn Rivenbark
Macon, Georgia

Printed by R. R. Donnelley
Harrisonburg, Virginia

Contents

PART TWO
Immigration, Terrorism, Internal Security: Related or Unrelated Phenomena?

PART THREE
Energy Policies: Between Environmental and Power Politics

PART FOUR
The New Frontiers of Economic Development for Europe

FRANCO FRATTINI

Foreword

The enlargement strategy and the frontiers of Europe are essential to the future of Europe. Over the years, the debate on the frontiers of Europe has gone hand in hand with the development of the European Union (EU) integration process. Enlargement remains an open issue that deeply affects the external role of the EU and its relations with other key international stakeholders, in particular the United States and Russia. In this context, I argue that the idea of geographic limits based on conventional criteria is not a suitable guide for the enlargement process. Instead, the EU should continue to offer the prospect of membership for those countries that share our principles of democracy, freedom, and the rule of law and are ready to assume the rights and obligations of membership, in accordance with the European treaties and the Copenhagen criteria.

It must be underscored that European integration was conceived to eliminate frontiers in all forms, ranging from physical, economic, and cultural frontiers to internal and external political ones. The European project thrived by focusing its energies on the realization of a common market, which in turn led to the creation of the Schengen area. In so doing, the European integration process was able to (re)unite the "old continent" in the name of liberal democracy and democratic values, which form the basis of our cultural identity and of the transatlantic relationship. Today the European Union is called upon to eliminate new frontiers, either by pursuing a true economic union by better coordinating the fiscal policies of its member states or by organizing a cohesive and effective external action policy and taking the first steps toward a common European defense framework.

Despite errors in the timing and manner of its gestation, enlargement to include the Central and Eastern European countries (CEECs) has proven to be a success. Enlargement was essentially a great stabilization operation conducted by using the European Union's civil "soft power" to best effect. The transforming power of the European model—with its political, economic, and value-oriented components—proved worthy of imitation. Brussels acted as a "magnet" by attracting its external neighbors and then transforming and integrating them. As a result, the enlargement of the European Union has brought peace, stability, security, and economic prosperity. This result is something we must never forget.

But is the Union's enlargement strategy still relevant today? Is it still in Europe's interest to take the enlargement project forward? Have the economic crisis and the speculative attack on the euro made the enlargement policy more uncertain or more necessary? In the medium and long term, what are the risks inherent to enlargement fatigue?

There is no doubt that some EU member states are increasingly skeptical of more enlargement. Italy's position on this matter, however, is very clear. It believes that it is in the European Union's interest to efficiently and rapidly complete the work it has begun, particularly in the Western Balkans and Turkey, as well as in Iceland. Reykjavik's decision to apply for EU membership demonstrates once again the power of attraction of the European project, and I will next put forward some considerations concerning the Western Balkans and Turkey.

Enlargement to the Balkans: The Political Vision of Thessalonica as a Political and Moral Duty

First, we need to ensure constant progress for future European accession for all the Western Balkan countries because of the strategic relevance of this area not just for the EU but also for the United States. In recent years, the prospect of full Euro-Atlantic integration has deeply changed this region, offering a political solution to eradicate the historical roots of instability and to bring peace, democracy, and economic development. However, despite all the progress achieved, this is no time for complacency.

This region continues to face political challenges related to the completion of its democratic transition. At the same time, outstanding bilateral issues continue to hamper regional cooperation. Moreover, the economic crisis that began in 2008 has deeply affected the economies of the Western Balkans, especially with regard to employment and social conditions. These effects may jeopardize the efforts already undertaken to consolidate stability and increase prosperity. Against this background, the EU accession process is the only way to ensure a sound recovery and prevent the risk of new social and economic strains at the EU's external borders, with negative repercussions for the Union's economy and society.

Fully aware of this, the Spanish EU presidency agreed to implement an Italian proposal and organized a high-level meeting in Sarajevo on June 2, 2010. This conference played a key role in renewing the EU's commitment to the Western Balkans and their membership prospects. It also further strengthened EU cooperation with the United States, which plays a strategic role in promoting the political and economic stabilization in the area, together with Russia and Turkey. However, it is now essential to envisage a concrete follow-up to that meeting. A more ambitious and proactive approach by the EU is required to keep the Western Balkan countries anchored to Europe, thus consolidating democracy and fostering the reconciliation process in the region.

At a time when international dynamics have led to the adoption of new strategic approaches in Asia, Africa, and the Persian Gulf, the enlargement process to the Western Balkans must remain a priority on the EU agenda in the years to come because of the region's strategic importance to European security and stability. It should be clear that the Union's ability to assume its full share of responsibility as a global player will be measured primarily by the success of its strategy toward that neighborhood. Our mission cannot be considered accomplished until all the Western Balkan countries have joined the European family, a family to which they naturally belong.

Alternatively, the EU member states must be ready to pay the costs of nonenlargement. What is at stake is the risk of undermining the credibility of the EU enlargement strategy as a whole, which would include losing political leverage over all the countries involved. Nonaccession of the Balkan countries risks jeopardizing their adoption of important reforms toward democratization and modernization. The lack of a concrete European perspective would, moreover, create a real danger of alienating local public opinion and of strengthening radical and nationalistic movements. It could also discourage a flexible and constructive approach to outstanding bilateral disputes and thus undermine any concrete possibility of overcoming the problems of the past once and for all.

In this light, the next steps to be taken are clear. We need to move forward on visa liberalization—a process that I launched in 2008 as vice president of the European Commission—for all the Balkan countries. Before the end of 2011 this measure must also encompass the citizens of Bosnia and Albania. Croatia is expected to join the EU in 2012. Accession talks with Macedonia should begin as soon as the dispute about its name finds a commonly agreed solution. Negotiations should also begin with Montenegro, which was granted candidate country status in December 2010. This status should also be granted to Serbia and Albania. And all of this needs to be done without leaving Bosnia or Kosovo behind.

Is Europe Losing Turkey? Ankara's EU Membership as a Strategic Objective

Some believe that Turkey is moving away from Europe. If so, does Europe have any responsibility for this change? The current framework of Turkey's EU accession process is not encouraging. The talks are at a standstill, mainly because of the lack of progress in the difficult normalization of Turkey's relations with Cyprus. At the same time, recent examples from Ankara's foreign policy decisions, ranging from the crisis in its relations with Israel and its rapprochement with Iran, are cause for significant doubts and questions.

Recent events notwithstanding, it is essential to re-launch the accession negotiations with Ankara in order to ensure Turkey's full integration in the EU. Turkey has committed itself to the EU integration process and has achieved remarkable progress in recent years, progress that has been encouraged by the European perspective. Any obstacles placed on Ankara's path toward Europe would compromise Turkey's adoption of important reforms and impact its democratization and modernization processes. They would also create a real danger of alienating Turkish society from the West and of strengthening radical and xenophobic movements, with negative repercussions not only for European security but for the international community as well.

The EU must not give Turkey any reasons or excuses to turn its back on Europe. The EU should maintain its commitments to Turkey's government and society and continue its talks with Ankara in good faith, according to the negotiating framework. Even in complicated times, the European Union must have the courage to grasp the challenge to its identity posed by Turkey's accession. We must be aware that Turkey's entry into the EU could have the same symbolic force for relations between the West and Islam as the French-German reconciliation or the fall of the Berlin Wall. Ankara's entry into the EU could be read as a sign of the compatibility between Islam, democracy, and human rights, and of the Union's ability to welcome different cultures without losing its own identity. Europe must not turn its back on this historic objective. The EU shares crucial strategic interests with Ankara, such as the stability of the southern Caucasus, the security of energy supplies, and the fight against terrorism.

There is no doubt that Turkey still has a long way to go before accession. It is equally clear that it will reach its destination only if it manages to respect the commitments and obligations it has signed up for. While the journey is difficult, its final destination cannot be opened up once again to question. Italy will do everything in its power not to "lose" Turkey, but rather to keep its "European outlook" open and avoid questioning Turkey's fundamental ability to proceed to full integration. Future EU membership for Turkey would be the culmination of a long modernization process for the country and would have a decisive impact on the prospects for stability in the entire Eastern Mediterranean and Black Sea region.

The entry into force of the Lisbon Treaty has made the European Union uniquely suited to take on its leadership responsibility. It strengthened the EU's role as a global actor able to seize the opportunities and face the challenges of the present international scenario with its fast changing developments that require a timely and unified response (for example, the recent revolts in the Arab world). The enlargement process is one such opportunity, one that Europeans cannot afford to miss if they want to make the EU a leading actor on the global stage. The European integration of the Western Balkans and Turkey would extend the EU's geopolitical weight, thus expanding its influence more directly to the east (the Caucasus and Central Asia) and to the south (the Mediterranean area). There will inevitably be challenges ahead, but we now have the means to tackle them—and win. An enlarged and stronger European Union will also be of key importance in giving new content to the transatlantic relationship.

Indeed, as I have written, with Carl Bildt, William Hague, and Alexander Stubb, the EU's enlargement process and its transformation from a (mainly) Western organization into a "truly pan-European Union" has been one of its greatest successes.[1] It is a mutually beneficial process for both the EU member states and the acceding countries, and one that should not be precluded from continuing.

Note

1. C. Bildt, F. Frattini, W. Hague, and A. Stubb, "Europe, Look Outward Again," *International Herald Tribune*, December 10, 2010.

Acknowledgments

We would like to extend a few words of gratitude to the people and institutions that made this publication possible.

This book is the result of three years of work in and around the Brookings Institution. It originated with a project led by a former director of foreign policy, Carlos Pasqual, together with then director of the Center on the United States and Europe Dan Benjamin: to both we extend our gratitude for pointing us in such an interesting direction! Other people at Brookings also provided valuable advice and support, including Jeremy Shapiro, Andy Moffat, and Fiona Hill. We must also mention the Brookings Institution Press—notably, Robert Faherty, Janet Walker, and Janet Mowery—whose excellent professional support once again guided us through the editorial process.

Outside Brookings, we thank the European Centre of Excellence at the University of Rome Tor Vergata—in particular Marco Amici and Valeria Contu—and the Italian National School of Public Administration and its president, Giovanni Tria, as well as Elena Cantiani for her administrative support. We acknowledge the generous support of the European Commission, namely Jean Monnet Action, not only for cofinancing the project, but also—in the person of Luciano di Fonzo—for giving us indispensable advice on how to better structure the research project. In addition, thanks go to the Italian Ministry of Foreign Affairs, and especially Minister Franco Frattini, for hosting the final conference in Rome in July 2010 and for taking the time to actively participate.

Last but not least, we express our appreciation to our families. To our parents—Donatella, Tatiana, and Luigi—for always believing in us and supporting us as we followed the sometimes tricky academic path. To our husbands—Giulio and Brian—and Federiga's son, Giorgio—for supporting us in our work and especially during the gestation of this book, even when this meant taking time away from them: we love you all the more (and now expect you to read it!).

FEDERIGA BINDI AND IRINA ANGELESCU

1

Introduction: Defining the Frontiers of Europe from a Transatlantic Perspective

The 2004–07 "Big Bang" enlargement of the European Union to include ten Central and Eastern European Countries (CEECs) as well as Cyprus and Malta was accompanied by a feeling of relief in Brussels. This moment marked the consolidation of the "new" frontiers of Europe, a continent no longer divided by the Iron Curtain of the cold war period. However, the post-enlargement euphoria was short lived. In hindsight, the enlargement of the European Union (EU) to the east did not so much settle the issue of Europe's frontiers as open a Pandora's box of questions about where the final borders of Europe will be set and what the EU's relations with its neighborhood should be.

As much as the EU would have preferred to enjoy its success and focus on its internal problems, its new neighbors to the south and east demanded that the process of enlargement be opened all over again. They are now "knocking at the EU gates" and asking to be let in as members. Consequently, after the adoption of the Lisbon Treaty and the issues raised by the economic crisis that began in 2008, the next hot topic on the EU agenda is the future of enlargement and relations with the neighborhood. The question of Europe's frontiers remains unanswered—and of great relevance to its neighborhood and to transatlantic relations.

The importance of future enlargements should not be underestimated. As the EU is trying to gain visibility and have a greater impact on the world stage, it cannot overlook the fact that until now enlargement has been its most successful form of foreign policy. The history of the European Communities (EC, now the EU) shows that waves of enlargement are usually followed by further integration and concentration of powers at the EU level. In other words, enlargement has a significant impact on EU domestic politics.

Defining the EU's frontiers is, however, not solely a domestic issue. Given the countries that could be involved in the next enlargements (Turkey, the Balkan states, and, in the long term, possibly countries in the Caucasus and even Russia), the EU's frontiers are a geopolitical decision with high stakes that will influence contemporary international relations: from transatlantic relations to U.S.-Russian relations. Europe's future borders are therefore likely to profoundly affect its bilateral and multilateral relations in the world. Since both the United States and Russia have strong preferences for how the enlarged EU should look, a new "battle over Europe" is likely to take place. This battle is clearly not only about geographic borders, but also—and mostly—about other issues and policies, ranging from energy security to the economy, development, and immigration.

The present volume aims to escape the usual EU-centric debates over enlargement and instead look at the issue of the future frontiers of Europe from a multidisciplinary and multi-faceted perspective. The chapters represent some of the most representative global voices in the academic and policymaking communities. The underlying idea of the book is that relations between the EU and its neighboring countries and debates about possible future enlargements of the EU should not center on "enlargement fatigue." Instead, the collected essays argue that any future enlargements of the EU are going to have greater geopolitical consequences than "domestic" ones. The contributors to this volume take into account the different interests of the United States and Russia, with a special eye on the future of transatlantic relations, as well as the effect on relations with other increasingly important international actors such as China and Latin America.

These ideas were discussed at an international conference that took place in Rome in July 2010, the second event in a series dedicated to the "Frontiers of Europe." The conference was organized by the Jean Monnet Centre of Excellence at the University of Rome Tor Vergata. It was co-financed by the EU Commission and supported by the Italian Foreign Ministry and the Italian National School of Public Administration (SSPA). The conference and present publication were made possible through the generous support of the European Commission.

Structure of the Book

The volume is divided into six parts, each addressing a set of issues that are of vital importance for the future of transatlantic relations and the EU's role in the world.

The book's foreword is by Franco Frattini, the foreign minister of Italy and a former EU commissioner for justice and home affairs. He argues that the frontiers of Europe are as much a matter of values and principles as they are a matter of geographic definition. Frattini takes a strong stance in favor of future enlargements and suggests that failure to enlarge further and successfully would undermine the EU's credibility on the world stage. He warns that without the inclusion of the Western Balkan states the EU "would not be complete," and he compares the symbolic importance of Turkey's possible EU membership to that of the fall of the Berlin Wall.

The chapter by Federiga Bindi offers an overview of the current state of accession negotiations and provides a historical perspective on all the waves of enlargement in the European Communities/ European Union history. She analyzes the EU history of enlargement from both the EU and the U.S. perspective and argues that until now the EC/EU enlargements—as well as the creation of the EC itself—have benefited from the strong support of the United States. The United States in fact saw European integration as a matter of national interest inasmuch as it ensured stability in Europe and in the transatlantic alliance. Bindi describes how the enlargement of the EC/EU evolved naturally as part of the European integration process. She warns that it is unclear whether the United States will remain supportive of future EU enlargements, an issue that is also addressed in other contributions to this volume.

Beginning part one, the chapter by Ferdinando Nelli Feroci discusses the current state of the accession negotiations. He reminds us that, at this writing in mid-2011, there are five official candidate countries (Croatia, Iceland, Macedonia, Montenegro, and Turkey) and many other aspirants to membership. In Nelli Feroci's view, the successful 2004–07 wave of enlargement will be remembered in history as "the reunification of Europe." He observes that although the EU is officially committed to enlargement, there is actually little enthusiasm among most member states and a general sense of enlargement fatigue. Nelli Feroci argues that such a frame of mind is counterproductive and could jeopardize the future of the European integration project.

The chapter by John Peet takes a broader view of the meaning of EU enlargement and of Europe's frontiers. His starting point is an attempt to best determine where the EU's frontiers end. He concludes by arguing that because the EU is defined in both geographic and political terms, it is to the EU's advantage to leave the question of its frontiers undefined. Peet emphasizes that any EU enlargement benefits not only the acceding countries but also the existing member states and the EU itself, given that most waves of enlargement were followed by further integration. Like Frattini and Nelli Feroci, Peet believes that in the medium term the EU should enlarge to include the countries of the Western Balkans and Turkey.

The contribution of Christoffer Kølvraa and Ian Ifversen focuses on the EU's relations with its neighborhood through the specific instrument of the European Neighborhood Policy (ENP), which was inaugurated in 2003. They look at the ENP in order to determine the underlying frame of mind that drives the EU's relations with its neighbors. On the one hand, Kølvraa and Ifversen suggest that the ENP can be seen as guided by geopolitical considerations focused on interests and geographic alignments. On the other hand, they argue that a civilizational discourse based on a transfer of values and principles best characterizes the EU's interactions with its neighboring states. They suggest that this latter approach should be chosen according to the preferences of the surrounding countries themselves.

Irina Angelescu's chapter opens the second part of the volume, which deals with the issues of immigration, security, and terrorism in the EU. She begins by offering a historical overview of how competencies in the field of immigration and asylum were granted by the member states to the EU. Angelescu argues that especially in the aftermath of the 2001, 2004, and 2005 terrorist attacks in the United States and Europe, there was a shift of paradigms in EU migration policies from human rights and development to security. Finally, she describes how the 2004–07 enlargement and the conditions imposed by the EU on the new member states in the field of immigration have strained these countries' relations with their neighbors and affected their labor markets. This dynamic is likely to characterize any future enlargements.

Gilles de Kerchove addresses three issues in his chapter: the nature of terrorism in Europe, the counterterrorism challenges that the EU has to respond to, and the changes and opportunities brought by the Treaty of Lisbon in this field. He observes that although the terrorist threat of organizations such as al Qaeda are still present, a recent dangerous phenomenon is that of the homegrown terrorist or "lone wolf" who operates in isolation from any terrorist organization. De Kerchove observes that there are some connections between diasporas and terrorism in Europe, but he warns against linking the two. Indeed, he argues that the fight against discrimination and social marginalization of migrants is a relevant and important counterterrorism tool, and further, that focusing on the community of migrants as the only potential source of terrorism is counterproductive and limiting.

The remaining chapters in this part are country-specific and elaborate on two specific issues associated with immigration: criminality and terrorism.

Umberto Melotti looks at the link between immigration and crime in Italy. According to him, the phenomenon is especially strong in this country because of shortcomings in law enforcement, inefficiencies of the judicial system, and lack of political will to deal with immigration. He argues against the culture of "denialism" that prevents politicians from taking necessary measures to address the immigration challenge. The attempts by Italy to address migration are similar to those by other European countries: a mix of border controls with crime and terrorism prevention and social measures aimed at integrating existing migrants. Melotti's concerns have been validated by the current crisis in the Arab world. The lack of European solidarity in dealing with the immigrants arriving on the southern Italian shores can be partially explained by Europe's fear that there is a link between diasporas and nonstate violence. The issue is complex and often extremely sensitive. Worst-case scenarios are made possible when prepositioned operational cells live within societies clandestinely. After analyzing the case of the Turkish diaspora in Germany, Jean-Luc Marret concludes that it is hard to see radical Turkish networks as a main source of threat. He suggests that Turkish organizations are currently operating in diasporas in the EU and that future enlargements could multiply opportunities for terrorist attacks. His contribution therefore raises the question of whether an enlarged EU would help better deal with terrorism—or, on the contrary, increase the risk of terrorist attacks.

The third part of the volume is devoted to the implications of possible future enlargements for the EU's energy security. The chapter by Alessandro Ortis outlines the energy issues of major concern in the global and European arenas, including those related to energy supplies and climate change. Ortis argues that the experience of 2007–09 shows that energy price security can only be attained by improving regulation and monitoring financial and energy markets. In the case of the EU, he argues for more investments in research and for efforts to improve EU-Russian relations. According to Ortis, the EU is carrying out a lonely battle against climate change. This situation is complicated by the fact that energy policies were not an original EC/EU competency and that the internal energy market is a very new project. Convergence toward a single European market was challenged by the 2004–07 enlargement and is likely to be further complicated by future accessions.

The contribution of Massimo Gaiani challenges the consensus that the 2004–07 enlargement has made the EU stronger and more dynamic. He argues that the EU's energy balance did not improve as a result of the enlargement because none of the new members is a major energy producer. At the same time, the EU affects the energy landscape of candidate and member states by imposing two requirements: shut down nuclear plants that do not meet international security standards and liberalize the domestic energy markets. In this sense, the EU had a positive impact by preventing a possible disaster like the one at Japan's Fukushima nuclear plant after the tsunami in March 2011. Furthermore, EU competencies in the field of climate change give it extra leverage in dealing with energy issues with these countries. Gaiani suggests that the Treaty of Lisbon gives the EU the task to ensure the proper functionality of the energy market, but also the security of the energy supply, the promotion of energy efficiency, and the development of renewable forms of energy and interconnected energy networks.

Luca Einaudi's chapter, in the fourth part of the book, is dedicated to the economic development of Europe. His contribution analyzes the origins of the euro, explains the underlying mechanisms of the euro crisis, and discusses the challenges of new economic governance. Einaudi argues that commentators not familiar with EU history too often do not see that the euro is a major political project, part of a long-term strategy to adapt Europe to globalization. Because of this fact, he says, the costs of dissolving the euro are too great to even be considered by EU member states. In the remainder of the chapter he addresses the way euro rules were conceived and how they failed and illustrates how these rules have been reinvented.

The contribution by Giovanni Andornino discusses the EU's relations with one of the most dynamic economies of the world, China. He argues that relations between these two actors are affected by their different approaches to foreign policy: Chinese politics is more pragmatic, while the EU is postmodern, preferring to link human rights issues to trade relations. This link has strained relations between the two actors, with China insisting on mutual respect for each other's sovereignty and territorial integrity. Andornino warns that the EU enlargement and its dynamics will lead to further complications in the EU-China dialogue. Despite its success in stabilizing the European neighborhood, enlargement also runs the risk of making Brussels increasingly reliant on regional, rather than global, strategies and approaches.

The fifth section of the book analyzes the security dynamics of any possible future enlargements. Jan Techau focuses on the NATO enlargements after the end of the cold war. He views NATO's expansion to the east as the biggest geopolitical shift in Europe since 1989, fundamentally changing the function of the transatlantic alliance. He argues that in the post–cold war world, NATO evolved from a military coalition to an agent of political change. At the same time, he questions whether enlargement to so many new member states affected the defensibility of the alliance. Techau projects that any future NATO enlargement would not rank high on the political agenda of many of its member states and would strain relations with Russia.

Mark Entin provides an unorthodox perspective on the EU's and NATO's recent waves of enlargements. In his view, neither organization has fully grasped the complexities of the new international environment because they have been too self-absorbed. He argues not only that the two organizations did not understand the nature of the post–cold war world but also that, through their actions, they prolonged the cold war reality by shifting the borders of the Western alliances to the east. Entin suggests that both organizations should stop ignoring Russia and consider the Russian president's proposals for a new Euro-Atlantic alliance. He says that media engagement in this endeavor on both sides would increase the chances that such negotiations would succeed.

The chapter by Kurt Volker presents the U.S. perspective on the EU enlargements, describing how U.S. views of EU enlargement have evolved over time. He says that the American position evolved from strong support in the early days of the European integration process to less enthusiasm after the cold war—only to then change again toward a pro-enlargement approach. Volker argues that the lack of EU commitment to incorporate the Western Balkans and Europe's current eastern neighbors is a liability to the United States. He says that, from the U.S. perspective, the EU's "enlargement fatigue" is of great concern because it could lead to instability and would require the deployment of further U.S. security resources in Europe to the detriment of other areas of U.S. engagement in the world.

The sixth part of the volume addresses European development policies, the rule of law, and the promotion of democracy. Amichai Magen argues that the extraordinary process of the EU's democratic enlargement to the east has now largely stalled, and that the future of democracy in North Africa and the Middle East is still uncertain, particularly given the recent unrest in the region. In his view, the EU's reluctance to engage its neighborhood, a resurgent Russia, and the weakening of the "EU magnet" as a result of the euro crisis, as well as the lack of concrete membership perspectives for Europe's eastern neighbors, could undermine the prospect of democratic consolidation in this region. Magen suggests that it is necessary to understand the EU's "transformative engagement" philosophy and approach to democracy promotion and compares it with the democracy promotion philosophy and strategies of the United States.

Joaquín Roy looks at how future EU enlargements could affect European–Latin American relations. He begins by emphasizing the historical importance of the relationship between the two regions, as symbolized by the attempts to apply the European model of regional integration to Latin America. Roy argues that a future step-by-step enlargement of the EU to the east is unlikely to have noticeable effects on relations with Latin America. Turkey's accession, on the other hand, would send a signal that the EU has dramatically changed. In his view, EU–Latin American relations are affected by a number of factors, such as the will and success of Latin American entities to develop an institutional framework for regional integration, the EU's future integration, and the attitude of the main EU actors in shaping relations with Latin America.

Maurizio Carbone looks at the EU's development policy, one of the most dynamic policy areas in the European Union since the turn of the twenty-first century. He argues that, on the one hand, EU development policy has focused on eradicating poverty and making foreign aid more efficient while, on the other hand, it incorporated new issues such as security, migration, and trade liberalization. The accession of the CEECs provides a good preview of any future enlargements of the EU. New member states are required to embrace the development *acquis communautaire*. Given the fact that none of the CEECs had a tradition of providing development aid, this requirement proved rather challenging. It also led to a paradoxical situation in which the new member states contributed to development aid while being themselves recipients of aid. According to Carbone, the new CEEC member states slowly adapted their development policy to the new environment. All in all, he argues that the implications of future enlargement rounds for the EU's development policies are unlikely to be significant.

In their conclusion, Federiga Bindi and Irina Angelescu assess the recent EU enlargement and the EU's present relations with the neighborhood, discussing the most immediate international challenges and possible future scenarios. They emphasize that the question of Europe's frontiers is not solely a domestic issue, but will be likely to dramatically affect transatlantic relations and international relations at large. They argue that it is to the EU's advantage to leave the question of its frontiers open while at the same time remaining fully committed to future enlargements and to closer relations with its neighborhood. The challenging issue of the EU's frontiers will fundamentally affect and alter international relations in the twenty-first century.

FEDERIGA BINDI

2 A Brief History of EU Enlargements

The European Economic Community and the European Union (EEC/EU) have together witnessed four waves of enlargement, in 1971, 1981–87, 1995, and 2004–07. Each one had different motivations and implications both domestically and internationally. In three of them the United States had some role, for good or bad. The purpose of this chapter is to draw a picture of the process in order to understand challenges and implications of each of them. The main argument of this chapter is that, so far, EEC/EU enlargement—not to mention the very creation of the Communities—has been perceived as in the interest not only of the Europeans but also of the United States. Whether the same will be true in future rounds of enlargement remains to be seen and is the question at the heart this book.

The Creation of the European Communities

The creation in 1951 of the first Community—the European Coal and Steel Community (ECSC)—was strongly supported by the United States as it responded to the need to stabilize the recently pacified European continent and in particular to normalize the troubled French-German relationship. At the heart of the problem was the status of the Saar region—a territory rich in carbon mines, which France had managed to keep under its "supervision"—despite U.S. calls in 1949 for a solution. A solution was finally found by Jean Monnet, a close friend of the late U.S. president Franklin Roosevelt and of the American high commissioner in Germany, John McCloy; at the time, Monnet was general commissioner of the "Plan de modernisation et d'équipement" in France. Monnet's idea was to give back to Germany full sovereignty over the territory, while placing the management of coal and steel under a supranational authority—the first step toward a European Federation. As Monnet wrote in his memoirs, "Déjà tous était là. [Everything was already there.]: "L'Europe doit être organisée sur une base fédérale. . . . Le gouvernement français propose de placer la production franco-allemande d'acier et de charbon sous une Autorité internationale ouverte à la participation des autres pays d'Europe."[1] The French prime minister, Robert Schuman, endorsed the proposal and secretly sent a common friend—Judge Robert Mischlich—to talk with German chancellor Konrad Adenauer, who also enthusiastically endorsed it. Arriving in Paris on his way to London, U.S. secretary of state Dean Acheson was informed of the idea in a secret meeting with Schuman, Monnet, and McCloy at the U.S. ambassador's residence, and he, too, strongly supported it. On May 9, 1950, at the Quai d'Orsay in the Salon de l'Horloge, the so-called Schuman Declaration—a proposal for the first supranational organization in history—was presented to the press. Six governments welcomed the proposal and began negotiations: France, Germany, Italy, Belgium, the Netherlands, and Luxembourg. The Treaty of Paris creating the European Coal and Steel Community (ECSC) was signed on April 18, 1951. Its "High Authority," chaired by Jean Monnet, was established in Luxembourg on August 10, 1951.[2] The next day, William Thomlinson was nominated as American ambassador to the ECSC; in contrast, fearful of U.S. influence, it would take the USSR thirty-four years to recognize the European Communities as an international organization with a juridical personality.

The Creation of the EEC and Its First Enlargement

The United States continued to support the creation of the European Economic Community (EEC) and, later, its enlargement to nine members. Much to the surprise of the British—the United Kingdom had declined to join—the ECSC proved a big success, enhancing coal and steel production and lowering costs, thus conspicuously contributing to Western European reconstruction. In a meeting in Messina on June 1–3, 1955, the foreign ministers of the six ECSC member states decided to take an additional step by creating a common market—a favorite idea of the Germans, the Italians, and the Dutch—and cooperating in the field of atomic energy, as France was requesting. Negotiations were difficult, however, and it was the personal engagement of the negotiators that ultimately made the difference.[3] The United States also supported the new enterprise but—after having been heavily involved in the failed negotiations over the European Defense Community in 1954)[4]—this time kept a lower profile. International events finally provided the necessary impetus for the conclusion of the negotiations: the invasion of Hungary (November 4, 1956) and, most important, the nationalization of the Suez Canal (July 20, 1956). The economic instability following the conflict did not last long, though it proved enough for the Europeans, especially the French, to become aware of the risks of their economic dependence and political fragmentation on the international scene. On March 25, 1957, the treaties giving birth to the European Economic Community (EEC) and EURATOM were signed in Rome (hence the name Treaties of Rome). The first president of the new European Commission, whose headquarters were located in Brussels, was a German, Walter Hallstein; Robert Schuman was elected president of the European Assembly (later the European Parliament).

Once again, the United Kingdom chose not to join, proposing instead the creation of a free trade zone called the European Free Trade Association (EFTA), in 1960.[5] The process for the creation of a customs union again proved successful, contributing to the growth of intracommunity exchanges: a common market for many agricultural goods actually came into being before the end of the transitional period. Similarly, for industrial goods, a somewhat imperfect customs union was achieved by July 1, 1968, with the elimination of taxes and quantitative restrictions and the introduction of a common customs tariff. The free circulation of workers was achieved in December 1968, with the adoption, however, of a long list of "precautions."[6] The EEC began to present itself as a compact and a united bloc, and many states followed the example set by the United States and accredited their own diplomatic missions in Brussels. In 1963 the Yaoundé Convention—one of the first major programs for the EEC's cooperation on development policy—was concluded between the EEC and eighteen former colonies.

However, with the success of the European Agricultural Policy, the first disagreements with the United States started to emerge. U.S. support of the European integration process waned after the end of the Kennedy administration in 1963.[7] By the early 1970s, the United States perceived the EEC as an economic competitor and held it responsible for the U.S. deficit in its balance of payments. Transatlantic relations became strained and the U.S. approach to the EEC became rather contradictory. From the U.S. perspective, UK membership in the EEC was a possible advantage for the United States. However, the process of enlargement to the United Kingdom was to be a difficult one. In 1958, following the Algerian crisis, General Charles de Gaulle was called back into French government. He accepted on the condition that a new constitution would be prepared. The new constitution, approved by referendum in September 1958, marked the beginning of the Fifth Republic, of which de

Gaulle was elected the first president. Although he respected France's engagement in setting up the common market, he supported the idea of a European "concert" (Europe Européenne or Europe des Etats) formed by sovereign national states—with France playing a central role—that could counterbalance the United States and the Soviet Union on the international scene. Therefore, while refusing further pooling of sovereignty, he sponsored a greater coordination between "the Six" in the field of foreign policy. In 1958 he proposed to hold monthly meetings of EEC foreign ministers, a proposal that was carried out beginning in 1960. He also proposed meetings at the level of heads of state and government, the first of which was held in Paris, on February 10–11, 1961, with the participation of the foreign ministers.

He saw a possible UK membership in the EEC as a U.S. Trojan horse, however. The United Kingdom's attitude did not help, either: when, in 1961, the UK government, led by Harold Macmillan, applied for EEC membership, followed by Ireland, Denmark, and Norway, the conditions set down by the British were so uncompromising that it felt to the other members as if the EEC was joining the United Kingdom, rather than the other way around.[8] To make matters worse, at least from de Gaulle's point of view, on July 4, 1962, then U.S. president John F. Kennedy launched his "Grand Design"—an idea for enhancing cooperation between the (enlarged) EEC and the United States. Things worsened again when, in Nassau on December 18 of the same year, Kennedy offered Polaris missiles to Great Britain. Indeed, he made the same offer to France, but was rebuffed because de Gaulle saw in the American proposal a means to dominate Europe with regard to nuclear weapons. In his eyes, Britain's acceptance was a clear demonstration that the British had no real interest in Europe. De Gaulle thus abruptly ended membership negotiations—for which unanimity was required—offering instead an Association Agreement, which Macmillan took as an offense because it would have put the United Kingdom on the same "level" as Greece and Turkey.[9] In addition, a historic Friendship Treaty was signed between France and Germany on January 22, 1963.

The years 1967 and 1968 were eventful for Europe. In 1967 Kurt Kiesinger was elected German chancellor; former Berlin mayor Willy Brandt, architect of Ostpolitik, became foreign minister. On April 21 the colonels' coup d'état in Greece led to the freezing of its Association Agreement with the EEC. Also in 1967, Harold Wilson's Labour Party won the election in Great Britain and soon announced that Great Britain would again seek EEC membership. De Gaulle at first expressed reservations, and then, despite the Commission's positive opinion, again vetoed the idea in November. Yet the Soviet Union's occupation of Czechoslovakia in August 1968 spread doubts about de Gaulle's policy toward Eastern Europe.

On November 13, 1968, following a British initiative, the Eurogroup was created as a part of NATO (it ceased to exist in 1994). Unexpectedly, after losing a referendum on the reform of the Senate, de Gaulle resigned on April 27, 1969; his vice president, George Pompidou, was elected president on June 15. To mend fences with fellow Europeans, he proposed the so-called Triptique. Approved at a summit in The Hague on December 1–2, 1969, the Triptique consisted of three main lines of action for the relaunching of European construction: completion, deepening, and enlargement. This involved completion of the common market by January 1, 1970, with particular attention to financing the Common Agricultural Policy (CAP) using the resources of the Community; deepening the Community, with special reference to progress in the field of economic and monetary policy; and enlargement to Great Britain and other countries, with the condition that the Community would adopt a common position before undertaking negotiations.

Accession negotiations were thus divided into two phases: the first phase among the Six (in the first half of 1970), the second phase with the four candidate countries beginning on June 30, 1970. In this phase, the general positions of the Six were to be expressed by the president in office, while the Commission was given a mandate to work with the candidate countries on finding solutions to the problems that emerged during the negotiations. The Accession Treaty was signed on January 22, 1972. Thus the United Kingdom, Denmark, and Ireland became members of the Community on January 1, 1973: it was then a Europe of Nine. Norway, however, in a referendum held on September 25, 1972, rejected membership with a 53.5 percent vote. Norway joined the other EFTA countries in a free trade agreement with the EEC.

From Nine to Twelve

Ironically, once the EEC grew from six to nine to include the United Kingdom—the United States' closest ally—transatlantic relations worsened instead of improving, leading to further intra-European cooperation in the field of foreign policy. The U.S. president, Richard Nixon, affirmed the principle of American leadership over NATO, while asking Europeans to contribute more to the organization's expenses. Secretary of State Henry Kissinger called 1973 the "year of Europe," underscoring that the United States had global responsibilities and interests while Europe's interests were, and would continue to be, only regional. In response, in Copenhagen on December 14, 1973, the EEC foreign ministers adopted the Declaration on European Identity. Its objective was to better define the EEC's relations with and responsibilities toward the rest of the world and clarify Europe's place in it. In the declaration, the Nine affirmed:

> European Unification is not directed against anyone, nor is it inspired by a desire for power. On the contrary, the Nine are convinced that their union will benefit the whole international community. . . . The Nine intend to play an active role in world affairs and thus to contribute . . . to ensuring that international relations have [a] more just basis. . . . In pursuit of these objectives the Nine should progressively define common positions in the sphere of foreign policy.[10]

It was also decided that the country holding the presidency should consult with the United States on behalf of its partners.

The EEC and the United States disagreed on a number of issues, including the Middle East, with the EEC leaning in support of the Palestinian cause and approving (in November 1973) a common declaration regarding the legitimate rights of the Palestinians. The Nine greeted the Camp David peace talks in 1977–79 without any noticeable enthusiasm. In the Venice Declaration of June 12–13, 1980, they reaffirmed the Palestinians' right to self-determination and the need to include the Palestine Liberation Organization (PLO) in the negotiations. When on November 4, 1979, the U.S. embassy in Tehran was seized and sixty-three hostages were taken, the United States immediately responded with a boycott on imports of Iranian oil and froze Iranian assets in the United States. While the EEC called several times for the release of the hostages, it did not support the U.S. call for sanctions. Only on April 22, 1980, did the EEC agree to sanctions, although only if they were implemented by the individual states.[11]

Relations with Eurasia were also a matter of strain in transatlantic relations. The EEC and the United States clashed over the question of Poland when martial law was declared on December 13, 1981. While the United States imposed sanctions on both the USSR and Poland and pushed the Europeans to do likewise, the Europeans agreed, but only to a limited number of restrictions on the USSR (on imports). It took three weeks for the European Political Cooperation (EPC) to formulate a response to the Soviet invasion of Afghanistan in December 1979. Moreover, the Europeans disagreed with the U.S. decision to boycott the 1980 Moscow Olympics. The United Kingdom supported the U.S. position, but France and Germany opposed it, worried that it would undermine deterrence.[12]

Meanwhile, the geography of Europe was beginning to change with the end of the dictatorships in Greece, Portugal, and Spain. The "regime of the colonels" came to an end in Greece in 1974, the same year that the long dictatorship of Antonio Salazar in Portugal was overthrown in the Carnation Revolution. In 1975, with Franco's death, Spain also began its démarche toward democracy. All three countries quickly introduced a request for EEC membership. It was politically impossible for the EEC to close the door on these new democracies, which needed institutional support to consolidate, especially politically and economically, though the enlargement would have imposed major costs on the EEC; all three candidate countries were characterized by low wages, high inflation rates, unstable currencies, low-cost agricultural products, and underdeveloped industrial sectors. The United States also supported their inclusion in the EEC. The worry, and pressure on the EEC, was in particular directed toward Greece, given its geopolitical position. A first overlap between NATO and EEC membership also emerged with this new round of negotiations.

As a result of strong pressure from the United States—whose interests for once coincided with those of France, which desired a southern rebalancing of the EEC—Greece was quickly admitted as the tenth EEC member on January 1, 1981, despite the unfinished status of the negotiations. That decision proved to be a big mistake: as the new Greek government led by the Socialist Andreas Papandreou rose to power, it began asking for special economic benefits, which led, in 1985, to the creation of the Integrated Mediterranean Program, to provide support for Mediterranean agricultural production. As a direct consequence, negotiations with Spain and Portugal stalled, and those two countries did not become members until January 1, 1986. In addition, although Portugal and Greece were already NATO members, Spain was not. In his election campaign for prime minister, Felipe Gonzales had spoken against Spain's inclusion in NATO. But after he took power in 1982, U.S. pressure contributed to making the issue of NATO membership a precondition of EEC membership. When Gonzales changed his mind, the government led a campaign to convince the Spanish people of the usefulness of membership and monitored public opinion until a referendum was held, March 12, 1986, in which Spaniards approved the country's membership in the Atlantic alliance.

As for Portugal—whose Carnation Revolution had a Marxist flavor—two positions were debated in the United States: on the one side were those who believed Portugal should be helped in its fight against communism, and on the other side those, such as Henry Kissinger, who thought that there was no solution for Portugal and that a Portugal with Communists in power would be a "Communist lesson" for the rest of Europe—a warning of particular concern to Italy, where the so-called *compromesso storico* between the Communist Party and the Christian Democrats was being negotiated as a way to exit the political and economic crises of the time. Eventually, the first view prevailed and the United States warned its Western allies about the risks of having a communist country within NATO—the Portuguese government had in fact made clear it would not leave it. The United States therefore began to support Spanish and Portuguese EEC membership as a way to consolidate democracy and promote economic development. Negotiations stalled, however.

A turnaround finally came after 1983. Meanwhile, nine elections had taken place between 1980 and 1983, changing the European political scene. In 1981 François Mitterrand was elected president in France; in Germany, Helmut Kohl became chancellor in 1982. Despite political and personal differences, the two leaders were able to establish a strong alliance that would influence European history. The French presidency of the EEC in 1984 and the Italian one in 1985 finally allowed for the closing of negotiations over the membership of Spain and Portugal, giving birth to the Twelve in 1986. During the six and a half years of negotiations there had been twenty-seven ministerial level sessions, as well as thirty-one substitute level and dozens of technical meetings. The signing took place on June 12, 1985, in the morning in Lisbon, and in Madrid in the afternoon.[13] In foreign relations, the southern enlargement led to a renewed interest and strengthening of relations between Europe and Central and Latin America—traditionally the United States' backyard— and to an important EEC contribution to the pacification of conflict zones.[14]

The End of the Cold War

By the end of the 1980s, the EEC felt it had reached a size that was likely to remain set for a long time. The other non-EEC European countries seemed unlikely to seek membership, either because they were under Communist rule (the CEECs) or because they were restrained in their international strategies by the legacy of the cold war (Finland, Sweden, and Austria, for example). Others, including Switzerland, Norway, and Iceland, showed no interest in joining. Everything unexpectedly and rapidly changed after November 9, 1989, the day the Berlin Wall collapsed. After a first reaction of happiness and hope, European leaders started to worry. Not only were the CEECs in need of economic support, but also and most of all the end of the cold war would mean a reunified Germany.

On November 18, Francois Mitterrand invited fellow EEC heads of state and government to the Élysée Palace to discuss future international settings. On November 28, Helmut Kohl presented a ten-point program to the Bundestag outlining the road toward German reunification. The European partners were forced to accept reunification.[15] In exchange—as Kohl himself suggested—they decided to proceed toward further European integration. On December 8–9, 1989, the European Council in Strasbourg summoned an Intergovernmental Conference (IGC) to revise the EEC treaties: support for the process of German reunification was thereby strictly linked to further progress on European integration.[16] The year 1990 was one of preparation, while in 1991 two IGCs would deal, respectively, with economic and monetary union (EMU) and with political union. As EEC Commission president Jacques Delors told the European Parliament, "We need an institutional structure that can withstand the strains."[17]

The treaty establishing the European Union was signed in Maastricht on February 7, 1992. It formalized the steps needed to achieve EMU no later than the end of 1999. Indeed, on May 2, 1999, the heads of state and government established that eleven countries would be the first to join the economic and monetary union: Portugal, Spain, France, Luxembourg, Belgium, the Netherlands, Ireland, Italy, Germany, Austria, and Finland. Although this step succeeded, the question of political union was different. What it would mean remained vague, though it was understood to mean the institution of a common European defense (including a possible European NATO pillar) and further institutional progress.

However, when the Gulf War of 1990–91 deeply divided the United Kingdom and France, it showed that the time had not yet come for a unified EU defense. The Maastricht Treaty therefore established the Common Foreign and Security Policy (CFSP) as well as cooperation on Justice and Home Affairs (JHA), but it was certainly not the European defense that people had spoken of initially.

The U.S. reaction to European developments in the early 1990s was multifaceted. The United States at first felt uneasy about the possible limitations on U.S. troops on German territory after reunification.[18] The U.S. press stressed the differences among Europeans[19] and underlined that the goal was "said to be political union, but there is no consensus on what that means" and that "France's idea of giving the community a security role has found little echo among governments anxious to preserve a strong United States presence in Europe through NATO."[20] The United States closely followed the European debates, especially in the field of defense, in which France was advocating a stronger European ownership—for instance, revitalizing the moribund Western European Union (WEO)—and others, especially the United Kingdom, were resistant to the idea.[21]

As time passed, the EU member states got bogged down in how to better handle the new round of enlargements that were on the horizon. Still, three waves of enlargement resulted from the end of the cold war: 1995, 2004, and 2006. The 1995 enlargement was a (relatively) easy one. Austria (July 17, 1989), Sweden (July 1, 1991), Finland (March 18, 1992), Switzerland (May 20, 1992), and Norway (November 22, 1992) soon applied for EU membership. All of these countries were democratic and rich and had free market economies. Negotiations were therefore quickly opened (April 5, 1992) and closed (March 30, 1994), bringing the EU to fifteen member states.[22]

The story of enlargement to the east was different. Economic and trade agreements had been signed with Hungary and Czechoslovakia as early as 1988, with Poland in 1989, and with Bulgaria and Romania in 1990. The EU also created ad hoc programs such as Phare and Tacis to help these countries. However, EU member states were worried by both the institutional and the economic implications of such a massive enlargement. From an institutional point of view, the EU still had essentially the same framework that had been designed for six member states, and it was doubtful whether it would continue to work well for a membership of more than twenty-five. Furthermore, the ten prospective members were poor and would be recipient countries (that is, countries receiving more from the EU budget than what they would contribute), while the traditional main contributor, Germany, was deeply involved in financing and reforming its four new eastern *Länder*.

After timid and soon-abandoned suggestions that the CEECs should create their own organization, the EU offered the CEECs a new kind of Association Agreement—a so-called second-generation, and more political, agreement—which would help those countries prepare for membership. The new agreements were signed with Hungary and Poland in 1992; with the Czech Republic, the Slovak Republic, Bulgaria, and Romania in 1993; and with Slovenia in 1996. But the path to full membership was left unclear.

In an effort to clarify, the European Council meeting in Copenhagen in June 1993 decided on a set of criteria—now known as the Copenhagen criteria—required for a country to be eligible for EU membership: these included a free market economy, a democratic system, rule of law, and respect for human and minority rights. In addition, prospective members are to import into their legislation the *acquis communautaire*, that is, the whole body of EU legislation produced over the years.

It would take years to negotiate the details of membership and for the prospective member states to adapt their administrative and economic systems, as well as to insert and enact EU legislation into their national legislation. That was essentially good news to the worried EU members, less so for the prospective ones. Unfortunately, the process was badly managed and, even worse, badly communicated by the EU, as it embarked on a never-ending and never-achieved process of internal reforms that left the prospective members questioning the EU's real intentions.[23] This political vacuum was quickly filled by the United States, which stepped in to offer NATO membership to the newly free countries. NATO had created the North Atlantic Cooperation Council, a forum for discussing security, disarmament, and political questions with the former East-bloc republics, in December 1991.[24]

U.S. president Bill Clinton's commitment to NATO expansion dated back to early 1993, when he was pressed on the subject by President Vaclav Havel of the Czech Republic and Lech Walesa, then the president of Poland. Without a formal policy review, Clinton decided to announce during a European visit in January 1994 that it was no longer a question of "if" but "when" NATO would expand to the east.[25] That same year NATO created the Partnership for Peace (PfP), a program of bilateral cooperation between individual countries and NATO that allowed partner countries to build an individual relationship with NATO, choosing their own priorities for cooperation.

In 1995 NATO carried out and published the results of a study on NATO enlargement that considered the merits of admitting new members and how they should be brought in. It concluded that the end of the cold war provided a unique opportunity to build security in the entire Euro-Atlantic area and that NATO enlargement would contribute to enhanced stability and security for all. The decision was not, however, unanimously welcomed in the United States, where both the administration and the foreign policy community—Democrats and Republicans alike—were deeply divided on the issue. To those who argued that there was no clear U.S. national interest or payoff in the NATO enlargement process, those in favor—including Secretary of State Madeleine Albright and her deputy, Strobe Talbott—replied that "NATO enlargement has given Central and Eastern Europe greater stability than it has seen in this century."[26]

Despite these divided views, the Czech Republic, Hungary, and Poland were invited to begin accession talks at NATO's Madrid summit in 1997 and on March 12, 1999, they became the first former members of the Warsaw Pact to join the alliance. In parallel, in April 1999 the Membership Action Plan (MAP) was launched to help countries aspiring to NATO membership with their preparations; Bulgaria, Estonia, Latvia, Lithuania, Romania, Slovakia, and Slovenia joined it. All seven were subsequently invited to begin accession talks at NATO's Prague summit in 2002. On March 29, 2004, they officially became members of the alliance, making this the largest wave of enlargement in NATO history, much to their delight and triumph.

But Western Europeans were not crazy about NATO enlargement. As the *New York Times* reported at the time:

> Despite deep misgivings, the Europeans had no choice. . . . Their highest priority is keeping the United States engaged in Europe, and if the expansion of NATO was the price for that, they had no choice but to pay. Furthermore, it would ease the pressure on them to integrate Eastern and Western Europe by taking the new democracies into the European Union, which would entail major economic sacrifice.[27]

The timing of enlargement did not help either, with NATO always arriving one step ahead of the EU in the enlargement process. The EU incorporation of the ten new countries finally happened on May 1, 2004. The highest price for the EU members was therefore a political one: the belief that the CEECs owe their democratic and economic development to NATO has since become part of the U.S. narrative—and part of the CEECs own narrative—thus leading to an understatement of the actual leading role in and enormous expenditure of the EU on the enterprise. Another consequence was an underestimation of the success of enlargement within EU foreign policy.[28]

In conclusion, at this writing the rounds of EEC/EU enlargement are perceived as a matter of importance not only for the concerned parties but also for the United States, which has supported them in a variety of ways. Whether this will be the case for the next rounds of enlargement is in question and is the question at the core of this book.

Notes

1. Translation: Europe needs to be organized on a federal basis. The French government proposes to place French and German steel production under a supranational authority, open to the participation of other European states. J. Monnet, *Mémoires* (Paris: Fayard, 1976), p. 427.

2. The ECSC was arranged into four organs: the High Authority, the supranational body in which six members were nominated by a general agreement by the governments of the member states, but were independent; the Council of Ministers, formed by government representatives of the member countries; the Assembly formed by seventy-eight parliamentary delegates from their respective national governments; and the Court of Justice.

3. R. Marjolin, *Le Travail d'une vie: Mémoires 1911–1986* (Paris: Laffont, 1986), pp. 296–97.

4. Federiga Bindi and Palma D'Ambrosio, *Il Futuro dell'Europa* (Milan: Franco Angeli, 2005).

5. It was joined by, besides the United Kingdom, Norway, Denmark, Portugal, Switzerland, and Austria; Finland became an associate member in 1961.

6. Regulation (EEC) No. 1612/68 of the Council of 15 October 1968 on freedom of movement for workers within the Community.

7. See also Bindi and D'Ambrosio, *Il Futuro dell'Europa*.

8. Marjolin, *Le Travail d'une vie*, p. 330.

9. The Association Agreement with Greece was signed on July 9, 1961, and became effective on November 1 the following year. The agreement with Turkey is still being negotiated.

10. EEC, "Declaration on European Identity," December 14, 1974, point II.9 (www.ena.lu/declaration_european_identity_copenhagen_14_december_1973-020002278.html).

11. Marjolin, *Le Travail d'une vie*, p. 317.

12. Ibid., p. 259.

13. The Portuguese signatories were Mario Soares, Rui Machete, Jaime Gama, and Ernani Rodriguez Lopes.

14. J. Roy, "Relations between the EU and Latin America and the Caribbean: Competition or Cooperation with the United States?" in *The Foreign Policy of the European Union*, edited by Federiga Bindi (Brookings, 2010).

15. E. Di Nolfo, *Storia delle Relazioni Internazionali, 1918–1999* (Bari: Laterza, 2002), p. 1342.

16. F. Bindi, "La Fine della Guerra Fredda," in *Il Futuro dell'Europa*, pp. 77–88.

17. J. Delors, *Le nouveau concert Européenne* (Paris: Edition Odile Jacob, 1992).

18. F. Lewis, "France Returns to NATO," *New York Times*, March 27, 1990.

19. A. Riding, "Britain 'Deeply Skeptical' of Plan by France and Germany on Unity," *New York Times*, April 25, 1990.

20. A. Riding, "West Europeans Near a Consensus on East-Bloc Ties," *New York Times*, April 1, 1990.

21. "At East-West Crossroads, Western Europe Hesitates," *New York Times*, March 25, 1992.

22. Norway again rejected membership by referendum.

23. The EU in fact started a long process of internal reforms leading to the treaties of Amsterdam (1996) and Nice (2000). As neither of them resolved the institutional problems, European countries thought of an alternate way to amend the treaties, opting for a European Convention, optimistically imagining the type of convention that led to the U.S. Constitution. The European constitution that was approved and finalized in July 2003 was a sensible and readable document. European diplomats, however, in "finalizing it," downgraded the innovations included in the text to then finish killing it in December 2003. After the terrorist attacks in Madrid on March 11, 2004, which led to the election of José Luis Zapatero as prime minister of Spain (the former Spanish prime minister, José Maria Aznar, was among those responsible for the sacking of the European constitution in December), a new European constitution was approved on June 18, 2004. This text, too, was soon abandoned, after being rejected by referendums in France and the Netherlands in 2005. The 2004 enlargement took place anyway, under

the Nice Treaty rules. See Bindi and D'Ambrosio, "Gli sviluppi recenti," in *Il Futuro dell'Europa*, pp. 89–122.

24. In 1997 the North Atlantic Cooperation Council was replaced by the Euro-Atlantic Partnership Council (EAPC).

25. R. W. Apple, "Road to Approval Is Rocky and the Gamble Is Perilous," *New York Times*, May 15, 1997.

26. Ibid.

27. Ibid.

28. Federiga Bindi and Jeremy Shapiro, "Conclusions," in *The Foreign Policy of the European Union*, edited by Federiga Bindi (Brookings, 2010).

PART ONE

The State of EU Negotiations and Enlargement Perspectives

FERDINANDO NELLI FEROCI

3

EU Enlargement Policy: From Success to Fatigue

Enlargement has been one of the most successful policies of the European Union, as shown by the spectacular progress in the increase of the number of member states. Since the first enlargement in the early 1970s until now, membership has increased from the original six countries to twenty-seven, and from 200 million to almost 500 million EU citizens.

The fifth enlargement of 2004 and 2007 was by far the most politically significant, both for the number of new members and for its historical importance, and will be remembered as the reunification of Europe. The accession negotiations helped to create common ground and to consolidate democracy and the rule of law in countries that previously were at very different stages of social, economic, and political development.

The fifth enlargement is considered a political and economic success. The European Union acquired a truly continental dimension, and the stability provided by accession resulted in an increase in trade and investments. At the same time, the increase in the number of member states has also significantly increased the complexities of EU decisionmaking.

The European Union seems to have maintained its appeal despite the economic and financial crisis that began in 2008, with four new applications having reached the EU mailbox, from Montenegro (December 2008), Albania (April 2009), Iceland (July 2009), and Serbia (December 2009). Membership in the European "club" is considered good insurance against downturns in the economic cycle, as suggested by the application of Iceland, a small state that for many years ranked among the wealthiest nations in Europe.

At present, enlargement faces a complex and difficult phase within the EU. Officially the EU is still committed to enlargement, but enthusiasm has sharply decreased. This is particularly true in some decisive countries like France, Germany, and the Benelux countries (Belgium, the Netherlands, and Luxembourg), where an attitude of prudence—if not of open reluctance—prevails. As a result, the EU is sending contradictory signals to the candidate and potential candidate countries.

This new phenomenon has been described as "enlargement fatigue." It has many explanations, including the economic crisis, a more general attitude of fear of massive inflows of foreign workers, preoccupations related to the future of EU common policies and the future destination of EU funds. Some of those concerns may be justified, while others do not seem to be on solid ground judging from the experience of previous enlargements. Public opinion polls register concern, and politicians tend to exploit people's worries.

In such a context it would be advisable to have a clear perception of the actual costs and benefits of enlargement, as well as the prospects of accession of individual countries in the neighborhood, and to be able to manage the expectations and the possibly growing frustrations of candidate and potential candidate countries. It is also necessary to provide the public with correct facts and figures on the results of the past enlargement rounds and on the likely effects of the accession of new member states.

The Making of Enlargement: Current Negotiations

The EU in 2011 conducted accession negotiations with two countries: Croatia and Turkey. Negotiations with Iceland were formally opened on July 27, 2010, although at this writing in mid-2011 the talks on the different "chapters" (the areas of EU law and policy that new member states have to adopt at the date of accession) have not yet started. A fourth country, the former Yugoslav Republic of Macedonia, is officially considered a candidate, but the opening of negotiations has been delayed because of a bilateral dispute with Greece.

Croatia

Croatia obtained the status of candidate country in June 2004, and accession negotiations were opened in October 2005. In November 2008 the European Commission proposed an indicative roadmap for reaching the final stage of negotiation by the end of 2009. It was not possible to meet the planned deadline because of Croatia's bilateral dispute with Slovenia about the delimitation of land and maritime borders and delays in the pace and implementation of the reforms in Croatia in some crucial fields, such as justice. Croatia and Slovenia resolved the border issue in September 2009, and Croatia's prime minister, Jadranka Kosor, gave fresh impetus to the reforms required to move the negotiations forward.

These developments made possible the opening of the three remaining negotiation chapters, on competition, the judiciary, and foreign and security policy, at the end of June 2010. Now all the chapters related to EU law and policy are open, while two-thirds have already been provisionally closed. The EU Council therefore decided that Croatia's level of alignment with the *acquis* is good and does not require further talks. The ambitious goal of Zagreb was to conclude the technical negotiations in spring 2011 and to sign the Treaty of Accession by the end of the Hungarian presidency of the EU in June 2011. This goal has only been missed by a few months. At the European Council held June 23–24, 2011, it was decided that the Accession Treaty will be signed before the end of the year, which means that Croatia will become the twenty-eighth EU member as of 2012.

The accession of Croatia will have a positive role in reaffirming EU commitment to enlargement and will send an encouraging message to the other countries of the Western Balkans to pursue the reforms needed to consolidate democracy and the rule of law and to stabilize the economy.

Turkey

The Turkish case is more complex. Ankara signed an Association Agreement with the European Economic Communities (EEC) in 1963 (the second country to do so after Greece) and formally applied for membership in 1989. Ten years later, at the Helsinki European Council, the heads of state and government of the then fifteen member states granted Turkey the status of candidate country. This decision triggered a period of ambitious reforms in Turkey that allowed the country to satisfy the political criteria for the opening of accession negotiations—together with Croatia—in October 2005.

The momentum associated with the beginning of the negotiations was overshadowed only one year later, following the accession of the Republic of Cyprus and nine other new member states in May 2004, by the failed attempt to reach a settlement on the island with the "Annan Plan," which was rejected by the Greek Cypriots in a referendum. Since then, Turkey has refused to open its ports and airports to Cypriot ships and planes, in violation of the obligation it assumed under the so-called Ankara Protocol (an agreement to extend to the ten new member states the EU-Turkey Customs Union).

As a reaction to the Turkish decision, in December 2006 the EU Council suspended the closure of all negotiating chapters and "froze" the opening of eight of them, covering areas linked to the Customs Union. Furthermore, after his election in 2007, President Nicolas Sarkozy of France clearly stated his position in favor of offering Turkey a "privileged partnership" instead of full membership. Subsequently, France blocked negotiations on five chapters that implied the recognition of the prospect of accession. Another group of six chapters is being held back by Cyprus on the same grounds as the Council's decision of 2006. In total, at this writing eighteen chapters are blocked. Since thirteen chapters had already been opened, negotiations are possible in only a limited number of areas.

As a result, negotiations are proceeding at an extremely slow pace. The open reluctance of important member states such as France and Germany to grant full membership to Turkey, as well as the slowing rhythm of accession talks, has created a vicious circle. Frustration is growing in Ankara, where EU accession has become a highly politicized internal issue in the confrontation between the ruling AKP Party and the Kemalist and nationalist opposition, and it is more difficult for the government to push through reform bills. This, in turn, has the effect of further slowing the progress of the accession negotiations.

Turkish public opinion has pushed many political leaders to consider alternatives to accession, building on renewed self-confidence in the economic strength of Turkey, which has a growth rate far higher than that of the EU. The activism of the foreign policy of Turkey toward Central Asia and the Middle East is evident, but it is also manifest in the Western Balkans. However, it does not always appear in line with the external policies of the European Union.

The approval by a large majority of a confirmative referendum on a package of amendments to the constitution on September 12, 2010—most of which are in line with accession requirements—may be a good sign. However, a renewed commitment to accession would also be necessary on the EU side.

Iceland

Against this background of enlargement fatigue, the EU has recently decided to open accession negotiations with Iceland. This Nordic island recognized the merits of EU membership rather late, and only as a consequence of the financial crisis. Its decision to submit an application in July 2009 met with a surprising degree of support by member states, which decided in only a few months to open negotiations. In fact, Iceland is already integrated, as a member of the European economic area, in the EU internal market and is already associated with the Schengen *acquis*. Major problems to be solved in the context of the negotiations will likely be limited to fisheries and agriculture. Nevertheless, public opinion in Iceland remains hesitant about, if not openly opposed to, the prospect of accession, thus creating a situation of uncertainty over the final outcome of the negotiations.

The Future of Enlargement: Candidate and Potential Candidate Countries of the Western Balkans

The Former Yugoslav Republic of Macedonia

In 2005 the EU granted candidate status to the Former Yugoslav Republic of Macedonia (FYROM), but has not been able so far to open accession negotiations. The Commission made a recommendation in this regard in October 2009, following a positive evaluation of the progress made by the government in Skopje in a number of important areas. However, the Council has not been able to make a decision because the bilateral dispute with Greece on the name issue—which is dragging on since the early 1990s—continues to stand in the way of a consensus.

Despite increased consultations between the two parties (with a number of bilateral meetings between Prime Minister Nikola Gruevski and Prime Minister Georgios Papandreou), so far no breakthrough has been reached. There is a risk that a prolonged stalemate could have repercussions for the relations between the two main ethnic components of the population (Slav Macedonians and Albanian Macedonians). The stalemate is also due to different perceptions on the issues at stake for the future of the country. According to recent polls, while the majority of Slav Macedonians are not ready to accept what they see as a compromise (with Greece) on national identity for the sake of joining the EU and NATO, the vast majority of Albanian Macedonians are ready to accept any solution that would deliver that goal.

In such a climate, the European Commission has underlined the need to keep the reform momentum going, voicing concern that slowing down the government's European agenda would negatively affect the accession process. To allay those concerns, Skopje has reassured the EU of its commitment to reforms and to the European integration process. In any case, a persistent stalemate of the European perspective may have repercussions on the stability of the country.

Montenegro and Albania

In 2009 the Council transmitted the membership applications of Montenegro and Albania to the Commission, and the Commission prepared its opinion. Following the European Council meeting on December 14, 2010, Montenegro was granted the status of candidate country. Regarding Albania, in its opinion released in November 2010, the Commission recommended the beginning of accession negotiations once the country meets the necessary degree of compliance with some membership criteria.

The chances that Montenegro will receive a positive recommendation from the Commission on the opening of accession negotiations are quite high: the country is stable and its government is vigorously pursuing a pro-European agenda. Montenegro has no major problems with its neighbors; on the contrary, it has been playing a conciliatory and constructive role, representing a factor of stability for the region since its independence in 2006.

According to the European Commission, Montenegro has to concentrate its efforts on the rule of law, notably the fight against organized crime and corruption, the reform of the judiciary, and the strengthening of its administrative capacity. There is a strong possibility that the Commission will recommend the granting of candidate status, refraining nonetheless from proposing accession negotiations and calling instead for the government in Podgorica to implement a number of reforms before further steps can be taken.

The situation is much more complex in the case of Albania, owing to a political crisis that could potentially have serious consequences for the European integration process. Albania nevertheless has made impressive progress in recent years, considering that as recently as the 1990s it was still one of the most secluded and totalitarian regimes in the world. Since September 2009 there has been a continuous boycott of parliamentary activity by the opposition. It did not recognize the result of the general elections held in June of that year, in which the Democratic Party of the incumbent prime minister, Sali Berisha, prevailed by a small margin, in coalition with the Socialist Movement of Integration of Ilir Meta (a breakaway party from the Socialists). Notwithstanding the positive judgment by international observers,[1] the leader of the Socialist Party, Edi Rama, refused to acknowledge the result and blocked all attempts to bring an end to the deadlock. While the EU officially abstained from intervening, stressing that "it is the responsibility of the Albanian Government together with the opposition to find a solution,"[2] members of the European Parliament (MEPs) Joseph Daul and Martin Schulz, on behalf of the European People's Party (EPP) and the Progressive Alliance of Socialists and Democrats (S&D) political groups of the European Parliament, tried to facilitate a compromise in May/June 2010. They were not successful, but the Socialist Party (SP) consented to return to Parliament, even though there is little chance that political life will return to normal, unless Rama and Berisha agree on the most vexed question concerning the last elections: the reopening of ballot boxes in order to investigate alleged frauds and irregularities.

As the European Commission will be called to assess the performance of Albania primarily on the Copenhagen political criteria, there is little doubt that this longstanding political crisis will have a bearing on the opinion. The

Commission could act in two ways. First, it could forward a "critical" opinion, conditioning any future step on the European integration process to the fulfillment of a long list of conditions (first and foremost the political dialogue, but also reforms concerning the rule of law, the judiciary, administrative and enforcement capacity, and other issues.). Second, it could take a more nuanced approach (linking the granting of candidate status to a solution of the political crisis and then condition further steps on the accomplishment of a long list of reforms).

Serbia

In the case of Serbia, relations with the EU have long been hindered by questions related to the legacy of the 1990s, notably the obligation to apprehend and extradite officials charged with heinous crimes committed during the war to the International Criminal Tribunal for the former Yugoslavia in the Hague.

Already in 2009 prosecutor Serge Brammertz was able to report on the "satisfactory cooperation"—even if not yet "full cooperation"—of Serbia with the tribunal. This assessment paved the way in December 2009 for the Council decisions on the coming into force of the Interim Agreement on trade measures, and in June 2010 for the start of national ratification of the Association and Stabilization Agreement signed in 2008. After the "unfreezing" of the Interim Agreement on December 22, 2009, the Serbian president, Boris Tadic, presented the candidature of his country to join the EU. After fugitive Ratko Mladic's arrest in 2011, cooperation with the International Criminal Tribunal for ex-Yugoslavia (ICTY) has substantially improved.

However, while the application has been forwarded to the Commission, in the meantime the question of Kosovo has come again to the fore. The International Court of Justice responded to Serbia's request for advice on the legitimacy of Kosovo's unilateral declaration of independence on July 22, 2010, by stating its opinion (which is nonbinding) that the declaration is legitimate under international law.

As a follow-up to that opinion, Serbia agreed—after some complex negotiations with the EU—to present together with the EU a draft resolution in the UN General Assembly that calls for dialogue with Kosovo on all issues that was approved by consensus. The purpose of the dialogue would be "to achieve progress on the path to the EU and improve the lives of the people," thereby excluding the reopening of the "status" issue. Dialogue in the meanwhile has started under the auspices of the EU. In the meantime, in light of the constructive approach taken by the Serbian government, the Council decided to transmit the Serbian application to the Commission for its *avis*, so that Serbia can achieve candidate status in 2011.

Kosovo

Kosovo has been included in the Stabilization and Association Process, but the nonrecognition by five member states (Spain, Greece, Cyprus, Slovakia, and Romania) has so far prevented any real progress toward the EU perspective. Nonetheless, the Commission has started a process aimed at monitoring the level of Kosovo's preparation on trade-related matters, so as to make it possible, once conditions are met—and maybe in connection with Serbia's future steps toward the EU—to ask the Council for a negotiating mandate for a trade agreement.

The Commission intends to launch a visa dialogue as well, with the eventual aim of visa liberalization. The position of the five "nonrecognizers" should be more flexible on this issue because freedom of circulation would directly benefit the citizens, not the state. In any case, apart from the status issue and the difficult relations with Serbia, it is clear that Kosovo still has a long way to go in the process toward European integration. As the youngest state in the world—with still limited recognition—it has first to consolidate its institutions and rule of law and prepare the ground for sustainable economic and social development. Only then will it be able to fully join the process of *rapprochement* with the European Union.

Bosnia

The situation is just as complex in Bosnia as it is in Kosovo, but for different reasons. The 1995 Dayton Agreement was successful in ending the war, but it implied a cost, which has become evident over the years. Dayton provided strong decentralization and clear guarantees to the three ethnic groups that on sensitive questions they would never overrule each other. That is why today Bosnia has a weak central state and a decisionmaking process that is basically held hostage to the will of the constituent peoples and the two entities (the Bosniak-Croat Federation and Republika Srpska). Furthermore, the international presence foreseen by the Dayton Agreement (a High Representative endowed with executive powers) contributed to the creation of a "quasi-protectorate," which is not consistent with the development of a partnership with the EU aimed at accession. Accordingly, the Council decided in December 2009 that "it will not be in a position to consider an application for membership by Bosnia until the transition of the OHR [Office of the High Representative] to a reinforced EU presence has been decided."[3]

Therefore, there are a number of basic conditions to be fulfilled before a real process of accession to the EU can start for Bosnia: the closure of the OHR (linked to specific objectives and conditions, called "5+2") and a constitutional reform aimed at a functional state and at empowering it with the capacities needed to steer the EU agenda and the implementation of the *acquis communautaire.*

Conclusions

The enlargement process is characterized by a number of paradoxes. The first is that of Iceland. Europeans are ready to provide Iceland with a sort of fast track to rapid accession negotiations. And this is logical and natural given Iceland's significant degree of integration in the EU internal market, and considering that the only serious problems to solve are those related to the fishery regime and agriculture. But public opinion and the majority of political parties in that country are clearly against accession. There is therefore a serious risk that negotiations could be started, only to have Iceland's voters reject the prospect of accession.

The second paradox is the countries of the Western Balkans. A long time ago Europeans promised a "European perspective" to the countries of this region, but they have postponed this target so long that the EU's credibility will be soon at stake. The EU approach to these countries has changed from previous rounds of enlargement. Its policy has become cautious and somewhat ambivalent, reflecting the growing skepticism and doubts of some member states about the wisdom of further accession. In turn, this situation casts doubts over the real will of the EU itself to engage in further enlargements, with negative effects for the countries concerned.

These countries are indeed steering through a difficult process of reform and change, which is driven by the European perspective. If that is called into question, they would lose the primary incentive to make difficult decisions at home and convince their populations to accept them. In a way, "enlargement fatigue" is mirrored by "reform fatigue," or what has been called "fatigue with enlargement fatigue." Europeans risk losing the strongest incentive for cooperative behavior. Hopefully, new enthusiasm will be injected with Croatia's accession.

In contrast, the Western Balkan countries have shown a clear capacity to deliver when provided with the right incentives and clear goals. A case in point is the visa liberalization process, which has been a success by all standards: the "roadmaps" set by the Commission, based on clear benchmarks, have been a potent driver for change. There is therefore a need to seriously consider how to fill the gap between expectations and deliverables, in the awareness that accession, if ever possible, will not happen tomorrow.

The third paradox is Turkey. The case of Turkey is the most politically sensitive. There again Europeans are faced with a political dilemma. They have promised Turkey the prospect of accession and have opened accession negotiations. But at present no one is certain that the process will have a successful outcome. There is broad agreement that Turkey is a strategic partner of the Union, but different conclusions are drawn from this shared assessment. A relative majority of member states are convinced that the process should continue until it reaches a positive conclusion. A growing minority of member states, which include France and to a certain extent Germany, consider that the only practicable solution is a sort of special privileged partnership but certainly not full membership. There is a serious risk that the decreasing degree of support in Turkey for full accession may become stronger as it perceives itself to be unwelcome in the club. For its part, Turkey can help its chances through cooperation. An insufficient commitment to finding a solution for the Cyprus question—witnessed by Turkey's refusal to fully apply the dispositions of the Custom Union Agreement to Cyprus—is considered proof that Turkey lacks an authentic desire to be a member of a Union that includes Cyprus. A certain amount of ambiguity about the way internal, including constitutional, reforms are being conducted and implemented in Turkey has left some justified doubts over its determination to fully respect European and Western standards. The moment of truth is approaching because Europeans will soon have no more chapters to open for negotiation. It is urgent that the EU define a clear strategic position toward Turkey because ambiguity in the long run is not sustainable, and could be harmful.

Notes

1. According to OSCE-ODIHR, the elections met "most OSCE commitments." "OSCE-ODIHR Election Observation Mission Final Report on the Parliamentary Elections of 28 June 2009 in Albania," Warsaw, September 14, 2009, p. 1.

2. Foreign Affairs Council, "Council Conclusions on the Western Balkans," June 14, 2010.

3. General Affairs Council, "Council Conclusions on Enlargement/Stabilisation and Association Process," December 7–8, 2009.

JOHN PEET

4 EU Enlargement: Benefits and Obstacles

From the beginning of the European project, the treaties have always been very clear: any European country that meets the necessary criteria should be eligible to join the club. That seems a sensible policy that I believe the EU should retain.

This argument raises three immediate questions, however. First, what is a European country? Second, who should set the criteria for membership and evaluate whether they have been met? And third, even if these first two questions are answered successfully, do eligibility to join and fulfillment of the criteria lead automatically to membership?

The first question—what is a European country?—is not at all easy to answer. The only definitive point is that Europe does not extend to North Africa, which the club made clear by turning down an application for membership from Morocco in 1987. It has also made clear, despite some subsequent comments by leading European politicians, that Turkey is deemed to be a European country. Indeed, it has done this repeatedly: when it signed an Association Agreement in 1963, when it established a customs union in 1995, when it accepted Turkey as a potential candidate for membership in 1999, and then when it opened accession negotiations in 2005. The admission of Cyprus as a member in 2004 also carries the implication that Turkey is geographically part of Europe: the bulk of Turkey's population lives to the west of Cyprus.

It is broadly understood now that Belarus, Ukraine, and Moldova are also part of Europe. What is less clear is whether Russia is in Europe, and likewise, what the position on the three Caucasus countries is. I would submit that all of these countries ought, in principle, to be considered sufficiently European to be candidates for EU membership one day. But not everyone would agree.

Nor would everyone necessarily exclude the whole of North Africa—parts of which were central to the Roman Empire, for instance—but most analysts do not consider North Africa to be part of Europe.

Sometimes there are demands to establish clear limits or boundaries for EU membership; countries outside those boundaries would be ineligible. But as Europe is ill-defined in both geographic and political terms, I would argue against doing this. Other organizations tend to avoid any clear definition, with the result that there is a certain fuzziness about where Europe begins and ends. The Organization for Security and Co-operation in Europe (OSCE), for example, includes Kazakhstan and the other four Central Asian countries of the former Soviet Union (indeed, Kazakhstan was chair of the OSCE in 2010). The Council of Europe includes Russia, as well as Turkey, but not Central Asia. The Eurovision song contest has featured not only Israel but also, in the past, Morocco.

The European Neighborhood Policy, broadly defined, includes countries that might qualify as part of Europe, but it also extends to North African countries that do not. The EU's new Eastern Partnership comes closer to counting only those countries that might one day become members of the EU. But none of this answers the question of what Europe is specifically. And some would argue that the question should be about values as much as about geography. It seems sufficient now to assert that some countries (Kazakhstan, for instance, and probably Israel and Lebanon too) will never be considered part of Europe, though people may quarrel with this. At all events, one should be prepared to argue about the merits and values of individual cases and countries.

The other two questions, on membership criteria and whether eligible countries automatically have a right to join, are simpler to deal with. On the criteria, the treaties assign to the European Commission the task of judging whether a candidate fulfills the requirements of membership. The broad criteria were famously established by the Copenhagen European Council in 1993: democracy and the rule of law, a functioning market economy, and the ability to take on the obligations of membership. For negotiating purposes, accession talks are usually broken down into thirty-five chapters, constituting the *acquis communautaire* that an applicant must implement. Some applicant countries have formed the view that entering into a negotiating process implies the ability to bargain; but in reality, the 100,000 or more pages of the *acquis communautaire* are not flexible: applicants must accept and implement the rules in their entirety (subject only to transition periods) before they can be admitted.

The answer to the third question is that membership is not automatic even if a country is eligible to join and has fulfilled all the necessary criteria. A candidate country's membership still has to be approved unanimously by all of the existing members, each of which has to ratify the resultant accession treaty, as well as by the European Parliament. The applicant must also agree that it wants to join. Many applications in the past have not led to full membership, starting with Britain's in 1961, which was vetoed by President Charles de Gaulle of France in 1963. Switzerland has applied to join the EU too, but froze its application after a negative referendum. Norway has twice applied and even agreed on the terms of membership, only then to see its decision overturned by national referendums. But, so far at least, no country that has opened accession negotiations has failed, eventually, to be offered full membership in the club.

Benefits of Enlargement

What are the benefits of enlargement? I would suggest that there are three principal ones. The most obvious benefit is to the applicant country itself. It gains membership in the world's largest single market and trading bloc. It also wins greater political weight inside the EU. In most cases it secures significant budgetary transfers from the EU (but not always—Britain, Austria, Finland, and Sweden have all been substantial net contributors to the EU budget from the day that they joined). Membership in the EU cements and underpins democracy, the rule of law, and the operation of a free-market economy in countries where some of these things may have been fragile, to say the least. There is in addition a security dimension to EU membership. Most countries that have successfully applied to join have also joined the NATO military alliance, although four countries (Ireland, Austria, Finland, and Sweden) have not. There is thus some link to Western security arrangements, an especially important consideration for countries that were formerly under Soviet domination.

A second, and perhaps less obvious, benefit from enlargement is to the existing members of the club. Some countries are surprised by this, given that enlargement usually costs money and brings new competition into the EU. But it is a fact that the current members of the EU have a great interest in preserving the stability and prosperity of their immediate neighbors—and EU enlargement has proved to be by far the most effective way of delivering these things. In the 1970s and 1980s, it was a crucial tool in entrenching the shift away from military rule and dictatorship in Greece, Spain, and Portugal. At the turn of the century it performed a similar function in relation to the former communist countries of Central and Eastern Europe. Indeed, enlargement can truthfully be said to have been the European project's single most successful foreign policy.

I would draw a contrast here with the experience of the United States with its neighbors to the south, including Mexico and Central America. Repeated American efforts to secure stability and prosperity, often accompanied by large amounts of money, have produced little in the way of success. The North American Free Trade Agreement (NAFTA) has yielded economic benefits, but Mexico's political and social development has continued to lag. Europe's own experience with North Africa has been similarly dismal. In both these examples, policies to promote democracy, the rule of law, and functioning market economies have often failed lamentably—quite unlike the success with the same objective in the Mediterranean countries and later in Central and Eastern Europe.

The third and perhaps least appreciated benefit of enlargement, I would submit, is to the European project itself. Without enlargement, the EU would have less foreign policy and trade clout, pull much less economic weight, and simply be less important. Enlargement has helped to deliver European relevance in all of these areas, partly by simply making the club bigger and partly by importing into it both new thinking and new ideas. The European economy has clearly done better as a result of enlargement, which has brought into the EU faster-growing countries and markets.

As a global political and economic actor the EU would, in my view, be a lot worse off now without Spain and Portugal, which joined in 1986; also worse off without Poland and Hungary, which joined in 2004; and even worse off without Britain, which joined in 1973. And, contrary to the thinking of some opponents of enlargement, there is no zero-sum game involved in this. Taking in new members does not necessarily imply a slowdown of European integration either: indeed, past enlargements have often been followed by new treaties that push the European project forward. In short, the EU, its existing members, and the applicants for membership can all draw substantial benefits from the enlargement of the club, and many have already done so.

Current Problems with Enlargement

Given all of these past and potential future benefits, why is the current enlargement process in such difficulty? It is true that negotiations are continuing with Croatia and Turkey and were opened with Iceland in July 2010. Macedonia has been recognized as a candidate since 2005, but the opening of negotiations is blocked because of its name dispute with Greece. Elsewhere in the Western Balkans, Albania and Montenegro have both formally applied for membership in the EU. And Brussels has also formally recognized that Bosnia, Serbia, and Kosovo are all countries with the status of potential candidates. Yet with the possible (and only partial) exception of Croatia, which opened all of its negotiating chapters and concluded its talks in 2011 with a view to joining as a full member in 2012, none of these prospective candidates is having a smooth or speedy ride.

I would offer four explanations for this situation. The first is generalized enlargement fatigue. The enthusiasm with which European leaders prepared to welcome the ten former communist countries of Central and Eastern Europe in 2004 has largely disappeared. The process of digesting these new countries has been drawn out longer and perhaps more painfully than the optimists hoped (though it should be noted that those who forecast that an EU of twenty-seven would be quite unable to function efficiently were largely proved wrong even before the Lisbon Treaty came into effect in late 2009). In many quarters there is some feeling that it would be good to pause before admitting additional member countries.

Those who favored deeper integration of Europe before any further widening also argue that their position has been vindicated following the big expansion of 2004 and 2007. Experience with Bulgaria and Romania—which joined in 2007—has been particularly disappointing. Problems with corruption, organized crime, and the rule of law have led many neutral observers to conclude that these two countries were admitted to the EU in 2007 before they were really ready. As a result, the natural reaction was to erect a higher bar for current and future applicants.

A second and related reason for the present problems is a popular backlash against enlargement, aggravated by the current economic and financial crisis within the eurozone, which is affecting the entire EU. The truth is that public opinion in Europe was never particularly enthusiastic about enlargement (though it is worth recalling that, in a referendum in 1972, the French people voted strongly in favor of British entry). Most ordinary voters saw the accession of Spain in 1986 and Eastern Europe in 2004 as a threat to their jobs and their living standards. In particular, there was widespread hostility to free movement of labor from these countries, especially when it turned out that far more people had migrated in search of work than had been expected.[1]

Popular misgivings about enlargement played a big part in the French and Dutch rejections of the draft EU constitution in 2005. The "no campaign" in France played on the myth of the Polish plumber who was said to be stealing good jobs from Frenchmen. Opposition to the 2004 enlargement was a significant influence on voters, as was the prospect of Turkey as an EU member. Indeed, President Jacques Chirac of France tried unsuccessfully to defang this last issue before the vote by amending the French constitution to require a national referendum before Turkey could be admitted (though this requirement has since been watered down). Unfortunately, rather than try to sway public opinion in favor of enlargement by emphasizing its benefits, many political leaders in Europe, including Mr. Chirac's successor, Nicolas Sarkozy, have played along with voters' negative sentiments.

Third, I would suggest, there is a specific worry about the Western Balkans. This is widely believed to be a lawless region that has all too often sucked outsiders into its internal conflicts. Such fears have again been made worse by experience with Bulgaria and Romania inside the EU. There is a perception that difficulties with the rule of law, with official corruption, and with organized crime are widespread across the Balkans, and a worry that some of the countries in the region may be trying to join the EU before they are fully able to take on the obligations of membership.

The legacy of the 1990s wars—and especially the problems of Kosovo and Bosnia—also increases resistance to the notion that the EU should become further embroiled in this troubled region by actually letting the countries in it join the club. Croatia just about makes the grade with informed opinion-makers, though the experience of its bitter border dispute with Slovenia held up its membership talks for several months.[2]

In contrast, Albania and Bosnia do not yet seem to be anywhere near ready. Talk of admitting Serbia and Kosovo to the EU raises the bad memories of admitting Cyprus in 2004 without first settling its internal boundary dispute to its north, something that most EU policymakers now admit was a huge mistake (it happened only because there was a fear that unless Cyprus was admitted, Greece might block all other candidates). Trying to persuade people to be more positive about the Balkans by arguing that if their membership were delayed or rejected they might relapse into war, crime, and other troubles is hardly a good way of reassuring the worriers about the stability of the region.

Fourth, I would argue that most of these objections and concerns apply with even greater force to Turkey. Hostility to Turkish membership runs deep in Europe. Turkey is big, it is relatively poor, it has a foreign policy orientation that seems nowadays to be leaning as much (or more) toward the East as to the West, and it is mainly Muslim. On all these grounds, public opinion in many European countries is strongly against Turkey ever joining the EU. Some political leaders, notably President Sarkozy of France, and less vociferously Chancellor Angela Merkel of Germany, have made clear that they are against Turkish accession at any price. Talk of "privileged partnership" may have stopped, but the fact is that no fewer than eighteen of the thirty-five chapters in Turkey's accession talks are currently blocked—some by Cyprus, others by France, and the rest by the EU as a whole because of Turkey's refusal to open its ports and airports to Cypriot vessels. And France and Austria are still threatening to put Turkish membership, if it is ever offered, to a referendum, which would likely produce a no vote in both places.

These four explanations for today's enlargement problems ought not to constitute insuperable obstacles to creative and forceful politicians. But to surmount them would require much stronger political leadership among the existing EU members, especially in the countries that are most fiercely against enlargement, such as France, Germany, Austria, and the Netherlands. Unfortunately, there is little sign of any such leadership at the moment. To the contrary, in most of these countries leaders are pandering to rather than trying to change voters' anti-enlargement instincts. Until this changes, enlargement as a policy goal of the EU will continue to be in trouble.

Despite these obstacles, the natural force of momentum should slowly but steadily carry the Western Balkan countries forward toward Brussels. It is hard, when simply looking at a map, to see any principle that could be invoked permanently to exclude any of these countries from EU membership. Indeed, Balkan diplomats now like to refer to the inclusion of their countries in the EU not as an enlargement at all, but rather as a completion of Europe's integration, a way of filling in the missing piece of the continent, and as a finishing touch to the European project. For all their difficulties and their testy bilateral disputes, of which the EU is understandably wary, these countries are also small and thus relatively easy, at least in principle, to absorb into the EU's structure.

The Case for Turkey

None of this can be said of Turkey. On present trends, Turkey's population will overtake Germany's soon after 2015, so by any realistic timetable for its accession it would be the biggest EU member (and thus be entitled to the most members of the European Parliament (MEPs) and to the largest voting weight in the Council of Ministers). Although, as explained earlier, it has been accepted as a European country for many years, and it even has in Istanbul the biggest city in Europe (larger now than Moscow), the bulk of its landmass (and population) lies on the Asian side of the Bosphorus Strait. And although it is not the only Muslim country that might one day become a member of the EU (both Albania and Kosovo are mainly Muslim, and Bosnia also has a substantial Muslim population), it would be by far the biggest.

Yet if the EU or any individual country were to reject Turkey's application completely, the consequences would be disastrous, not only for Turkey but also for the European project as a whole. A hostile but economically successful country on the edge of the EU could hardly be seen as an advantage to Europe. A Turkey that leaned more toward Syria, Iran, Russia, and the Turkic world could easily turn into a strategic (and military) loss to the West (hence a recent stream of articles in the international press on the theme of "who lost Turkey?"). It is worth remembering that for several centuries Ottoman Turkey was an implacable foe of Western Europe.

A rejection of Turkey would also be seen in the Middle East, the Arab world, and even inside the EU as a rejection of Islam, however much those who are against Turkish membership might deny this. That would be bad not only for the EU's relationship with the entire region but also for the position of the 20 million or so Muslims who already live in EU countries and can sometimes feel socially and politically excluded. And if the door were ever slammed for good on Turkey, it seems highly unlikely that any way could be found of settling the problem of Cyprus, divided between a Greek-Cypriot south and a Turkish-Cypriot north, which would accordingly continue to fester inside the EU as well as damage relations between the EU and NATO.

On the other hand, a Turkey that was admitted to the EU would bring substantial advantages with it. A dynamic economy and a young workforce are rarities inside today's Europe. A Europe that faces serious demographic decline would surely find the addition of a country with a fast-growing population and a median age of only 28 a big asset. Turkey's military clout (it has the biggest army in Europe) would lend weight to the EU's aspirations to a bigger defense role in the world. The EU's ambitions to play a bigger foreign policy role would also benefit from the inclusion of the world's seventeenth biggest economy, with a strategic role in the Caucasus, in relations with Iran and the Arab countries, and also in dealing with Russia.

Turkish diplomats used to moan to Westerners that they were living in a bad neighborhood. Today Turkey has a new policy labeled by the Turkish foreign minister, Ahmet Davutoglu, as "zero problems with the neighbors." In pursuit of this new policy goal, Turkey is playing an increasingly important economic and diplomatic role with Syria, Iraq, and Iran, in the Caucasus, and with Russia. Its unique position as a member of NATO and of other Western clubs such as the Council of Europe and the OECD, and as a member of the Organization of the Islamic Conference, serves to reinforce Turkey's strategic significance.

Almost every day brings reminders of the growing importance of Turkey as an energy corridor. The Baku-Tbilisi-Ceyhan oil pipeline, and its equivalent for gas, is an important route from the Caspian basin to the West. The 2009 signing of an agreement to build the Nabucco pipeline between Turkey and Austria, which may be hugely important in reducing the EU's dependence on Russian gas by providing new possibilities for oil and gas from the Caspian basin and perhaps from Turkmenistan and Iran, was a further important development. In addition, Turkish entry into the EU would surely offer the best, and perhaps the only, chance to settle the Cyprus dispute.

For all these reasons, I see the future of Turkey in the EU as a crucial issue for the EU's own future. Economically and in foreign policy the EU needs to find some way of accommodating Turkey if it is to sustain its present strength as a global player. If it cannot manage this, its economic and diplomatic weight will decline and its position in the Muslim and especially Arab worlds will deteriorate sharply. The Turkish question is thus now as much about the future of the European Union as it is about the future of Turkey.

Conclusion

Enlargement has been one of the European Union's most important and beneficial single projects, perhaps coming behind only the single currency and the single market. It is the EU's most successful single foreign policy by far. It had a critical influence in securing democracy, prosperity, and the rule of law in the countries of the Mediterranean after they threw off autocracy in the 1970s. It then did the same for the countries of Central and Eastern Europe after the collapse of communism in the 1990s. Now the lure of possible membership in the EU is proving just as crucial in driving forward reform and promoting stability in the Western Balkans, Turkey, and even such far-off places as Moldova and the Caucasus.

So much for the advantages that enlargement can bring to aspirants or potential aspirants. But it is also the case that the EU has benefited internally from admitting so many new members. The European economy has been strengthened by the arrival of fast-growing emerging markets that have been eagerly catching up with the West. Europe's foreign policy and trading clout have been reinforced. European business has gained a lot from the increased competitive pressure, and from the ability to outsource production to cheaper locations in Eastern Europe. And the sclerotic, somewhat inward-looking nature of the Brussels bureaucracy has been shaken up, to everyone's advantage, by the need continually to redefine itself along with the growing membership of the EU.

For all of these reasons, enlargement continues to be an essential plank in the future building of Europe. And that is why the crisis of confidence in the euro and even in the EU and the problems this creates for further enlargement are so worrying. If Europe's leaders cannot raise their heads above the parapet to defend and support further enlargement, often against an instinctively hostile public opinion at a time of great economic difficulty, the health of the European Union itself could begin to suffer.

Notes

1. Most notably, the British government, which unlike most other EU governments eschewed transitional protection against labor migration in 2004, hugely underestimated the number of Poles who would choose to leave Poland to find work in Britain.

2. Iceland, incidentally, also meets with broad approval as a potential candidate for the EU, but the chances of early entry for that country are receding at this writing in 2011, and there is every possibility that in the end Icelandic voters might, like their Norwegian counterparts, decide against joining.

CHRISTOFFER KØLVRAA AND JAN IFVERSEN

5 The European Neighborhood Policy: Geopolitics or Value Export?

With the accession of the Central and Eastern European Countries (CEECs) to the European Union in 2004, the EU acquired new neighbors to the east. The European Neighborhood Policy (ENP) was formulated as a way of coping with these new neighbors, as an alternative to additional enlargement. It signaled a new and innovative external policy based on offering a privileged relationship to specific third countries. "Neighborhood" forcefully entered the language of the EU's foreign policy. In addition to meaning "those next door," the concept of neighbors and a neighborhood carried certain geopolitical connotations. "Neighborhood" can be synonymous with the "near abroad," which would be of particular interest for any state acting internationally. But neighborhood also points in a different direction. We are expected to have a special relationship with our neighbors. Neighbors are of more concern to us than countries farther away.

The ENP is based on the assumption of a privileged relationship and couched in the language of responsibilities and expectations. Responsibility and obligation point toward a moral discourse based on the recognition of universal values. However, values are not simply introduced into the ENP through references to the international norms and standards that are the backbone of liberal theories of international relations. The articulation of responsibilities and duties also involves specific kinds of positioning. It opens up the question of who is entitled to endorse universal values and export them. In the ENP, we argue, these questions are dealt with in a civilizational discourse. Civilization entails more than just recognition of universal values. It is also about who is in a position to export them and why.

We believe that the formulation of the ENP draws from two competing discourses, a geopolitical and a civilizational discourse. With the tools of discourse analysis, we look at how the two discourses shape the official presentation and justification of the ENP. We first describe the ideal types of each discourse, drawing support from the extensive scholarly debate on the ENP, which in many ways confirms our choice of framing. We hope to show that some of the problems encountered by the ENP are rooted in its discursive setting and can be explained by a constant and unresolved tension between the two discourses.

The Geopolitical Discourse

Geopolitics is no doubt inescapable. Politicians reason geopolitically. They make assumptions about places and territories in their policy formulations.[1] Geopolitical discourse is basically about the ordering of territorial space and the state's ability to secure its interests in that space. This is true even if current scholarship under the heading of critical geopolitics has expanded its scope to include all possible links between geographic imagination and state policies.[2] A similar tendency to broaden the understanding of territoriality has been under way for several decades within international relations (IR). A programmatic text from 2001 announced a grand theoretical redirection of IR theory through a reconceptualization of the links between identity, borders, and political order.[3] Since then it has become commonplace to view geopolitical reasoning as interwoven with identity politics. A new subdiscipline, border studies, has even emerged to study the links between borders and identities.[4]

However, when scholars today speak of a "return of geopolitics" in foreign policy, they most often seem to mean the return of a classical mode of geopolitical reasoning. Even if the scholarly literature on geopolitics contains abundant views of what should be included under the label, it tends to be rather more spare in tracing out the semantics of geopolitical discourse. Virginie Mamadou and Gertjan Dijkink condense the "geopolitical codes" to "characterize the map of friends and foes to evaluate places abroad in the national interest of the state."[5] Obviously, geopolitical discourse implies a subject, often in the shape of a state that acts on an external territory. There seems to be agreement that the essence of geopolitics is control of territory.[6] It furthermore follows from Mamadou and Dijkink's definition that the control of territory relates to state interests, which become the basis for legitimating external policies. Beyond the abstract level of "reasons of state," the articulation of such interests varies according to the geopolitical context of a particular space, but access to necessary resources and security issues typically loom large. Geopolitics can even be seen as "the construction of security in spatial terms."[7]

Controlling a territory logically involves setting borders. Geopolitical discourse is thus also a border constructing operation. If we claim that territory is the main nodal point, these borders are primarily defined in spatial terms. But most scholars of geopolitics also include cultural and political boundary markers in their analyses. Klaus Dodds lists "borders, resources, flows, territories and identities" as the main features of geopolitics.[8] Although we do not doubt that territories and borders—in short, ideas about geography—are intimately related to identity issues, we believe that basic geopolitics concerns the "pure" relation between state and territory. In geopolitics, states define territories, and vice versa. States control territories in different ways depending on their political order; and territory is a crucial factor in determining this order, as traditional scholars of geopolitics untiringly claimed. Geopolitical discourse creates and upholds this relation, which involves a differentiation between "places of greater or lesser importance" for the state within a "spatialized" world.[9] Geopolitics orders space, sets priorities, and configures vital interests in relation to the relevant geography. The "near abroad" is simultaneously an external space—on the other side of the border—and a space of utmost importance to the state. Spaces of lesser importance have no subject position in the discourse. In their most dramatic form, as in the case of buffer zones, they can become anonymous spaces used for resource procurement or the transit of goods. The subject position is restricted to those deemed "major powers," whose competing interests are played out in their "buffer zones" or "near abroad."

We are aware that phenomena such as globalization seem to seriously challenge the concept of territoriality. It is in vogue to talk about deterritorialization as an effect of globalization. As we see it, however, deterritorialization does not mean the elimination of territory—which would be absurd—but is just another way of understanding the link between territory and state, which is typically captured by scholars of geopolitics by including "flows" in their definition.

Despite the challenges involved, geopolitics has not been absent from EU studies. The challenges obviously stem from the fact that the EU is not a typical state, and it does not control its territory in the way that a single state does. Broadly speaking, the geopolitical perspective was introduced to help explain the security situation in "post-Wall Europe."[10] The role of the EU's "near abroad" and the growing "fuzzyness" of the borders with countries in the waiting line for membership were emphasized.[11] Enlargement was seen as a sort of geopolitical trap that posed embarrassing questions about who was in and who was out. As Christopher Hill warned in 2002, in an analysis of the impact of enlargement, "the EU will not be able to avoid geopolitical reasoning."[12] This is certainly also true for the ENP.

We claim that two perspectives have dominated analyses of the ENP. The first relates to the EU's power and obligation to project its ideals and policies to external recipients, the second to the geopolitical "entrapment" of the EU. The first perspective has dominated a scholarly debate about the EU's specific civilian or normative power and its capacity to act externally; the second has primarily revolved around the new security issues associated with the EU's neighborhood. Below, we discuss how the former perspective can be related to a civilizational discourse. For now, we will concentrate on the latter.

Although it is not that unusual to refer to geopolitics in studies of the ENP, it seems to be a doxa to stress that this perspective should be avoided when dealing with the EU's external policies. There is probably a straightforward reason for this. Geopolitics still has a rather questionable reputation as being cynical and amoral. Pointing to geopolitical reasoning is thus often accompanied by a claim that one is uncovering underlying factors or hidden motives. Geopolitics is a part of the EU's foreign policy reasoning, but rarely a very evident one.

The first analyses of the ENP followed immediately after its introduction.[13] The notion of a "wider Europe," which prepared the ground for the ENP, also captured the interest of scholars. Already the wider Europe framework was seen as a way of coping with the EU's neighborhood in two ways, geographically and normatively.[14] Emerson coined the term "a friendly kind of European Monroe Doctrine" to play down the geopolitical connotations when speaking of geography and to avoid the "smells of hegemonic possession and old style *Realpolitik*."[15] But a Monroe Doctrine is still geopolitically tinged. William Wallace, in his account of the initiative from the following year, did not refer explicitly to geography, but still emphasized the EU's "vulnerability to its neighbours" as "the background threat of disorder spilling across its borders."[16] In one of the first lengthier studies, aimed at exploring the geopolitical background of the "wider Europe" initiative, Sandra Lavenex concluded that the new policy was to a large extent "driven by strategic possession goals."[17]

Seeing it as primarily a response to security issues arising from new unstable neighbors has been a dominant strand in the debate on the ENP. Often the link between security and geopolitics is taken for granted. One scholar even sees the whole enlargement process as a way for the EU to approach "geopolitical issues" from a "soft security template."[18] Some scholars have focused on border issues by highlighting the creation of "new dividing lines between insiders and outsiders."[19] Others have endorsed the rhetorical and conceptual balancing proposed by Emerson in speaking of "soft" or '"postnational" geopolitics.[20] Soft or not, the framing of the ENP as geopolitics means focusing almost exclusively on issues of "instability," "crises," "conflict prevention," and "security risks," as Robert Aliboni does in his impressive listing of possible threats arising from the neighborhood.[21] Such lists can be followed by more explicit uses of geopolitical metaphors and images, including "buffer zones," "concentric circles," and "hubs and spokes."[22] This does not leave much doubt about the conclusion: the ENP is a manifestation of geopolitical reasoning.

In a fascinating analysis from 2007, Christopher Browning and Pertti Joenniemi epitomize the whole debate on geopolitics in the ENP. They focus on "the geostrategic discourses" forming the ENP.[23] The term "geostrategy" is borrowed from William Walters, who used it to designate different ways of "organising the space of the border."[24] In fact, Walters was one of the first to introduce conceptual tools explicitly targeted at analyzing the EU's geopolitical discourse. In their analysis of the ENP, Browning and Joenniemi discuss whether the border space the ENP is concerned with has been conceptualized as a "networked non-border," such as those within the EU crisscrossed by all kind of flows and movements; as a "march" akin to the classical zone between competing powers or the buffer zone around the primary territory of a major power;[25] as a "colonial frontier," across which a transformation of the periphery is carried out often in the form of a civilizing mission; or finally as a "limes" (boundary or line of fortification), which relates to an understanding of external territory as a source of threats to protect oneself from. This is the type that resonates best with the focus on security. If the ENP is seen mainly as motivated by the growing threat of disorder from the neighbors, efforts to fence the EU off from these threats would seem logical. The fencing off, or limes, is forcefully captured in metaphors like "gated community" and "fortress Europe."[26]

It can be questioned whether the "networked non-border" is, in fact, a geopolitical strategy for controlling the border space, since it seems exactly to involve a common agreement to relinquish control of borders, if not to simply eliminate them. Likewise we question whether the colonial frontier is best understood as a mode of geopolitics. With its language of duty and obligation, rather than of state interests, security, and resources, we would instead place it within a civilizational discourse unbound by territory in a way that geopolitical modes or strategies can never be. In their evaluation of the ENP, Browning and Joenniemi disregard the possibility that the neighborhood is conceptualized through the geostrategy of the networked non-border, which would make it indistinguishable from the EU's internal space. Instead they follow the dominant trend of seeing the ENP as primarily resulting from a rather cynical geopolitical reasoning ("the policy's initial overriding logic and rationale has arguably been one of limes geostrategy"), although they hasten to add that the other strategies "have also played important roles."[27] In this way they reproduce Emerson's balancing between the normative and the geographic.

We see the concern with geopolitics within the scholarly evaluations of the ENP as a manifest illustration of the importance of the geopolitical discourse. From the reading of these evaluations, as well as from a broader reading of the meta-reflections within the academic field of geopolitics, we are confident that we can identify the nodal points and the main positions articulated within a geopolitical discourse as it emerges in the political documents of the ENP.

The Civilizational Discourse

If geopolitical discourse is essentially about the separation of spaces and about state interests in controlling territory, the civilizational discourse is about differences in time and about a civilized center transforming a less-civilized periphery. Underlying the civilizational discourse is a basic historical teleology first formulated by Enlightenment philosophers.[28] Civilization is here essentially the conclusion of a civilizing process: "Civilization is something which happens to a community . . . whereby it approaches nearer to an ideal state [of civility]."[29] This is contrary to the popular understanding of civilization as only a macro-cultural unit confronting other units of the same kind.[30] Civilization—in the singular—concerns values rather than culture. Value is a nodal point in this discourse. Civilizational discourse therefore centers on the transfer of values in a process of "educating."[31] The civilizing mission rests on a claim that the difference between the civilized and the less so is of a temporal nature.[32] The values of the center do not represent a particular culture, but a more advanced stage of history. They are therefore to be viewed as universal.

In being universal, they can legitimately be transferred to others without employing any particularistic notion of state interests. The transfer is viewed instead as a duty, an obligation, or indeed as an altruistic act.[33] The bringing of civilization must take place for the sake of the less-civilized. In the act of civilizing, the particular interests and priorities of the center must be suppressed and replaced by a language of duties, responsibilities, and—in its most pathetic form—self-sacrifice. Following discourse analysis, we can say that the civilizational discourse constructs a subject that always acts on behalf of the grateful other. It is from his position that the duty to civilize "for the savages' own sake" can draw its ultimate legitimacy. The periphery is given a position in the civilizational discourse, but it is severely limited and only allows the articulation of the calling for or expectations of the benevolent gift of universal values.[34]

It should be clear by now that neither the geopolitical nor the civilizational discourse can be identified solely by its conceptual architecture. A reference to values or to territories is not enough to identify a civilizational or geopolitical discourse. We must also show the presence of certain modes of legitimation and the presence of certain kinds of subject positions. It is certainly possible to argue geopolitically for the spread of democratic values—for example, by conceiving of such an action as a way to safeguard one's own security, interests, or indeed hegemony. "Hegemony through democratization" is no more an oxymoron than its opposite, "Bombing for democracy," where a civilizational discourse employs means that at first seem antithetical to it.

This confusion between what pertains to the conceptual architecture and what concerns the discursive structure proper is in fact a persistent issue in the literature, which since the early 1970s has attempted to come to terms with the particular nature of the EU's international power. François Duchêne's conceptualization of a "civilian power Europe" is often taken to be the first analysis of a common European foreign policy in a framing drawing on civilizational discourse.[35] But even a cursory reading of Duchêne reveals that the "civilian means" he advocates (trade, diplomacy, international organizations) are motivated by clearly geopolitical arguments. These means, he argues, are Europe's only hope of securing its interests and autonomy in a world of superpowers. Duchêne's power might be "civilian," but there is nothing selflessly civilizational about it.

It was only as the concept of "civilian power Europe" experienced a renaissance from the 1990s onward that it started to become more civilizational in the true sense of the word.[36] Being "civilian" (that is, nonmilitary) was no longer the determining factor in being a "civilian power." What mattered more were the "civilized" goals that such a power would pursue—by whatever means necessary. Stelios Stavridis could, for instance, state the common view that "thanks to the militarizing of the Union, the latter might at long last be able to act as a real civilian power in the world, that is to say as a force for the external promotion of democratic principles."[37] As regards perhaps the most influential theory of Europe's international power to have emerged in recent years—Ian Manners's "normative power Europe"—we can initially detect the same tension.[38] Manners's argument centers on norm diffusion as the core mode through which Europe influences the surrounding world. But norm diffusion is not civilizational per se. It is also part of what Joseph Nye famously conceptualized as "soft power"—and which he considered a core branch of American foreign influence, but which did not carry any "altruistic" ambitions or connotations.[39] There is nothing inherently enlightened or altruistic about diffusing norms—in its most brutal form this is what totalitarian propaganda aims to do. Manners's argument only becomes clearly civilizational when he argues that the EU's norm diffusion is based on universal values and not motivated by a desire to dominate, which would go against the recent European history of transcending the geopolitical manoeuvering of the Westphalian system. It is the implication of Europe's advanced historical state (that is, post-Westphalian) linked to the claim that Europe embodies universal values, and the denial of selfish motives of domination, that indicates the presence of a civilizational discourse. Thus when Manners points out that this history and the current value-based form of European Community "predisposes it [the EU] to act in a normative way in world politics," this implies acting in "a civilized way"—or indeed in "a civilizing way."[40]

If a civilizational discourse has already been articulated in scholarly debates over the EU's foreign policy activities in general, then it is perhaps no surprise to also find it present as a dominant frame for the ENP. Many scholars argue that the ENP is legitimated and formed by the real or imagined "attraction" of Europe for its neighbors. The neighbors' "great expectations" for the EU are exactly what legitimizes a civilizing mission concerned with spreading European/universal values. Understood in this way, the ENP is not born from geopolitical concerns about controlling territories, but caused by the need to respond to these expectations: "it [the EU] has, after all, been a success story, and others want to share in that."[41] The neighbors are, however, expressing hopes for a "full civilizing mission," which includes the prospect of full membership, as in the case of Ukraine. The ENP is therefore premised on the pull or attraction of the EU, but simultaneously it is a strategy to divert these desires of the periphery away from their original object: EU membership. Karen Smith has forcefully argued that the ENP is designed to handle a situation where on the one hand "enlargement fatigue" in the Union prevents it from opening up a candidate track for the neighbors, while on the other hand it must seek to handle or "half-satisfy" the expectations of the outside.[42] In this reading, the ENP becomes a form of "ersatz enlargement,"[43] a "conciliation prize,"[44] or even "a placebo"[45]—an attempt to deliver just enough to avoid completely alienating the neighbors, while making no promises that the new privileged relationship formulated in the ENP might lead to accession. But neighborhood is still inscribed in a civilizational discourse, even if the center becomes something of a "reluctant empire," since the background assumption is that the ENP is an obligatory response to a set of expectations, a duty or a responsibility toward those who are privileged as neighbors. Scholars have been critical of the ENP. Most of the criticism has, however, been directed at its poor performance and has not targeted the basic assumption that the world beyond Europe is attracted to the European success story. There is thus a tendency to accept the basic civilizational framing.

One of the few authors who actually engage directly in a critical discussion of this framing of the ENP is Pertti Joenniemi.[46] Joenniemi draws inspiration from an argument made in more general terms by Thomas Diez about European identity construction becoming noticeably more spatial.[47] Diez claimed that a more geopolitical "othering" was replacing an earlier temporal focus on Europe's past as the other. Joenniemi agrees on the "return of geopolitics," but insists that the temporal perspective has been intact and just transferred to the external other. Europe thereby emerges as a superior moral and civilized space, against a neighboring outside that is perceived as less developed and "located in the past."[48]

The civilizational discourse is indeed present in scholarly treatments of the ENP, even when it is not about the comparison with enlargement. A civilizational discourse is often implicated the moment a concept such as civilian or normative power is introduced. Esther Barbé and Elisabeth Johansson-Nogués see in the ENP the Union's ambition to illustrate that it is "a force for good" in the international realm, but also emphasize that it is continuously hampered by the need to balance values and utility—that is, to balance on the one hand the high-minded principles of a civilizational discourse and on the other hand the effectiveness of the policy in a concrete setting.[49] Ronald Dannreuther also implicitly invokes an image of temporal distancing when he claims that the "capacity for 'transformational diplomacy,' through imitation rather than imposition" is "central to the EU's claim for its distinctive role in international affairs."[50]

The ENP involves a temporal transformation of the neighbors, which presumably will bring them closer to the EU's standard. Already implicit in the concept of civilian power today—especially when moving toward the idea of normative power—is an assumption that this is not simply another kind of power, but an advanced and postmodern form of power. Indications of the EU's advanced stage—as regards its unique character as a foreign policy actor—can be found in the prevailing use of the prefix *post-*. Dannreuther, for instance, claims that the ENP will be "the principal testing ground for validating the EU's distinctive claim to be a transformative "post-"Westphalian power, gaining influence through encouraging the internal transformation of societies rather than through physical or military coercion."[51] The EU has in a way left behind the modern techniques of military coercion and is exercising its *mission civilisatrice* with means appropriate to its stage of development. Not only are the neighbors "backward"—ready and calling for a transformative gesture from the European center—but so are other major international actors, which are stuck with modern means. Michael E. Smith distinguishes the EU's approach to the neighborhood from the heavy-handed American policies for securing influence. He goes so far as calling it a "benevolent imperialism" because it is aimed at the diffusion of democratic standards.[52]

Another interesting element in Dannreuther's argument is the reference to the neighborhood as a "testing ground." This is typical of what happens when the civilizational discourse is applied to the ENP at the expense of the geopolitical one. In geopolitics space is specific in the sense that geography, location, and resources of a certain territory take on prime importance. In a pure civilizational discourse the spread of universal values is not conditioned by the contingencies of a specific space. The endeavors of civilization are universal; the values are good and applicable anywhere and everywhere. The designation of the neighborhood as a "testing ground" transforms this space from a distinct geopolitical border zone into a seemingly arbitrary starting point for a missionary activity of universal ambitions. As a testing ground the neighborhood is reduced to just one instance of a much larger uncivilized outside.

As shown, the tension between the particularities of *our* neighborhood—inadvertently a geopolitical content—and the universal qualities and ambitions of Europe's civilizing external endeavors runs through the analyses of the ENP. We now turn to the concrete articulations of the policy to demonstrate that civilization and geopolitics are co-present in it, and that this overlapping and juxtaposing of two different discourses explain the distinctive form and mode of legitimation that characterize the policy.

Geopolitical and Civilizational Discourse in the Formulations of the ENP

Around the year 2000 the European Council and the Commission began to reflect on the future situation of the EU after the planned entry of the CEECs that were negotiating membership. In a speech in March 2000 on the coming enlargement, the president of the EU Commission, Romano Prodi, expressed concern about the "new neighbors" bordering the new member states and called for a "neighborhood policy."[53] Two years later, High Representative for the Common Foreign and Security Policy Javier Solana, and Commissioner for External Relations Chris Patten formulated a letter to the Council (at the request of the latter) entitled "Wider Europe," laying the groundwork for a proximity policy toward Europe's new neighbors to the east.[54] The neighbors treated in the letter become meaningful in a geopolitical discourse in which they are primarily understood in geographic terms. In a way, this resonates with a literal understanding of neighbors as defined by geographic proximity.

Neighbors are neither family, which indicates closeness and sameness, nor enemy. To be geopolitically framed, a discussion of neighborhood must, however, link to the question of controlling territory for the sake of securing oneself. Neighbors can also be viewed as the source of risks and threats. In presenting the objectives of a new "neighborhood policy," Patten and Solana wrote: "There are a number of overriding objectives for our neighborhood policy: stability, prosperity, shared values and rule of law along our borders are all fundamental for *our own security*. Failure in any of these areas will lead to increased *risks* of negative spillover on the Union."[55]

Here the objectives presented are justified by their alleviation of risks for the EU. These risks are identified as "illegal migration, trafficking and spillover from local or regional crises." The neighbors are thus positioned as places of instability. Solana and Patten initially define the eastern neighbors through their ambivalent position in relation to the possibility of future membership. For these countries such prospects have been neither denied (as they were for the countries of North Africa) nor guaranteed (as for the Balkans). But it soon becomes clear that the priority is to "shape further relations with the countries of the wider border in a manner of our choosing." The East is thoroughly geopolitical and born from the "new geography" of the Union: "When the frontier of the Union shifts eastwards, the opportunities and challenges raised by our eastern neighbors will affect us more directly than today." Even if "shared values" are articulated both as the basis for and as one of the priorities in the cooperation, the broader argument is never civilizational. Even if this geopolitical orientation toward different spaces is to some extent covered over by the grand claim that the policy is designed to avoid creating "new dividing lines in Europe,"[56] Solana and Patten frame a process that stresses the security, interests, and possibilities of the EU in the particular space of the eastern neighbors.

Although this letter is an internal document, not immediately produced for public consumption, one should not conclude that a civilizational discourse is simply "public" rhetoric while geopolitics reigns supreme only behind closed doors. If one reads the European Security Strategy (ESS) of 2003—certainly a public document—there is initially an almost blatant civilizational framing at work. Europe's history is described as one of transcending violence and authoritarian power in favor of a community around the universal values of "rule of law and democracy."[57] Solana, the author of the strategy paper, begins with an appraisal of the universal and selfless ambitions of Europe's external activities: "Europe should be ready to share in the responsibility for global security and in building a better world."[58] However, in the section of the security strategy directly devoted to the ENP, geography makes an abrupt comeback: "Even in an era of globalization, geography is still important: It is in the European interest that countries on our borders are well-governed."[59]

The strategy paper is a document that seems caught in the tension between, on the one hand, geopolitical claims about the dangers close by—for example, insecurity spillover and transiting threats—and, on the other hand, grander claims about Europe's responsibility to the world, its duty to become a global player, and its unique civilian methods and civilized goals.

The geopolitical framing of the neighbors is also co-present with a more civilizational one in other speeches and documents from the ENP's first years. Metaphors and semantics with a geopolitical connotation such as "near abroad" (cautiously supported by quotation marks),[60] "gates of Europe,"[61] or "zones of instability"[62] reappear with some regularity in the documents and speeches concerning the ENP. However, the geopolitical framing is not reducible to semantics. The presence of a geopolitical discourse is also indicated by the way neighbors are positioned in relation to the European subject. The neighbors are not accused of being directly responsible for the threats subsumed under the heading of "instability." The neighborhood is viewed as a site of insecurity, but the neighbors are not perceived as the actors producing it. The perpetrators are said to be somewhere else, if they are named at all. Most often threats are conceived of as flowing and transiting through the space of the neighborhood. Even the threats themselves are designated as movable. In one of the first communications on the ENP, they are listed as "the trans-border dimension of environmental and nuclear hazards, communicable diseases, illegal immigration, trafficking, organized crime or terrorist networks."[63] In the geopolitical discourse neighbors are thus reduced to being transit countries between a Europe to be protected and the dangers on the other side. In classical geopolitics this was characterized as a buffer zone. The buffer has meaning only for those in need of protection. Living in a buffer zone is devoid of meaning. The geopolitical spatialization of the neighborhood as transit and buffer is at the same time a process of deculturalization. It is not really important whether the neighbors share "our values" if their primary role is to be transit countries. This is, however, a crucial issue in the civilizational framing of the ENP.

It was between the Patten-Solana letter and the Security Strategy that the ENP received its perhaps most unambiguously civilizational framing. In a speech in late 2002 that served to officially launch the ENP, the president of the EU Commission, Romano Prodi, almost completely suppressed its geopolitical dimension. Although some geopolitical semantics slipped through, the speech's framing neutralizes their effect. When Prodi at one point speaks of the neighbors as "our backyard," the geopolitical reading of such a metaphor—a space of unrivaled control—is undermined because the passage in which it occurs is all about the attraction that the neighbors feel for Europe.[64] In fact, the selfless and duty-bound construction of the activities of the central subject proper to a civilizational discourse is an ever-present feature in Prodi's speech. His proximity policy is much more about the desires and expectations of the neighbors than it is about the security interests of the Union: "Lasting and sustainable stability in the European region has been the crowning achievement of the European Union. This is what we do best, if I may say so. . . . We should recognise that this success creates legitimate expectations in the EU's future neighbours."[65]

Terms such as "duty," "responsibility," and "hope" (on the part of the neighbors) appear often in the speech; it contains no references to the EU's interests. The question that frames Prodi's speech is not the same as that in the Solana-Patten letter. If the Solana-Patten letter revolved around the issue of how to protect the Union from potential threats from the new periphery, then Prodi's speech, in his own words, is about "what we have to offer to our neighbors." What is on offer is "everything but the institutions." The ENP will transfer the very "essence" of the Union—its values and principles—to the neighbors.[66]

This theme of treasures selflessly offered to the periphery is so dominant that it ultimately transforms even core geographic concepts. When Prodi at the end of his speech states, "We should be prepared to offer them a reasonable degree of proximity," it is clear that proximity is no longer a stable and unchanging geopolitical fact to be dealt with, but has itself become a metaphor for transformations inherent in the Union's civilizing endeavors in the neighborhood. The geopolitical particularity of the neighborhood thus progressively evaporates. In the end it is indeed no more than a "testing ground" or a "starting point" for a mission of properly universal proportions: "We have to assume our role as a global player. The development of a substantive proximity policy should be one of the first steps. We need to institute a new and inclusive regional approach that would help keep and promote peace and foster stability and security throughout the continent, ultimately promoting the emergence of better global governance."[67]

It is this kind of civilizational discourse that dominates many of the official declarations on the ENP, even if geopolitics can never be entirely suppressed. The reason is not simply the realist argument that the EU lacks the hard power of a classical geopolitical hegemon to actually dominate adjacent "zones of influence." The unavailability of the geopolitical discourse to EU actors is also—if not primarily—born from the fact that such formulations are rendered ideologically unavailable because they would conflict with a core dimension of the Union's very identity. The EU as a grand political project is fundamentally legitimized as a departure from an earlier disastrous European history dominated by internal wars, genocides, and brutal and uncompromising geopolitical maneuvering by European states in relation to each other and to the outside world.[68] Geopolitics, in this ideological framing, is thought of as the international dimension of a morally vacant *realpolitik*, which the European project imagines itself to have transcended. High-ranking EU officials, in fact, often only mention geopolitics in order to deny its relevance for Europe today. In a speech on enlargement in early 2003, Prodi emphatically declared, "We have left behind us that *realpolitik* that we ourselves invented,"[69] and as early as 2001 Patten, addressing a Russian audience, emphasized that the EU "has no use for geopolitical zones of influence."[70]

This means, however, that trouble predicatively ensues when the EU has to deal with actors who understand themselves as geopolitical powers and expect to be treated as such. As mentioned earlier, geopolitical discourse does not only entail a strict hierarchy between the center and its "sphere of influence"; it also articulates a set of differences in the international space between "buffer zones" or "minor powers" and the level of major powers acting geopolitically. In short, geopolitical discourse simultaneously articulates a conflictual equality between major powers and a stark hierarchy between these and the territories "in between" that they compete to dominate. Whereas geopolitical discourse can therefore deal with "equal but different" powers, civilizational discourse—in its pure form—cannot easily accommodate a position for "other civilizers" because such a presence challenges the universality of the civilized values. There can be only one civilization—those outside that civilization, it is implied, are to varying degrees "less civilized." In the more geopolitical framing of the Solana-Patten letter, Russia was carefully marked out as a special case that could not simply be lumped in with the rest of the neighbors.[71] When Prodi, however, chose to ignore Russia's special status, this placed it on a par with Morocco and Ukraine and thus not distinguished from the other "minor countries" in the peripheral European "ring of friends."[72] In Prodi's first great legitimizing articulation of the ENP there was no room for geopolitical pragmatism. The policy had to be founded on the secure ideological ground of a grand civilizing mission in tune with Europe's transcendent self-understanding. But the price to pay was that the other major power of the neighborhood suddenly found itself on the receiving end of a rather patronizing "rescue mission" from Brussels.

Scholars such as Christopher Browning and Dmitri Trenin have convincingly demonstrated how Russia reestablished itself as a major geopolitical power under Vladimir Putin, which meant perceiving itself as a center of influence different from, but equal to and to some extent in competition with,

Europe and the United States.[73] It is perhaps not surprising therefore that when addressed as part of a "less-civilized" periphery to be salvaged by Europe, Russia's reaction was swift and harsh. As Derek Averre reports, the Russian deputy foreign minister, Vladimir Chizhov, openly insisted that Russia "must be considered as an equal partner and not as the object of a civilising influence exercised by other countries or groups of states."[74]

At the 2003 St. Petersburg summit between the EU and Russia it was made clear that Russia would not participate in the ENP as just another neighbor.[75] In an effort to salvage the policy it was instead agreed to develop the EU-Russian strategic relationship through the creation of four "common spaces," distinct from the framework of the ENP.[76] After the 2003 summit, the EU certainly tried to downplay Russia's refusal to participate in the ENP on par with the other neighbors.[77] But as Hiski Haukkala points out, the difference between a policy of value-dissemination and "spaces of cooperation" is that the EU de facto retracted any claim or implication that Russia needed to be educated about the universal democratic values of the EU.[78] In fact, in an October 2003 speech, Commissioner for Enlargement Günter Verheugen, trying to justify Russia's new special status, became pointedly geopolitical in his characterization of Russia as "much more than a neighbor, since it is a strategic partner; but it is also a neighbor." The relationship was now articulated in a way that emphasized Russia's status as an equal geopolitical power: "Our strategic partnership rests on the common values to which we are committed, on our mutual interests as major international players, and, increasingly, on convergent views."[79]

On closer inspection, however, the civilizational framing had not been abandoned completely. Both in the Joint Statement issued at the 2003 summit and in Verheugen's speech cited above, it was stressed that the "strategic partnership" with Russia would be developed on the basis of "common values."[80] It is interesting to note that Russia here is seen to possess the same values as Europe, in stark contrast to Prodi's earlier ambition to extend European values to a neighborhood that included Russia. Both in the Joint Statement after the summit and in Verheugen's speech, a meeting point between the civilizational language of value dissemination and the geopolitical language of major and minor players is precariously constructed. Russia is afforded the geopolitical privilege of "more than a neighbor," but is in the same move included in the civilizational discourse as a (potential) civilizer alongside Europe.

This balance between civilizational and geopolitical discourse in the ENP and especially as regards Russia was, however, easily upset when the discussion revolved around classical geopolitical issues of external access to essential resources. While speaking about the EU's external energy policy, José Manuel Barroso's commissioner for external relations and neighborhood policy, Benita Ferrero-Waldner, did not mince her words: "Our European Neighborhood Policy was developed as a response to the new geopolitical situation following the May 2004 enlargement."[81] She did not hesitate, either, to designate the neighbors as "transit countries," important mainly for hosting the pipelines through which the EU's energy flowed. In a later speech on the same topic she went so far as to state that "energy issues form a central part of the European Neighborhood Policy. A significant part of the 'great game' in energy is being played out in our backyard."[82] Here there is no longer any secret made of the fact that the ENP—besides its civilizational endeavor to spread European values—is also a "game," whose winners will have influence, resources, and security. Along the same lines, Russia is described as "a key geopolitical actor."[83] The relationship is seemingly no longer about shared values or about the spread of those values. Indeed, as a final irony, Ferrero-Waldner, in the same speech in which she seems to fully accept Russia's status as a major geopolitical power, also berates Russia for its interference and intervention in the Georgian conflict: "[This] remains unacceptable, and we cannot share the principles of foreign policy recently articulated in Moscow, including the resurgence of spheres of influence."[84] In effect, Russia is accepted as a geopolitical power—as long as it does not act as one.

Conclusion

The ENP was conceived in 2002 and vigorously launched the following year. As we have shown, the policy articulations were, from the beginning, manifestly marked by a tension between a geopolitical and a civilizational discourse. In the geopolitical discourse, the EU positioned itself as a rather traditional international player safeguarding its interests. The neighbors were discussed primarily as spaces of instability to be controlled. The civilizational discourse intended to neutralize this geopolitical framing by emphasizing the altruistic and duty-bound relations to the neighbors. The shift from interests to universal values, and from protection to norm diffusion, produced a completely different subject position. For the neighbors, it meant that they changed status: no longer a zone of instability, they became a testing ground for the EU's universal pretentions. The existence of the two discourses has allowed the EU to act as a doppelganger. The neighbors were, however, left with no role to play. With the complete absence of any cultural discourse in the ENP, they were not given the means to make themselves visible. In a cultural discourse, the EU officials could have addressed either the Europeanness of their neighbors or, conversely, their affiliations with other non-European cultures. Then the neighbors would at least have been granted an identity. This option was, however, made impossible by the ersatz character of the ENP, on the one hand, and the distancing involved in calling the neighbors non-European, on the other hand.

The civilizational discourse of the ENP was strongest from 2003 to 2007. Since then, geopolitics seems to have gained an upper hand in dealing with the neighbors. In writing an epitaph for the ENP, Georgia should figure prominently. It was, in fact, the total lack of European response to the Russian invasion of Georgia in 2007 that exposed the vulnerability of the civilizational undergirding. Neighborhood did not count much in the conflict. Perhaps this is why the EU has launched the new Instrument for Stability (IfS), in which neighborhood is no longer in play. In branding this new initiative, Karel Kovanda, deputy director of the Directorate General for External Relations, equates the Georgian conflict with the 2004 Asian tsunami.[85] There is no mention of neighborhood whatsoever. The IfS only works with catastrophes and recipients of aid, in which case the EU no longer portrays itself as a civilizer, but as a conventional donor.

Notes

1. John Agnew and Gearóid Ó Tuathail, "Geopolitical Discourse: Practical Geopolitical Reasoning in American Foreign Policy," *Political Geography* 11, no. 2 (1992): 190–204.

2. Gearóid Ó Tuathail, *Critical Geopolitics: The Politics of Writing Global Space* (London: Routledge, 1996); Virginie Mamadouh, "Geopolitics in the Nineties: One Flag, Many Meanings," *Geojournal* 484 (1998): 237–53; John Agnew, *Geopolitics: Revisioning World Politics* (London: Routledge, 1998); Mark Bassin, "The Two Faces of Contemporary Geopolitics," *Progress in Human Geography* 28, no. 5 (2004): 620–26.

3. Yosef Lapid, "Identities, Borders, Orders: Nudging International Relations Theory in a New Direction," in *Identities, Borders, Orders: Rethinking International Relations Theory*, edited by M. Albert, D. Jacobson, and Y. Lapid (University of Minnesota Press, 2001), pp. 1–21.

4. David Newman and Anssi Paasi, "Fences and Neighbours in the Post-Modern World: Boundary Narratives in Political Geography," *Progress in Human Geography* 22, no. 2 (1998): 186–207.

5. Virginie Mamadouh and Gertjan Dijkink, "Geopolitics, International Relations and Political Geography: The Politics of Geopolitical Discourse," *Geopolitics* 113: 355.

6. Simon Dalby, "American Security Discourse: The Persistence of Geopolitics," *Political Geography Quarterly* 9, no. 2 (1990): 172.

7. Ibid.

8. Klaus Dodds, *Geopolitics: A Very Short Introduction* (Oxford University Press, 2007), p. 3.

9. Agnew, *Geopolitics*, p. 2.

10. Ola Tunander, Pavel Baev, and Victoria I. Einagel, *Geopolitics in Post-Wall Europe* (London: Sage, 1997).

11. Thomas Christiansen, Fabio Petito, and Ben Tonra, "Fuzzy Politics around Fuzzy Borders: The European Union's 'Near Abroad,'" *Cooperation and Conflict* 35 (2000): 389–415.

12. Christopher Hill, "The Geopolitical Implications of Enlargement," in *Europe Unbound: Enlarging and Reshaping the Boundaries of the European Union*, edited by J. Zielonka (London: Routledge, 2002), p. 103.

13. Michael Emerson, "The Shaping of a Policy Framework for the Wider Europe," *CEPS Policy Brief* 39 (Brussels: Centre for European Policy Studies, 2003), pp. 1–14; William Wallace, "Looking after the Neighbourhood: Responsibilities for the EU-25," *Policy Papers* 4 (2003): 1–30; Sandra Lavenex, "EU External Governance in 'Wider Europe,'" *Journal of European Public Policy* 11, no. 4 (August 2004): 680–700.

14. Michael Emerson, "The Wider Europe as the European Union's Friendly Monroe Doctrine," *CEPS Policy Brief* 27 (Brussels: Centre for European Policy Studies, 2002), p. 2.

15. Ibid., p. 20.

16. Wallace, "Looking after the Neighbourhood," p. 19.

17. Lavenex, "EU External Governance in 'Wider Europe,'" p. 695.

18. John O'Brennan, "'Bringing Geopolitics Back In': Exploring the Security Dimension of the 2004 Eastern Enlargement of the European Union," *Cambridge Review of International Affairs* 19, no. 1 (2006): 156.

19. Karen E. Smith, "The Outsiders: The European Neighbourhood Policy," *International Affairs* 84 (2005): 758.

20. James Wesley Scott, "Bordering and Ordering the European Neighbourhood: A Critical Perspective on EU Territoriality and Geopolitics," *Trames* 13, no. 3 (2009): 233.

21. Roberto Aliboni, "The Geopolitical Implications of the European Neighbourhood Policy," *European Foreign Affairs Review* 10 (2005): 1–16.

22. Ruben Zaiotti, "Of Friends and Fences: Europe's Neighbourhood Policy and the 'Gated Community Syndrome,'" paper presented at the 47th Annual International Studies Association Conference, San Diego, California, March 22–25, 2006, pp. 2–27.

23. Christopher S. Browning and Pertti Joenniemi, "Geostrategies of the European Neighbourhood Policy," DIIS Working Paper 9 (Copenhagen: Danish Institute for International Studies, 2007), pp. 1–37.

24. William Walters, "The Frontiers of the European Union: A Geostrategic Perspective," *Geopolitics* 9, no. 2 (2004): 675.

25. Ibid., p. 684.

26. Zaiotti, "Of Friends and Fences," p. 4; Browning and Joenniemi, "Geostrategies of the European Neighbourhood Policy," p. 538.

27. Browning and Joenniemi, "Geostrategies of the European Neighbourhood Policy," p. 531.

28. Jean Starobinski, *Blessings in Disguise or, The Mortality of Evil* (Harvard University Press, 1993); Bruce Mazlish, *Civilization and Its Contents* (Stanford University Press, 2004).

29. R. G. Collingwood, *The New Leviathan or Man, Society, Civilization, and Barbarism* (Oxford University Press, 2003 [1942]), p. 283.

30. Samuel Huntington, "The Clash of Civilizations?" *Foreign Affairs* 72, no. 3 (1993): 22–49; Samuel Huntington, *The Clash of Civilizations and the Remaking of World Order* (New York: Simon and Schuster, 1996).

31. Jan Ifversen, "The Meaning of European Civilization—A Historical-Conceptual Approach," *European Studies Newsletter* 1, no. 2 (1998): 20–38.

32. Johannes Fabian, *Time and the Other—How Anthropology Makes Its Object* (Columbia University Press, 1983); Bernard McGrane, *Beyond Anthropology—Society and the Other* (Columbia University Press, 1989).

33. Lars-Henrik Schmidt, "Mer-villen," *Slagmark*, no. 22 (1993): 7–17.

34. Christoffer Kølvraa, "Imagining Europe as a Global Player: The Ideological Construction of a New European Identity within the EU," Ph.D. dissertation, Aarhus University, 2009.

35. François Duchêne, "Europe's Role in World Peace," in *Europe Tomorrow—16 Europeans Look Ahead*, edited by Richard Mayne (London: Fontana, 1972), pp. 32–47; François Duchêne, "The European Community and the Uncertainties of Interdependence," in *A Nation Writ Large—Foreign-Policy Problems before the European Community*, edited by Max Kohnstamm and Wolfgang Hager (New York: Macmillan, 1973), pp. 1–21.

36. Richard Whitman, "The Fall, and Rise, of Civilian Power Europe?" National Europe Centre Paper 16, paper presented to "The European Union in International Affairs," a conference at the National Europe Centre, Australian National University, July 3–4, 2002; Hans Maull, "The New Civilian Power: Germany and Japan," *Foreign Affairs* 69, no. 5 (1990): 91–106; Karen E. Smith, "The End of Civilian Power EU," *International Spectator* 35, no. 2 (2000): 11–28; Karen E. Smith, "The Outsiders: The European Neighbourhood Policy," *International Affairs* 84 (2005); Stelios Stavridis, "Militarising the EU: The Concept of Civilian Power Revisited," *International Spectator* 36, no. 4 (2001): 43–50.

37. Stavridis, "Militarising the EU," pp. 43–44.

38. Ian Manners, "Normative Power Europe: A Contradiction in Terms?" *JCMS* 40, no. 2 (2002): 235–58.

39. Joseph S. Nye, "Soft Power," *Foreign Policy* 80 (1990): 153–71.

40. Manners, "Normative Power Europe," p. 252.

41. Judy Batt, Dov Lynch, Antonio Missiroli, Martin Ortega, and Dimitrios Triantaphyllou, "Partners and Neighbours: A CFSP for a Wider Europe," *Chaillot Papers* 64 (2003): 119.

42. Smith, "The Outsiders."

43. Carmen Gebhard, "Assessing EU Actorness towards Its 'Near Abroad': The European Neighbourhood Policy," EU CONSENT Network of Excellence Occasional Paper 1 (2007), p. 15 (http://www.eu-consent.net/content.asp?contentid=1459).

44. Michelle Pace, "The European Neighbourhood Policy: A Statement about the EU's Identity," *Internationaler Dialog* 12 (2005): 3.

45. Michael Emerson, "European Neighbourhood Policy: Strategy or Placebo?" Working Document 215 (Brussels: Centre for European Policy Studies, 2004), pp. 1–22.

46. Pertti Joenniemi, "From Enlargement to the Export of Norms: EU-Europe Re-articulated in Time and Space," paper presented at Brit IX Conference, University of Victoria, Canada, January 12–15, 2008, pp. 1–24.

47. Thomas Diez, "Europe's Others and the Return of Geopolitics," *Cambridge Review of International Affairs* 17, no. 2 (2004): 319–35.

48. Joenniemi, "From Enlargement to the Export of Norms," p. 13.

49. Esther Barbé and Elisabeth Johansson-Nougés, "The EU as a Modest 'Force for Good': The European Neighbourhood Policy," *International Affairs* 84 (2008): 81–96.

50. Roland Dannreuther, "Developing the Alternative to Enlargement: The European Neighbourhood Policy," *European Foreign Affairs Review* 11 (2006): 183–84.

51. Ibid., p. 184.

52. Michael E. Smith, "Governing Wider Europe: Eastern Europe and the EU's New Neighbourhood Policy," paper prepared for "International Relations in Eastern Europe," a conference at Humboldt University, Berlin, March 16–18, 2006, p. 17.

53. Romano Prodi, SP/00/112, "Towards the New Europe," Dialogue on Europe Forum, Berlin, March 30, 2000.

54. Chris Patten and Javier Solana, "Wider Europe," joint letter to General Affairs Council, April 2002 (http://www.lfpr.lt/uploads/File/2002-10/Letter.pdf).

55. Ibid., emphasis added.

56. Ibid.

57. European Council, "A Secure Europe in a Better World: European Security Strategy," December 12, 2003.

58. Ibid.

59. Ibid., p. 12.

60. Chris Patten, SP/02/430, "Statement on the European Parliament Report on Progress Achieved in the Implementation of Common Foreign and Security Policy," Plenary Session European Parliament Strasbourg, September 25, 2002.

61. Romano Prodi, SP/03/27, *The Mediterranean Islands at the Heart of Europe*, Sardinia Regional Council Cagliari, January 23, 2003.

62. Günter Verheugen, SP/04/33, *The Neighbourhood Policy of the European Union: An Opportunity for Tunisia*, Institut Arabe des Chefs d'Entreprises, Tunis, January 21, 2004.

63. European Commission, "Wider Europe—Neighbourhood: A New Framework for Relations with Our Eastern and Southern Neighbours," communication to the Council and the European Parliament, Brussels, COM (2003) 103 final, March 11, 2003, p. 5.

64. Romano Prodi, SP/02/619, "A Wider Europe—A Proximity Policy as the Key to Stability," speech at the Sixth ECSA-World Conference, Jean Monnet Project, Brussels, December 5–6, 2002.

65. Ibid.

66. Ibid.

67. Ibid.

68. Kølvraa, "Imagining Europe as a Global Player"; Jan Ifversen and Christoffer Kølvraa, "European Neighbourhood Policy as Identity Politics," paper presented at the EUSA Tenth Biennial International Conference, Montreal, Canada, May 17–19, 2007, pp. 1–33; Ulrik Beck and Edgar Grande, *Cosmopolitan Europe* (London: Polity Press, 2007); Ole Wæver, "Insecurity, Security and Asecurity in the West European Non-War Community," in *Security Communities*, edited by Emanuel Adler and Michael Barnett, pp. 69–118 (Cambridge University Press, 1998).

69. Romano Prodi, "Enlargement of the Union and European Identity," Florence, January 20, 2003.

70. Chris Patten, SP/01/11, "The EU and Russia—The Way Ahead," Diplomatic Academy, Moscow, January 18, 2001.

71. Patten and Solana, joint letter on "Wider Europe," April 2002.

72. Prodi, "A Wider Europe."

73. Dmitri Trenin, *Russia, the EU and the Common Neighbourhood* (London: Centre for European Reform, 2005), pp. 1–8; Christopher S. Browning, "The Region-Building Approach Revisited: The Continued Othering of Russia in Discourses of Region-Building in the European North," *Geopolitics* 8, no. 1 (2003): 45–71.

74. Quoted in Derek Averre, "Russia and the European Union: Convergence or Divergence?" *European Security* 14, no. 2 (2005): 179.

75. Pace, "European Neighbourhood Policy."

76. Ibid., p. 3; Dov Lynch, "The Security Dimension of the European Neighbourhood Policy," *International Spectator* 40, no. 1 (2005): 38.

77. Michele Comelli, "The Challenges of the European Neighbourhood Policy," *International Spectator* 39 (2004): 101.

78. Hiski Haukkala, "The Russian Challenge to EU Normative Power: The Case of European Neighbourhood Policy," *International Spectator* 43, no. 2 (2008): 35–47.

79. Günter Verheugen, "EU Enlargement and the Union's Neighbourhood Policy," Diplomatic Academy, Moscow, October 27, 2003.

80. Joint Statement, EU-Russia Summit, St. Petersburg, May 31, 2003; Verheugen, "EU Enlargement and the Union's Neighbourhood Policy."

81. Benita Ferrero-Waldner, SP/06/710, "Opening Address—Conference: Towards an EU External Energy Policy to Assure a High Level of Supply Security," Brussels, November 20, 2006.

82. Benita Ferrero-Waldner, SP/07/517, "European External Relations and Energy Policy: Towards an International Energy Strategy," EWI/F.A.Z. Energy Conference, Cologne, September 11, 2007.

83. Benita Ferrero-Waldner, SP/08/545, " *EU/Russia: A Challenging Partnership, but One of the Most Important of Our Times,*" EP plenary debate on EU/Russia, Strasbourg, October 21, 2008.

84. Ibid.

85. Karel Kovanda, "Interview: The EU's Role in Crisis Response," in European Commission for External Relations, *Making the Difference—What Works in Response to Crises and Security Threats—The Debate Continues* (Luxembourg: Office for Official Publications of the European Communities, 2009), p. 43.

PART TWO

Immigration, Terrorism, Internal Security: Related or Unrelated Phenomena?

IRINA ANGELESCU

6

One Frontier, Many Boundaries? European Union Migration Policies

When it comes to migration, the European Union's restrictive policies have earned it an (in)famous reputation as "Fortress Europe." Although the EU does not yet have the equivalent of the U.S.-Mexico border wall, it has designed "invisible walls"—restrictive policies ranging from border control to visas and readmission agreements—aimed at controlling the entry of all foreign nationals to its territory.[1]

This chapter discusses the competencies the EU has gained in the field of migration and asylum policies because of the member states' (security) concerns. It argues that the primary lens through which migration is addressed at the EU level is that of securitization (migration is seen as a threat, rather than as an opportunity) and that as a result, the EU has built several boundaries in order to protect its one frontier. This approach has already fundamentally altered the EU's relations with its neighborhood, and is likely to fundamentally affect any future wave of enlargement.

The chapter has three parts. The first section offers a historical overview of the EU's competencies in the field of migration and asylum, the acquisition of which was driven largely by security concerns. The Schengen Convention is illustrative of a trend within the EU whereby a few (big) member states design a policy outside the EU framework according to their preferences, and then incorporate it into the EU *acquis communautaire*. In the majority of cases, these initiatives are meant to prevent migration and have gradually led to a "shift of paradigms for migration" at the EU level from a human rights and development approach to a securitarian framework. The second part illustrates some of the boundaries designed by the EU in order to prevent migration, including restrictive visa policies and agreements with third countries to accept returned migrants. This component illustrates that migration is affected by and can significantly transform external relations between the EU and other countries. Indeed, fear of migration is one of the main arguments used against further enlargements of the EU.

The third section discusses the most recent wave of enlargement, in which the Central and Eastern European Countries (CEECs) were required to adopt the *acquis communautaire* related to migration and asylum, with few exceptions. This process has led to diplomatic and economic tensions between the CEECs and their non-EU neighbors, as well as to domestic resentment because of work restrictions imposed on the CEECs' citizens in the EU labor market. Their experience is relevant inasmuch as future accession negotiations are likely to be carried out according to similar dynamics.

Historical Perspectives: The Gradual Move toward a Securitarian Migration Approach

EU cooperation on immigration and asylum is new in comparison with other issues (such as agriculture and trade), and can be dated back to the Treaty of Maastricht in 1992.[2] However, these issues were always in the background, with discussions about freedom of movement dating back to the very beginning of the European project. Article 3c of the 1957 Treaty of Rome addressed the possibility of an eventual "abolition . . . of obstacles to the freedom of movement," but only for the European Communities (EC, future EU) citizens, not third-country nationals (TCNs).[3] Freedom of movement of people is one of the four fundamental freedoms of the European project (together with free movement of goods, capital, and services). With the gradual disappearance of internal borders between the EU member states and the creation of one external border to delimit and protect the territories of (most of) the EU, efforts were concentrated on consolidating the external borders in order to best protect freedom of movement within the common European space.

The EU has been granted some competencies in the field of migration because of the member states' inability to deal effectively with this challenge by themselves.[4] This is not to say that the member states always opt for multilateralism over unilateralism in migration matters. Unilateral and bilateral solutions are still the preferred path, but multilateralism is resorted to whenever "existing policies are deemed inadequate for the magnitude of the problem at hand."[5] Already in 1975 the so-called "Trevi Group," an informal intergovernmental body, addressed issues of cross-border terrorism and migration through more coordinated law enforcement efforts. The Single European Act of 1986 foresaw the abolition of internal borders and the harmonization of policies related to free movement of EU citizens and migration control of TCNs within the single European space. In the 1980s, the Schengen and Dublin Conventions were designed to limit the access of TCNs to the EU territory and to prevent asylum seekers from applying in more than one EU member state.

As pointed out at the beginning of the chapter, the Schengen Convention is an example of a policy designed (in 1984–85) outside the EC/EU framework by a few member states (France and Germany, soon joined by Belgium, Luxembourg, and the Netherlands) that was later incorporated into the EU *acquis*. The Schengen Convention, signed in 1990, has a double aim: on the one hand, to eliminate the internal barriers among its (EU) member states, and on the other hand, to increase security at the external borders through means such as policing and surveillance technologies. Some of the measures taken to achieve these goals are the creation of a common visa for all the Schengen member states as well as a Schengen Information System (SIS) that allows the exchange of relevant information among its members. The desire to abolish internal borders among the member states was driven by the goal to ensure economic growth, whereas the hardening of external borders was intended to ensure EU security (which became even more necessary where the internal borders between member states were abolished). All in all, the creation of the Schengen area resulted in a situation whereby "while internal borders among EU member states are gradually being abolished, external EU borders are being tightened up."[6]

Because EU membership does not automatically translate into Schengen membership, the adoption of the Schengen system has led to a situation in which "borders" were set between the Schengen and non-Schengen EU member states.[7] To complicate things further, some non-EU states are part of the Schengen area. As Figure 6-1 shows, four of the twenty-seven EU member states are not Schengen countries (Bulgaria, Ireland, Romania, and the United Kingdom), while three non-EU member states are currently part of Schengen (Iceland, Norway, and Switzerland).

According to Ivan Krastev and Mark Leonard, the end of the cold war played a significant role in the consolidation of the EU perception of migration as a security threat. After conducting interviews with the foreign policy elites of all twenty-seven EU member states in 2010, the two authors found a "surprising convergence" of the threat perception: at the top of the list were the economic crisis, uncontrolled migration, and climate change, not the more 'traditional' military threats:[8]

Figure 6-1. *Map of the Schengen Area as of 2011*

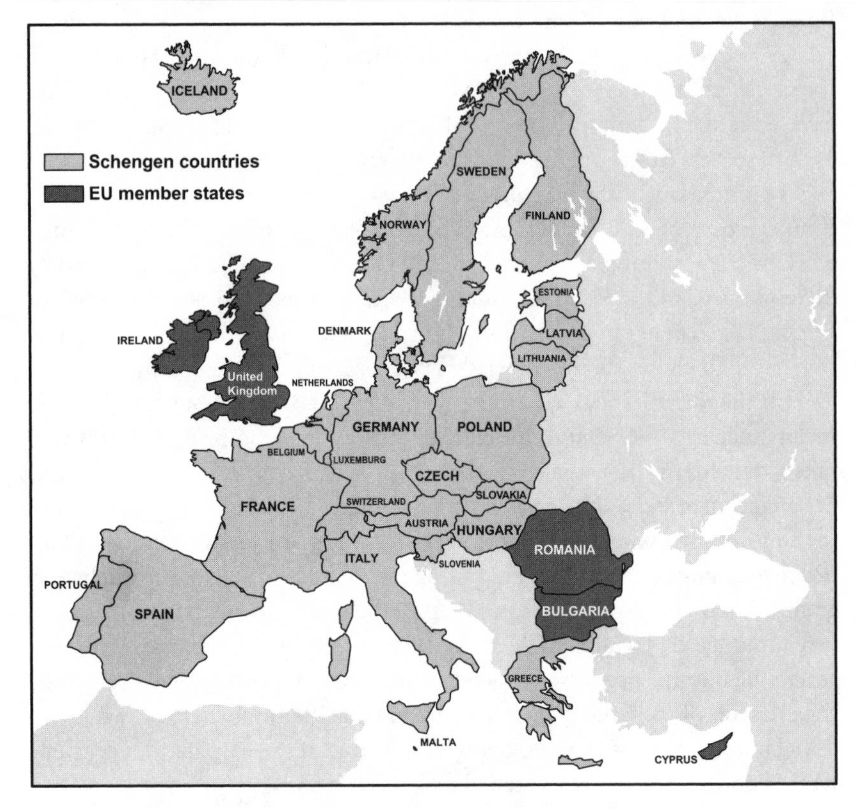

Source: AXA Schengen (www.axa-schengen.com/en/schengen-countries).

The vacuum left by the absence of war has been filled with post-modern fears. While Russia and Turkey worry about their borders and status, EU security elites are mainly concerned about defending their way of life. Apart from a nod at terrorism, our survey showed that *what EU security elites fear are threats to their standards of living: the impact of the financial crisis; energy insecurity; climate change; immigration.* This reveals a strong tendency to translate security problems into economic and social issues that can be dealt with by regulation, criminal justice or technology rather than classical foreign and military policies. Because the main threat they perceived was not of war between big European powers but of instability and chaos in between (the "internal abroad"), EU security elites generally fear weak neighbors as much as strong

> neighbors. Their strategic aim is to be prepared for the unexpected and therefore in general to increase governance capacity.[9]

Consequently, in 1992, when the Treaty of Maastricht created Justice and Home Affairs (JHA) as the third pillar of the EU, interior ministers became very active, permitting the EU to gradually accumulate competencies in this field. Thus, with this treaty the Schengen Convention became a part of the *acquis communautaire* (that is, part of the EU competencies). Later on, the Treaty of Amsterdam (1998) would create the Area of Freedom, Security, and Justice (AFSJ), which was to be implemented on the basis of five-year programs.

The fast development of the AFSJ "came as a surprise" to both external and internal observers, resulting in enhanced cooperation and EU competencies in matters as diverse as border control, immigration, asylum, European citizenship, and freedom of movement.[10] In relatively little time, the EU developed an Integrated Border Management (IBM) strategy, developed a Schengen Borders Code, coordinated border surveillance (Frontex), and coordinated prosecution (Eurojust); it also created a series of security agencies, ranging from CEPOL (European Policy College) to Sitcen (Joint Station Center), the Task Force of European Police Chiefs, and COSI (Standing Committee on Internal Security). This trend was consolidated by the Lisbon Treaty, which enhanced the role of the EU institutions in security matters.[11]

With regard to the AFSJ, the EU has so far adopted three programs for its implementation: the Tampere Program (1999–2004), the Hague Program (2005–09), and the Stockholm Program (2010–14). The gradual increase in securitization is evident in their constitutive documents of these programs. The Tampere document mentions the word "security" 14 times, the Hague Program 46 times (with 12 mentions on the first page alone), and the Stockholm document 102 times. The length of the documents varies substantially too: the Stockholm Program has more than twice the number of pages as the Hague Program.[12]

Apap and Tchorbadjiyska discuss "the distinctive lack of coherence and coordination among three principal areas of EU policy, namely external relations, enlargement, and justice and home affairs," with the first two wanting to maintain a certain degree of openness toward neighboring countries, and the latter afraid of more migrants and focused on limiting their numbers.[13] This was not always the case. The official documents of the three programs mentioned above suggests that the "true" split happened after the terrorist attacks in the United States on September 11, 2001, in Madrid on March 11, 2004, and in London on

July 7, 2005. Whereas the Tampere document begins by affirming the EU's "shared commitment to freedom based on human rights, democratic institutions, and the rule of law," the Hague Program professes its commitment to the AFSJ and discusses the "new urgency" of the security of the EU member states following the U.S. and Madrid attacks. Thus, in the aftermath of 9/11 "a sort of permanent state of emergency" was created where "borders are no longer defined in terms of the territory which they contained but of the people moving across them."[14]

Elspeth Guild and Sergio Carrera criticized the Hague Program for introducing the "balance" (between liberty and security) metaphor. According to them, striking the right balance between the two has not been possible. Instead,

> the political elements of the EU's AFSJ agenda have been vulnerable to political demands for 'more security' . . . without paying due consideration to the effects on and ethical implications of these very security policies for the liberal democratic principles, fundamental rights and liberties at the heart of the EU.[15]

The 2003 European Security Strategy identifies new security threats such as energy security, terrorism, proliferation of weapons of mass destruction, migration flows, demography, failing states, and organized crime that, even if they do not originate in the EU itself, could affect its security.[16] In 2009 the Stockholm Program introduced the phrase "a Europe of rights." While Guild and Carrera interpret it to mean that the EU is becoming more open to questions about its human rights policies (affecting both EU citizens and citizens of TCNs), Carrera and Merlino show that this interpretation is accurate only at the declamatory level, and that, in fact, the Stockholm Program emphasizes control and pays little attention to TCNs' rights.[17] Indeed, one priority of the Stockholm Program is to "foster the international dimension of Europe's irregular immigration policy" by promoting cooperation with non-EU countries on border surveillance and border controls and by facilitating the return of unwanted migrants and asylum seekers to their home countries.[18]

Setting Boundaries: The External Dimension of the EU Migration Policies

One of the most dynamic aspects of cooperation on asylum and immigration matters since the late 1990s has a foreign policy component through "partnerships" with countries of migrants' origin and transit in order to limit their number.[19] These partnerships had already been established by some member states before the Maastricht Treaty. In the 1980s, for example, individual member states applied the safe country of origin and transit norms in order to stem applications of asylum seekers and return them to their home countries.[20]

The EU migratory restrictions have led to the creation of "concentric" circles of countries or regions whose citizens receive different treatment based on existing policies: the innermost circle is represented by EU citizens, who enjoy freedom of movement within the European space; the second circle includes countries like Norway and Switzerland, whose citizens enjoy similar rights to those of the EU citizens in terms of freedom of movement; the third circle is that of the immediate neighbors to the east and the south (in the Mediterranean, North Africa, and the Middle East) with which the EU has completed readmission agreements in exchange for visa facilitation and liberalization negotiations; finally, the fourth, outermost, circle is represented by the rest of the countries whose citizens seek immigration and asylum in the EU.

For the EU, the first line of border control is located in third countries; the EU border itself is only the second line of control.[21] In this logic, visa policies play an important part and become a form of "policing at a distance." A distinction needs to be made between visa facilitation and visa liberalization. The main purpose of visa facilitation is to provide short-term visas (for stays shorter than ninety days). Only short-term visas are a competency of the EU; long-term visas remain the prerogative of individual member states. Visa liberalization refers to a process of easing the visa-granting process by, for example, clarifying which categories of people are eligible and reducing the processing fee and time. Visa liberalization—or visa-free travel—is the long-term goal of the visa facilitation regimes.

However, the EU soon realized that the "visa borders" were insufficient for migration control. Studies revealed that the EU visa-granting practices were perceived as "intransparent, expensive and troublesome," and the EU member states began to doubt the effectiveness of these policies.[22] Consequently, readmission agreements were brought into the discussion as a complementary strategy for migration control. This decision implied acknowledgment by the EU "of the insufficiency of the immediate domestic border controls," and the use of readmission agreements "underscored the external dimension of JHA policies."[23] This external dimension of the JHA aims to "step up international security by strengthening the resources and abilities of third countries to act in the field of security," based on the belief that "security is relational, and that the EU will be better off via intensive cooperation."[24] In so doing, it is trying to "balance two conflicting needs": on the one hand, the EU is trying to distance itself from the surrounding world; on the other hand, it is attempting to engage its neighborhood in order to ensure stability.[25]

The link between visa facilitation and readmission agreements was first made in the EU negotiations with Russia and Ukraine. Because these countries were reluctant to adopt the readmission agreement clause, the EU linked it to visa liberalization. Thereafter, visa facilitation and readmission agreements were negotiated "as a package" from the start with all the other countries, including Moldova and the countries of the Western Balkans. It was suggested that the link between visa facilitation and readmission agreements was a new standard in the EU's relations with its neighbors and that it could become an integral part of the EU's "global approach on migration."[26] By 2007 the EU had concluded visa facilitation and readmission agreements with Albania, Bosnia and Herzegovina, Macedonia, Moldova, Montenegro, Russia, Serbia, and Ukraine. Certainly, acceptance of readmission agreements—which, as pointed out earlier, are mechanisms that reflect the EU's securitarian approach to migration—has become a major part of conditionality applied to any member pursuing EU candidacy and accession, or even closer relations with the EU.[27] Just as in the case of the Schengen Convention, the EU gradually appropriated this practice from (some of) its member states, pushing the boundaries of migration further out. A study carried out by the European University Institute (EUI) in Florence of the readmission agreements adopted over the past four decades concludes that readmission agreements and forced return have gained great importance in Europe during this period of time.[28]

Looking Back to See the Future: The Enlargement Experience of the CEECs

The experience of the EU's 2004–07 "Big Bang" enlargement is relevant for the purposes of this analysis inasmuch as any future enlargements are likely to be guided by similar dynamics. In comparison with other waves of enlargement, the CEECs, as well as Malta and Cyprus, had to implement a more substantial *acquis* in the field of migration and asylum policies.[29]

To begin with, the EU actions showed a double standard. On the one hand, the CEECs were required to fully adopt the *acquis* related to the control of movement of people, even when some of the "old" member states had negotiated the right not to apply some of these rules (for example, the United Kingdom and Ireland are not bound by the decisions made under Title IV of the Amsterdam Treaty, but there is a provision that would enable them to contribute to and benefit from measures in the field of asylum and migration in the future, before or after the adoption of these measures/initiatives). On the other hand, the citizens of the CEECs encountered restrictive policies on the free movement of labor, even after accession.[30] Out of the thirty-one negotiations chapters, two concern migration and free movement of people: those related to the free movement of labor and to the JHA, which regulates visa, asylum, immigration, and border issues.

The EU used the enlargement process as a means to redraw its "paper borders" or visa policies. As part of the adoption of the *acquis*, the CEECs had to implement tighter border controls and introduce visa and passport control checkpoints at the border with their non-EU neighbors, thus damaging diplomatic relations and the local cross-border economies. For example, Lithuania was required to close down its "simplified" border crossings into Belarus. At the EU's request, candidate CEECs such as Estonia, Latvia, Poland, Slovakia, and Romania introduced visas for neighboring but non-candidate states Russia, Moldova, and Ukraine. Because of the close historical, cultural, linguistic, and economic links in the region, this measure produced many adverse effects.[31] In June 1999, Poland's president, Aleksander Kwasniewski, spoke out against the creation of border barriers in the EU integration process. He compared the imposition of visas to the construction of "a new iron curtain" at Poland's eastern border that would harm millions of people in Eastern Europe for whom the possibility of visiting a neighboring country is a measure of their "normality, trust, and good will in relations to other states."[32] One result of this limited freedom of migration was the so-called incomplete migration in Eastern Europe, a form of mass mobility of very short duration, often documented as tourism, which involves petty cross-border trade in border regions.[33]

Freedom of movement in the EU of the CEEC citizens was limited both before and after accession. In particular, after accession many CEECs encountered (temporary) restrictions in the EU labor market, which created domestic resentment and led to feelings of "second class EU citizenship." Even for a short-term stay, Bulgarian and Romanian citizens were required to possess valid visas to travel within the EU until as late as April 2001 and January 2002, respectively. As mentioned, neither country is now a member of the Schengen area. Both encountered delays in their accession to Schengen because of opposition from influential member states such as France, which were concerned about the two countries' "poor border and immigration controls."[34]

Another consequence of shifting the EU's "paper borders" to the east has been an increase in incentives for the new EU member states to grant citizenship (and hence EU citizenship) to nationals from neighboring non-EU countries. The securitization of borders makes travel to the EU more difficult. Consequently, citizens living in non-EU countries who are eligible to apply for the citizenship of their EU neighbors have an incentive to do so in order to be able to travel in the Schengen area (for example, historical minorities such as

Poles living in Ukraine, or Romanians living in Moldova). This fact resulted in an increase in the number of applications for EU citizenship—and in tense relations between EU member states.

Conclusion

Demographic aging is one of the most clearly discernible trends of the twenty-first century, and it will affect Europe disproportionately. The principal cause of this phenomenon is rising life expectancy, followed by low birth rates. It is projected that, without migration, the EU's population will decline by 57 million people by the year 2050. By contrast, the foreseeable development in the EU's neighborhood (North Africa, the Middle East, and Central Asia) will be characterized by a young and growing population.[35]

At present, it is estimated that the proportion of TCNs living in the EU represents 6.4 percent of the total population.[36] Despite this small number, migration is likely to remain an important part of the EU agenda, and the preeminence of the security paradigm in the field of migration is likely to continue for the foreseeable future. This will result in extending the EU's migration borders through the conclusion of readmission agreements and the implementation of additional security measures to protect its external borders by controlling migration. This security paradigm was reflected in a speech at the 2010 Munich Security Conference by the High Representative for the EU's Foreign Affairs and Security Policy, Catherine Ashton, in which she identified illegal immigration as one of the "wider issues" threatening the security of European citizens.[37]

As the EU was granted increased competencies in the field of migration and asylum policies, most of its policies were concentrated on managing and controlling this migration. The securitarian paradigm (that is, migration seen as a threat) prevailed over its alternative, development and human rights promotion. Ironically, it is likely that the latter approach—by tackling the root causes of migration—would lead with time to a reduction in the number of migrants, thus accomplishing the aims of the securitarian paradigm.

This securitarian paradigm is also very likely to be one of the main arguments used by the EU leaders against further enlargements. The recent political turmoil in North Africa and the Italian appeal to the other EU member states for assistance with the relocation and acceptance of incoming migrants has created tensions within the EU.[38] Indeed, discussions at the EU level are focused on how to reform the Schengen system by reinstating border controls among members, rather than on possible collective responses to such events.[39] This reaction is in line with the securitization paradigm in which immigration policies are designed to keep migrants out, putting security above human rights concerns. The events in North Africa have also heightened fears of unrest and more anti-immigrant attitudes among European citizens, who are likely to further support and encourage additional anti-immigrant measures.[40]

As pointed out by the Romanian foreign minister, Teodor Baconschi, some (Western) EU member states are "haunted by the ghost of mass migration" and are afraid of a big wave of immigrants after every round of enlargement.[41] This state migration-weariness is already affecting the EU's relations with its neighboring countries, including one current candidate country (Turkey). Visa liberalization negotiations are progressing rather slowly with three of the Eastern Partnership countries (Ukraine, Moldova, and Georgia) and have not even begun with the other three (Azerbaijan, Armenia, and Belarus). Meanwhile, Turkey has threatened to not begin a clampdown on people sneaking into the EU from its territory unless the EU begins visa liberalization talks with its government, just as it did with non-EU candidates Moldova, Russia, and Ukraine (and even more so since it lifted visa requirements for "remote countries" like Paraguay and Uruguay).[42]

All in all, the EU's restrictive migration policies have already significantly altered its relations with third countries. Perceptions matter greatly in foreign relations, and the feeling of rejection that the EU is currently sending to the citizens of third countries is likely to backfire with time. As pointed out by Bruce Jones, migration policies—and in particular, visa-free travel—are *the* best form of foreign policy that the EU can enact for "ordinary citizens."[43] In this sense, TCNs who are subjected to humiliation during the visa application process, or are unable to obtain a visa because of costs and conditions, are likely to perceive the EU as applying "consular sadism."[44] Such sentiments will make populations more reluctant to accept the EU's requirement that they make costly reforms in future accession negotiations.

Notes

1. A development worth following on this point is the fence that Greece plans to build on its border with Turkey to stop the flow of immigrants; see Suzanne Daley, "Greece Tries to Shut a Back Door to Europe," *New York Times*, January 31, 2011 (www.nytimes.com/2011/02/01/world/europe/01greece.html?_r=1&emc=tnt&tntemail1=y).

2. Sandra Lavenex and Emek Uçarer, "Introduction: The Emergent EU Migration Regime and Its External Impact," in *Migration and Externalities of European Integration*, edited by Sandra Lavenex and Emek Uçarer (Lanham, Md.: Lanham Books, 2002), p. 1.

3. Emek Uçarer, "Guarding the Borders of the European Union: Paths, Portals and Prerogatives," in *Migration and Externalities*, edited by Lavenex and Uçarer, p. 17.

4. Florian Trauner and Imre Kruse, "EC Visa Facilitation and Readmission Agreements: Implementing a New EU Security Approach in the Neighborhood," CEPS Working Document 290 (Brussels: Centre for European Policy Studies, April 2008) (www.ceps.eu/book/ec-visa-facilitation-and-readmission-agreements-implementing-new-eu-security-approach-neighbour).

5. Uçarer, "Guarding the Borders," p. 18.

6. Jan Zielonka, "Boundary Making in the European Union," in *Europe Unbound: Enlarging and Reshaping the Boundaries of the European Union*, edited by Jan Zielonka (London: Routledge, 2002), p. 1.

7. Uçarer, "Guarding the Borders," p. 23.

8. Ivan Krastev and Mark Leonard, "European Security: The Specter of a Multipolar Europe," European Council on Foreign Relations (ECFR) report, October 2010, p. 24 (http://ecfr.eu/page/-/documents/FINAL%20VERSION%20ECFR25_SECURITY_UPDATE_AW_SINGLE.pdf).

9. Ibid., p. 27, emphasis added.

10. Elspeth Guild, Sergio Carrera, and Alejandro Eggenschwiler, eds., *The Area of Freedom, Security and Justice Ten Years On: Successes and Future Challenges under the Stockholm Programme* (Brussels: Centre for European Policy Studies, 2010), p. 1.

11. Ibid., p. 1.

12. European Parliament, "Tampere European Council 15 and 16 October 1999: Presidency Conclusions" (www.europarl.europa.eu/summits/tam_en.htm); European Council, "The Hague Programme: Strengthening Freedom, Security and Justice in the European Union" (www.europol.europa.eu/jit/hague_programme_en.pdf - last visited on February 15, 2011); European Council, "The Stockholm Programme —An Open and Secure Europe Serving and Protecting Citizens," 2010/C 115/01 (http://eur-lex.europa.eu/LexUriServ/LexUriServ.do?uri=OJ:C:2010:115:0001:0038:EN:PDF).

13. Joanna Apap and Angelina Tchorbadjiyska, "What about the Neighbors? The Impact of Schengen along the EU's External Borders," CEPS Working Document 210 (Brussels: Centre for European Policy Studies, October 2004).

14. Joanna Apap, Sergio Carrera, and Kemal Kirişci, "Turkey in the European Area of Freedom, Security and Justice," CEPS EU-Turkey Working Paper 3 (Brussels: Centre for European Policy Studies, August 2004).

15. Elspeth Guild and Sergio Carrera, "Towards the Next Phase of the EU's Area of Freedom, Security and Justice: The European Commission's Proposal for the Stockholm Programme," CEPS Policy Brief 196/20 (Brussels: Centre for European Policy Studies, August 2009), p. 6.

16. European Council, "A Secure Europe in a Better World: European Security Strategy," Brussels, December 2003 (www.consilium.europa.eu/uedocs/cmsUpload/78367.pdf).

17. Guild and Carrera, "Towards the Next Phase," pp. 4–5; Sergio Carrera and Massimo Merlino, eds., *Assessing EU Policy on Irregular Immigration under the Stockholm Programme* (Brussels: CEPS, 2010), p. 4.

18. Carerra and Merlino, *Assessing EU Policy*, p. 5.

19. Lavenex and Uçarer, "Introduction," p. 7.

20. Uçarer, "Guarding the Border," p. 25.

21. Trauner and Kruse, "EC Visa Facilitation," p. 5.

22. Ibid., pp. 6–7.

23. Ibid., p. 7.

24. Thierry Balzacq, "The External Dimension of EU Justice and Home Affairs: Tools, Processes, Outcomes," CEPS Working Document 303 (Brussels: Centre for European Policy Studies, September 2008), p. 2.

25. Trauner and Kruse, "EC Visa Facilitation," p. 31.

26. Ibid., p. 16.

27. Apap, Carrera, and Kirişci, "Turkey in the European Area," p. 9.

28. For an inventory of the agreements linked to readmission, visit the project's website: www.mirem.eu/datasets/agreements/index?set_language=en.

29. For the sake of brevity, the abbreviation "CEECs" is used to refer to the 2004–07 candidates, but the elements analyzed are applicable to Malta and Cyprus as well.

30. Elena Jileva, "Visa and Free Movement of Labor: The Uneven Imposition of the EU Acquis on the Accession States," *Journal of Ethnic and Migration Studies* 28, no. 4 (2002): 686.

31. Ibid., p. 696.

32. Ibid., p. 687.

33. Ibid., p. 690.

34. *Euractiv*, "France Blocks Romania, Bulgaria's Schengen Bids," December 2010 (www.euractiv.com/en/future-eu/france-blocks-romania-bulgarias-schengen-bids-news-500445).

35. Rainer Münz, "Old Europe: A Look Ahead to the Twenty-First Century," *Eurozine*, April 25, 2007 (www.eurozine.com/articles/2007-04-25-munz-en.html).

36. Eurostat, "Les ressortissants étrangers dans l'UE27 en 2009," September 7, 2010 (http://europa.eu/rapid/pressReleasesAction.do?reference=STAT/10/129&format=HTML&aged=0&language=FR&guiLanguage=en).

37. Catherine Ashton, "The European Union's Role in Global Affairs," *Hampton Roads International Security Quarterly* 2 (Portsmouth), April 1, 2010.

38. Rachel Donadio, "Fears about Immigrants Deepen Divisions in Europe," *New York Times*, April 12, 2011 (www.nytimes.com/2011/04/13/world/europe/13europe.html?emc=tnt&tntemail1=y).

39. *Euractiv*, "Ministers Agree on Need for New EU Border Rules," May 13, 2011 (www.euractiv.com/en/future-eu/ministers-agree-need-new-eu-border-rules-news-504810?utm_source=EurActiv+Newsletter&utm_campaign=9229efe11e-my_google_analytics_key&utm_medium=email).

40. Rachel Donadio and Suzanne Daley, "Revolts Raise Fear of Migration in Europe," *New York Times*, March 9, 2011 (www.nytimes.com/2011/03/10/world/europe/10europe.html?emc=eta1).

41. *Realitatea,* "Baconschi: Aderarea Turciei la UE ar diminua imigra ia ilegalã," December 1, 2010 (www.realitatea.net/baconschi-aderarea-turciei-la-ue-ar-diminua-imigratia-ilegala_778249.html).

42. Valentina Pop, "Turkey to EU: No Visa-Free, No Clampdown on Migrants," *EUobserver*, January 27, 2011 (http://euobserver.com/15/31708).

43. Bruce Jones, "Islamic Radicalization in Europe and the United States," presentation at a workshop organized by the Center on the United States and Europe at the Brookings Institution, Washington, December 15, 2009.

44. Florian Trauner, "From Membership Conditionality to Policy Conditionality: EU External Governance in South Eastern Europe," *Journal of European Public Policy* 16, no. 5 (2009): 787.

GILLES DE KERCHOVE

7 Terrorism and Immigration in the European Union: Strangers in the Night?

This discussion of immigration, terrorism, and internal security from a European Union (EU) perspective addresses three broad themes: the nature of the terrorism threat faced by the EU; the challenges for the EU in responding to this threat; and the changes and opportunities presented by the Lisbon Treaty for EU counterterrorism efforts.

The Nature of the Terrorism Threat

The EU member states are faced with different forms of political violence, such as the separatist terrorism of Euskadi Ta Askatasuna (ETA) and the Kurdistan Workers' Party (PKK), but also domestic threats from extreme right-wing or left-wing parties, as well as animal rights extremists. However, terrorism inspired by al Qaeda remains the greatest threat to the Union from organizations with the intention and capability to launch mass casualty attacks such as the one so narrowly avoided in Detroit on Christmas Day 2009 or the Stockholm attack on December 11, 2010. No other terrorist movement is currently attempting mass slaughter on a similar scale. Even so, al Qaeda does not have a monopoly on politically motivated violence, and we need to be alert to other trends.

The threat of terrorism inspired by al Qaeda has evolved significantly over the past two to three years. On 9/11 we were confronted with a well-organized and well-structured organization that had command-and-control structures and was able to mount sophisticated attacks all over the world. Today the threat is more complex, diffuse, and diversified. Participation is also more opportunistic. The December 2009 attempt to blow up a plane flying from

Amsterdam to Detroit was carried out by a Nigerian educated in the United Kingdom and trained in Yemen—Umar Farouk Abdelmoutallab.

Today we see four main sources of the threat, which are described in the sections below.

The First Source of Threat: Al Qaeda Central

The core organization of al Qaeda is probably based somewhere on the borders of Pakistan and Afghanistan. Several factors have contributed to weakening al Qaeda's core. First, al Qaeda has been under enormous pressure from U.S. and Pakistani military action. It has been seriously hurt by the International Security Assistance Force and Operation Enduring Freedom military operations, as well as by operations by the Pakistani military forces and by U.S. special forces operations (in particular, drone strikes). Many of its sanctuaries and training camps have been destroyed, and many in the leadership have been arrested or killed.

Second, al Qaeda has also been destabilized by the election in the United States of President Barack Obama, who has mounted a visible challenge to its propaganda narrative. By moving from a global war on terror to a law enforcement–centered approach based on the rule of law, international law, and human rights, U.S. policy now treats terrorists as the criminals they are. This shift in paradigm, the end of "enhanced" interrogation methods and secret detention, as well as the planned closure of the Guantánamo Bay detention facility, removed an important recruitment and propaganda tool for al Qaeda. In his Cairo speech in June 2009, President Obama sought a new beginning between the United States and Muslims around the world, based upon mutual interest and respect. He reached out to partner with Muslim majority countries and Muslims against violent extremism.

Third, there is growing resentment of al Qaeda in Muslim countries. Most of the victims of Islamist terrorism are Muslim. Unlike Hamas or Hezbollah, al Qaeda does not provide any concrete answers for Muslims in coping with their daily lives. The practice of the late Osama bin Laden and his key adviser Ayman al Zawahiri of issuing *fatwas* and speaking authoritatively about Muslim religion is more and more challenged by Muslim scholars and clerics.

However, al Qaeda's core remains the most significant source of threat to Europe. Whatever organizational dislocation it has suffered, it is clear that the organization's propaganda still has the power to inspire and motivate individuals around the world—including in Europe—to get involved in terrorism as a solution to the problems of the world as they see them. Al Qaeda's core and its affiliates have sophisticated media operations that issue messages—via videos, written messages, a new online magazine, *Inspire*, which calls for jihad—to targeted audiences over the Internet. It is also using and creating online social networks and communities. As a result, young Europeans continue to travel to conflict zones, such as the Afghanistan/Pakistan border or increasingly Yemen and Somalia, in order to train as terrorists and to join al Qaeda. Others are only in touch with the organization through the Internet.

The Second Source of Threat: Franchised Groups

Al Qaeda is actively seeking out new sanctuaries in which to regroup and continue its campaign—at the moment most significantly in the African Sahel and Yemen—but this risk exists wherever there are weak states and poor governments. While the al Qaeda core has been weakened, new franchised groups have developed in failed and failing states or in areas where state control is weak. These groups are al Qaeda in the Islamic Maghreb (AQIM, primarily in Mali, Mauritania, and Niger), al Qaeda in the Arabian Peninsula (AQAP, Yemen) and al Qaeda in Mesopotamia (Iraq). In addition, other groups such as Lashkar e Taiba (Pakistan) and Al-Shabaab (Somalia) have aligned themselves with the goals of al Qaeda and have developed ties with one another. These groups have a local or regional agenda but gradually adopt al Qaeda rhetoric (jihad, caliphate) and its modus operandi.

Recent worrying developments suggest that these groups are starting to mount attacks outside their region. For example, two bombings in Kampala, Uganda, which left seventy-four persons dead and seventy hurt during the World Cup soccer matches in 2010, were claimed by Al-Shabaab, and the attempted Detroit Christmas plane bomb attack was claimed by al Qaeda in the Arabian Peninsula (and the perpetrator trained in Yemen).

The Third Source of Threat: Networks

Terrorist travel has become an increasingly important phenomenon. According to a Europol report, "Terrorism Situation and Trend Report TE-SAT 2010," a rather significant number of radicalized EU nationals and residents are traveling to conflict areas or attending terrorist training camps and returning to Europe. This must be a serious concern for member states. On return, these people may use their newly acquired experience and skill for terrorist actions and spread their radical ideas to others or give guidance to others to follow them on their path of violence. Those who stay to fight are endangering coalition forces in conflict zones and civilian populations. Several warnings and alerts in recent months have been linked to this phenomenon and have led to a growing public debate. We must face the fact that an increasing number of EU residents are seeking or have received training in countries such as Yemen and Somalia, and in the Afghanistan/Pakistan (AF/PAK) region. The majority of plots detected over the last few years have involved such "foreign fighters." Apart from the operational risk posed by these individuals, they also pose a radicalization threat, attracting new recruits to the terrorist cause.

Networks are facilitating this terrorist travel by providing false documents, money, and safe houses to help youngsters from Europe and the United States reach hot spots to attend training camps, to fight, or to return home and mount attacks there.

The Fourth Source of Threat: Home-Grown Terrorists

An increasing number of home-grown terrorists are in touch with al Qaeda through the Internet. The emergence of "lone wolves" (or small groups) that have no organizational connections but work entirely from material they find for themselves online is a particular example of the evolving terrorist threat societies face. This kind of home-grown terrorism requires few resources and is harder to detect because it may not have any physical links back to what one might call "al Qaeda central." The lone wolves have been educated in the EU or the United States and have become radicalized in a complex process. They decide to mount attacks without any link to or instruction by the al Qaeda core, but are inspired by al Qaeda's objectives and philosophy.

Are Immigration, Terrorism, and Internal Security Related Phenomena?

It is obvious that external and internal threats are closely intertwined. This is recognized in the European Security Strategy (ESS), which states that "Europe is both a target and a base for such terrorism." The EU's Internal Security Strategy, which complements the ESS, states: "a concept of internal security cannot exist without an external dimension, since internal security increasingly depends to a large extent on external security." In other words, there is a terrorist threat from outside Europe and a terrorist threat from within Europe.

One example of a threat from outside Europe is the Sauerland group, which established a presence in Germany and had planned attacks there. They had followed language and religious classes in Arab countries, participated in training in Pakistan, communicated via the Internet, and received direction from al Qaeda in Afghanistan/Pakistan.

Europe is also being used as a platform for mounting attacks abroad against European interests and as a base for attacks against third countries, such as by the PKK or the Liberation Tigers of Tamil Eelam (LTTE) based in Sri Lanka. These organizations do not plan attacks in Europe but raise money there through trafficking or racketeering, for example. The PKK sends funds to northern Iraq and Turkey, using couriers. The LTTE was sending money to Sri Lanka via Dubai and Singapore. These groups are clever enough not to mount attacks in Europe. Nevertheless, the EU has to be wary and tough regarding them, resisting the temptation, given the lack of attacks in Europe, to discount the threat they pose. Such groups can be a direct threat to European interests in the countries in which they do operate. Europeans have been victims of PKK attacks. There are also targeted attacks against European citizens outside the EU (for example, kidnappings in the Sahel by AQIM).

There are some links between diasporas in Europe and terrorist groups abroad, such as the Somalian diaspora in the United Kingdom, the Netherlands and Scandinavia with Al Shabaab, and between the Pakistani diaspora in the United Kingdom and Afghanistan/Pakistan. Algerian and Moroccan communities might also have ties to AQIM. But we have to be extremely careful not to link immigration and terrorism. This risk applies only to a marginal number of immigrants. In addition, we have seen a growing number of converts going abroad—for example, Germans who converted to radical Islam and who are fighting in Afghanistan/Pakistan. Therefore, the risk of homegrown terrorism is not to be found only in migrant communities. Instead of linking immigration in a general sense to terrorism, a better approach would be to focus on four key issues that need to be addressed: radicalization, travel, failed and failing states, and the Internet.

Challenges

The EU's action against terrorism is based on the EU Counterterrorism Strategy of 2005 and the three specific strategies (the EU Strategy on Terrorist Financing, the EU Strategy on Combating Radicalization and Recruitment, and the Media Communication Strategy). The EU decided to focus its efforts in the fight against terrorism on four main objectives:

—*Prevent* people from turning to terrorism by tackling the factors that can lead to radicalization and recruitment, in Europe and internationally.

—*Protect* citizens and infrastructure and reduce our vulnerability to attack, including through improved security of borders, transport, and critical infrastructure.

—*Pursue* and investigate terrorists across EU borders and globally; impede planning, travel, and communications; disrupt support networks; cut off funding and access to attack materials, and bring terrorists to justice.

—*Respond* by preparing in a spirit of solidarity, to manage and minimize the consequences of a terrorist attack, by improving capabilities to deal with the aftermath, the co-ordination of the response, and the needs of victims.

The EU's strategy is comprehensive, covering a wide range of measures. These aim to increase cooperation in fields ranging from information sharing to law enforcement and the control of financial assets in order to make it easier to find, detain, and bring terror suspects to justice. Furthermore, the criminal law of the twenty-seven member states is being aligned so that terrorism is prosecuted and punished in the same manner throughout the EU.

The strategy sets out how the EU adds value over and above the work done by member states domestically and sets out clear governance arrangements involving both the three main EU institutions (the Council, the Commission, and the Parliament) working closely together and the role of the Counterterrorism Coordinator in following up and monitoring progress. The fight against terrorism also features prominently in the Stockholm Program of 2009 and the Internal Security Strategy of 2010.

Rather than discussing the strategies in detail, here I explore what additional steps the EU should undertake to address the four problems mentioned above (radicalization, travels, failed and failing states, the Internet).

Invest More in Prevention

As mentioned above, the first of the four pillars of the EU strategy is "prevent"—the prevention of radicalization and recruitment, including by addressing factors conducive to the spread of terrorism. This is an important yet difficult task for several reasons, including member states' competences, which makes EU action more sensitive; different approaches in the EU member states, depending on the state/church relationship and the approach to the integration of immigrants. Extensive studies have looked into why people become terrorists. They have shown that the drivers of this kind of radicalization are not confined to one faith or political persuasion. Consequently, a particular challenge is to prevent terrorism without stigmatizing any community. We need to proceed with an open mind and great sensitivity in order to get the balance right. In doing so, we have to challenge our own thinking about what can be done to prevent violent radicalization in a way that falls outside the core counterterrorism (CT) focus, yet remains part of "counterterrorism-relevant" policies. Cross-cultural dialogue, community cohesion, and participation have an obvious CT dividend, but this is devalued if CT is seen as the main driver.

I am increasingly convinced that we need both to *prevent* radicalization and to *promote* good relations and practices in terms of community engagement. Again, this implies looking beyond core CT tasks toward CT-relevant policies and practices. That is why the EU is very engaged in improving cross-cultural relations through initiatives like the Alliance of Civilizations. We need more genuine cross-cultural dialogue to break the vicious circle and to find ways to understand our differences. Dialogue is of great value as a tool for preventing extremism because it constitutes a clear rebuttal of the propaganda of extremists.

I believe that in addition to the specific focus on fighting radicalization and recruitment—which is counterterrorism-specific—the issue of discrimination and social marginalization is also relevant and important in the context of the fight against terrorism. It is too simple to say that discrimination and marginalization lead individuals into terrorism. The actual processes at work are more complex. However, better social inclusion could contribute to reducing the pool of persons potentially inclined toward violence. Problems of social exclusion can also be exploited as part of the terrorist narrative. The EU legal framework already prohibits ethnic and racial discrimination in the field of employment as well as in areas such as social protection, education, and access to goods and services, including housing. By contrast, in EU legislation discrimination on the grounds of religion or belief is currently prohibited only in the field of employment. In 2008 the Commission submitted a proposal for a Council Directive on implementing the principle of equal treatment of persons irrespective of religion or belief, disability, age, or sexual orientation—COM (2008) 426 final—which would also prohibit discrimination on the grounds of religion or belief in areas other than employment. The Council's preparatory bodies are continuing their examination of the proposal, but no agreement has yet been reached.

Prevention is a field where the EU relies heavily on member states to take the lead. A number of them have already done so as "leading countries" for particular strands of work. At the moment six member states are pursuing flagship projects with regard to radicalization and recruitment. The Netherlands, with a concrete and practical focus on the role of local actors, has created a de facto experience-sharing network of local actors from some ten member states. It is through this kind of sharing of best practices and concrete operational tools that we need to proceed. Only by building on the first-hand experience of local professionals—be they teachers, youth workers, police officers, or community liaison officers—will we deal with the reality on the ground. Indeed, we need more of a multi-disciplinary approach to fully grasp the challenges and to identify real responses.

The German "Check the Web" initiative is aimed at intensifying EU cooperation on monitoring and analyzing Internet sites in the context of counterterrorism. Regarding material on the Internet, there is a debate as to whether material should be kept online to allow for intelligence collection and monitoring or whether it should be taken down to prevent further radicalization of those who read it. Most of the Internet service providers of the websites concerned are in the United States, where taking them down is very difficult given the First Amendment protecting free speech rights.

Another member state, Spain, has a project on imam training, while Belgium is active in community policing. Denmark works on deradicalization, and the United Kingdom on how to counter the al Qaeda single narrative.

More ought to be done. It would be good if those member states that have not yet done so, such as Italy, were to lead new initiatives.

Revisit EU Policies for Monitoring Suspicious Travels

The threat of Europeans traveling to conflict areas or attending terrorist training camps elsewhere and then returning home became even more apparent in 2010. Several warnings and alerts have led to greater public debate. We must face the fact that a growing number of residents of the EU are seeking or have received training in Yemen, Somalia, and the AF/PAK region. The majority of plots detected over the past few years have involved such "foreign fighters."

We have to keep in mind that terrorists are vulnerable when they cross borders. A lot has been done already in the EU: there is better border management (by FRONTEX), improved security of travel documents (biometrics, identity management), and new databases (the Visa Information System [VIS], the Schengen Information System II [SIS II], LSP Interpol).

However, given the significance of this threat, a more strategic approach at the EU level is also necessary. It will be important for the relevant institutions and structures to find a coherent approach, under the pillars of the Counterterrorism Strategy. Overall, it will be important to collect new types of data, a fact that requires a strategy and vision for the EU where there is a fear of creating a surveillance society. An example was the initial veto by the European Parliament of the EU-U.S. Agreement on the Terrorist Financing Tracking Program (TFTP). The EU should move forward in creating its own Passenger Name Record (PNR) and TFTP programs, while observing data protection standards. The EU and the U.S. watch lists should be aligned, but this can only be achieved if we have a level transatlantic playing field with regard to data protection. The two actors also have to improve the capacity to integrate data.

See box 7-1 for specific actions that the EU might take to improve the security picture.

Box 7-1. *Specific Recommended Actions*

Following are a series of actions that the EU might take to address counterterrorism challenges.

Prevent

Develop a counternarrative showing that the "armed struggle" is not as exciting as possible recruits might think. Support and spread information on the reality of life in training camps and in the terrorist theater of operations (including the reluctance of al Qaeda to involve Europeans in actual fighting).

Extend EU activities under the Prevent workstream projects to make diaspora communities more resilient—for example, by developing an EU/U.S. project with respect to Somali communities.

Protect

Improve document checks and document security.

Develop closer operational cooperation with the relevant authorities of the third states constituting target or transit countries with a view to disrupting terrorist travel; invite these countries and the EU member states to make more use of the Interpol Lost and Stolen Passports database. Step up technical assistance to third countries in the areas of document security and identity management.

Establish an EU PNR Directive. In conformity with the existing data protection regulations, using established measures (for example, PNR and biometric technologies to monitor and bar terrorist travel), I welcome the Commission's proposal for an EU PNR Directive in February 2011, which should ideally also cover intra-EU flights. We should also intensify law enforcement and judicial cooperation with countries of transit (such as Turkey) and destination (Pakistan, Yemen) and ask for PNR from these countries. This could also be a productive subject to discuss in the political dialogue between the EU and the Gulf Cooperation Council (GCC), representing countries that have seen their nationals travel to conflict zones and are hosts to aviation hubs and airline companies of growing international importance.

Ensure that EU member states are connected to the International Civil Aviation Organization (ICAO) Public Key Directory, which gives access to certificates and revocation lists, allowing electronic chip signature validation in biometric passports and speeding up the process agreed in the Toledo Joint Statement to work with the United States to enlist as many countries as possible in the directory.

Analyze the effectiveness of national visa policy and its practical application in preventing terrorism and take up the German initiative to strengthen the consultation procedure and the initiative under the French presidency, when the Council

(continued)

adopted conclusions proposing an alert system within the visa application procedure (referring to Art. 99 Visa Codex). Lifting visa requirements can pose a risk for terrorism and organized crime.

Start an initiative to further develop efficient forgery detection skills for border guards and consulate staff.

Pursue Information Exchange

Examine how we can better protect our borders by improving the cross-checking with data bases when someone enters the EU (making full use of the Schengen Information System, etc.).

Step up data sharing between the EU and the United States, and continue to work on the proposal to give the United States access to Europol Analytical Workfiles and to start a project for Afghanistan similar to the VENLIG project (in which the United States shares data collected with Europol), exploiting also data the United States receives from third countries such as Pakistan and Yemen in return for provision of the PISCES frontier control system.

Pursue Legislation

Initiate a discussion on whether the framework decision on terrorism should be amended so as to make it a crime to attend a terrorist training camp in the EU or abroad.

Pursue International Cooperation

Ask Europol to produce a specific report with FRONTEX on the link between Islamists and organized crime: look at the routes (the American Somalis were transiting through European hubs), modus operandi (disguising techniques such as tourism, pilgrimage, visiting relatives, and so on), means of transport, facilitation networks, and links with trafficking in human beings, travel hubs, and other aspects.

Stepping up EU Counterterrorism and Development Assistance to Fragile States

We need to respond to the problem of failed and failing states, which provide potential havens not only for terrorists but for all forms of crime. Without security, development is impossible. For example, we cannot achieve targets for female education if terrorists burn down all the schools that admit girls and women. This is increasingly recognized by the development community, but there is still a reluctance to use aid money to tackle the security challenges facing these countries. We need to work to make sure the causes of insecurity and conflict are given more consideration in developing programs to support sustainable development. We should also continue to improve the coordination between internal security instruments and Common Foreign and Security Policy (CFSP)/European Security and Defense Policy (ESDP) tools not only in sharing information but also in sharing expertise to make sure that the extensive contribution the EU makes to creating security and expanding the rule of law across the world has a visible dividend in terms of internal security. This is needed in particular to justify the continued contribution of domestic law enforcement personnel to these missions.

It is necessary to ensure that the EU has adequate resources to support its external counterterrorism effort. During my visit to Yemen in November 2010, I was struck by the fact that the government of Yemen's complaints were much harsher against European countries that had taken restrictive measures following the recent bomb scares than they were against the United States. A major reason for this was the way in which the United States was able to balance the restrictive measures needed to protect its internal security with an immediate and public gesture of support to the government of Yemen. John Pistole, head of the U.S. Transportation Security Administration, visited Yemen within days of the detection of the suspicious packages, and the United States was also able to send staff and equipment to Yemen within the same timeframe. If the EU were able to respond to future such events in a similar manner, it would significantly increase its influence in the countries where we most need to be effective in pursuing our internal security goals.

There needs to be a steep increase in the EU contribution to counterterrorism assistance. Terrorism is one of the major threats to international stability. In Pakistan and in Yemen it is directly challenging the state. In the Sahel, terrorists operate as if the states did not exist. If the EU is to be a serious actor in promoting global stability, and wants to promote a distinctive approach to CT based on the rule of law, it needs to put proper resources behind this. The sums of money potentially involved are not enormous by the standards of development programs: a lot is already being achieved with very little. It was a major step forward that the 2009–11 long-term Instrument for Stability (IfS) introduced even the possibility that the EU could start to get involved in supporting capacity building for CT. The sum of €10–14 million is clearly inadequate to the scale of the problem and the dimensions of the role the EU can and should play. But it has enabled a start to be made, in particular in the Sahel. In addition to this, the crisis management IfS has stepped in to fund programs in Pakistan (€15 million) and in Yemen (€15 million). These programs are by nature high risk, but the price of failure by the governments we are trying to assist would be borne directly by European citizens facing an increased threat of terrorist attack. It is essential that we learn the lessons from these first projects and use them to build expertise going forward. It is also essential for our credibility with the countries concerned that short-term actions are seen to have sustainable follow-up.

The European External Action Service (EEAS) needs to be able to use the short-term Instrument for Stability to intervene in Yemen or Pakistan, coordinated with the actions of other EU Institutions. Just as important, this immediate and coordinated action needs to fit into the broader engagement of the EU in the country concerned. If the short-term actions undertaken are to produce sustainable change for the better, they need to be integrated with a longer-term plan to develop the capacities of the country concerned to fight against terrorism. And both need to be informed by the reservoir of expertise on assistance in this area, which is only now being developed. This means that, to the greatest extent possible, both the short- and longer-term actions should be planned and implemented by the same people, ideally by people based in the countries concerned.

Recommended actions include:

—Increase the funding envelope for counterterrorism in the next Instrument for Stability.

—Programming of the IfS should be undertaken by the EEAS. Implementation of longer-term CT funding should be implemented by the same group that manages funding of the short-term Instrument for Stability.

—Posts should be funded within the EEAS in specific countries where counterterrorism forms a major part of the future relationship.

Impact of the Lisbon Treaty on Counter-Terrorism Policy

The good news is that the Lisbon Treaty helps us to address these challenges. In the area of Justice and Home Affairs, qualitative majority voting and joint decisionmaking with the European Parliament have become the norm. By abolishing the previous "pillars" of EU action, the Lisbon Treaty allows the Union to adopt more integrated policies. As stated above, connecting internal and external security is crucial for success, as almost every major terrorist plot has an international dimension. This is not necessarily a simple command-and-control connection, as seems to have been present in the terrorist attacks in Mumbai in 2008, but can include, for example, indirect encouragement and advice over the Internet. The Detroit attack had strong links to Yemen, as did, apparently, the shootings by a U.S. army psychiatrist at Fort Hood, Texas. Pakistan is a common connection in a large number of plots recently discovered. Even groups with domestic agendas, such as ETA, whose terrorism is largely confined to one EU member state, have extensive international connections. Recent experience shows that these connections can be a major vulnerability that good international coordination can exploit against them: an example in favor of better using the border management agency FRONTEX for security purposes, in addition to its main task of controlling the migration flow, would be to allow FRONTEX to process personal data.

The creation of the Standing Committee on Internal Security (COSI), which has the task to ensure operational cooperation on internal security, will increase high-level EU cooperation on internal security. Joint meetings with the Political and Security Committee are being envisaged to strengthen the internal-external links between EU policies.

The creation of the European External Action Service (EEAS) will allow for more coherence in EU external action. As the counterterrorism coordinator, I will be active in support of the High Representative of the European Union for Foreign Affairs and Security Policy and, in cooperation with the EEAS, on the whole spectrum of activity relevant to CT. CT-specific assistance and capacity building should be increased, as set out above. However, this is only a small part of the EU's overall international engagement relevant to CT. The EEAS should also:

—Coordinate the external action of other parts of the EU Council and Commission working on relevant issues. This is particularly important in sustaining the high-level political dialogues the Union conducts on CT, such as with the United States and Russia, and wishes to develop with other key global players, such as India and China (as recommended in the Stockholm Program). Issues such as the TFTP agreement, or the EU response to the Detroit and Mumbai attacks, have a major effect on our overall relationships with these countries, and the EEAS needs a proper overview to ensure coherence.

—Continue to deliver specific projects on countering terrorism, including using the Instrument for Stability for capacity-building projects, as mentioned above.

Take a lead in developing the approach of international law to counterterrorism, as mandated by Art. 3 (5) TEU. International law should be promoted as a policy goal and not be regarded as a constraint. Since 2006 the EU and the U.S. legal advisers have been engaged in an in-depth dialogue about the complex international legal questions related to counterterrorism. The U.S. shift away from the global war against al Qaeda is important and has to be supported. It is counterproductive to speak about a global war against al Qaeda in the legal sense, which would entail the application of international humanitarian law outside of conflict zones. The EU's consistent policy has been to promote a law enforcement approach outside of specific armed conflicts.

—Contribute to reforming the system of terrorist listing (where UNSCR 1904 marked a significant step forward, and the Union separately needs to decide how to implement Art. 75 TFEU). I am concerned that the EU needs to develop more flexible ways to use the listing instruments to produce the changes in behavior that the system was intended to achieve.

—Ensure the mobilization of all the available instruments—European Defense Force (EDF), Common Foreign and Security Policy (CFSP), Common Security and Defense Policy (CSDP), police cooperation, and criminal justice—in a more coordinated manner. Improving the effectiveness of the European Union Police (EUPOL) mission in Afghanistan is a particular current priority because such an integrated approach could not only improve the operation of the mission itself but also benefit the EU's own security. A positive impact on internal security will help justify devoting more resources from interior ministries. As a further example there has been a lot of work on security and development in the Sahel, mainly dealt with in the CFSP world, at the same time that the Justice and Home Affairs world has been dealing with West Africa, most notably in the Pact to Combat International Drug Trafficking; yet both are related and we need to prevent these two "arcs of crisis" from linking up.

—Develop the CT-relevant aspects of other programs. In particular, there needs to be a strengthened security dimension to development work, recognizing that development is impossible without security, just as security is impossible without development. And the EU needs to include in its efforts the full chain of criminal justice, including access to justice for all. It is no good, for example, building up an efficient police force if there are no courts in which suspects can be tried, and no prisons in which criminals can be held.

—Improve public diplomacy to make its case in the Arab World, such as the extent of our assistance to the Palestinians. In particular, the EU should appoint a dedicated Arabic spokesperson to raise the EU's profile in the Arab media.

—Structure itself in a way that will attract the relevant counterterrorism experts to its headquarters and delegations.

Conclusion

In conclusion, I would like to reemphasize one point: the risk of homegrown terrorism is not only found in migrant communities. Furthermore, even there the risk applies to only a small number of migrants. The threat is much more diverse and complex, and needs the tailored responses set out above. Focusing exclusively or predominantly on immigration would make our response to the threat less effective. However, better integration of migrant communities and projects for preventing the radicalization and recruitment of members of such communities should be important parts of our efforts against terrorism.

JEAN-LUC MARRET

8 European Union Enlargement, Violent Radicalization, and Terrorism

The security implications of an EU enlargement involving Turkey, in particular, are very complex and, by definition, overwhelmed with political implications. Some people would do anything for such an expansion. Others see Turkey's entry into the EU as a "clash of civilizations," or put more bluntly, the latest step toward the Islamization of Europe.

An EU enlargement can be based on a specific timetable and done to varying degrees (new members might participate in the "Schengen area" or not, adopt the euro or not, and so on). Radicalization is also a highly variable concept, ranging from nonintegrationist organizations to those that support violence. Some regard radicalization as the first step toward terrorism, while others that are opposed to such an "ideology" (for example, France), do not consider it terrorism but rather something that is linked to the issue of integration or the lack of it.

Essentially, however, the issue of the security consequences of such an enlargement would be real (and substantial) only if the violence that emanates from the new member country did not exist before the enlargement of the European Union territory. This assertion can be easily demonstrated, but it could have extreme political consequences: all diasporas tend to be infested with violent organizations that replicate the conflict taking place in the country of origin. The various forms of Turkish Islamism, including Turkish moderate, secularist, and laicist actors that counterbalance Islamism, those related to Kurdish separatism, as well as far-right and far-left sympathizers, can already be found in Europe. Consequently, an eventual EU enlargement to include Turkey might not create a new nexus of terrorism per se, but would probably act as a multiplier of opportunity.

Diasporas and "Glocal" Violence

The link between diaspora and nonstate violence is complex and sometimes extremely sensitive.[1] At once, to avoid ambiguity, it is imperative that we emphasize that a diaspora is a priori peaceful. However, it can be contaminated in many ways—sometimes attenuated, sometimes dramatically intense—by the same causes that may strike the country of origin. In the worst-case scenario, a diaspora can be used by radicalized individuals or active groups to penetrate, influence, or dominate communities and networks in order to obtain, sometimes forcibly, real or symbolic support. On the other hand, terrorist cells should never be considered in isolation, as not indicative of the broader picture. Some relevant questions and remarks are thus necessary:

—First, how does one define a "radical actor"? There is probably no easy or single answer to this. Do diasporas of immigrants come from countries affected by conflict, guerrilla warfare, or terrorism?

—What are diasporas' sociocultural practices? Do some radical doctrines or actors exist everywhere?

A diaspora can *a minima* be defined as a community that is self-identified as having a link with its country of origin. This dimension is both psychological and subjective—a feeling of having a shared history. It is also embodied in tangible material elements (for example, imported cultural practices such as food, clothing, and all things analyzed by anthropology).[2] Diasporas certainly have different forms. However, they seem to have similarities, too. A diaspora consists of individuals living outside their native (or imagined as such) countries. They believe that their "homeland"[3] is reflected in the language they speak, the religions they practice, and the culture they produce—in short, their cultural identity.[4]

A functional typology of diasporas can make a distinction between:

—victimized diasporas (composed of individuals who fled from conflict or genocide)

—working diasporas

—imperial diasporas (consisting of a kind of "colonization" by population)

—commercial diasporas (for example, those very economically active populations of Indian origin on the east coast of Africa);

—cultural diasporas

All of these aspects can obviously coexist.

Finally, it must be noted that a phenomenon as complex as globalization has multiple, and sometimes conflicting, implications for diasporas, which are by definition themselves globalized.[5] Communication opportunities and strengthened exchanges of information between a country of origin and migrant populations contribute to the maintenance of individual relationships.[6] It is possible that diasporas are much more vulnerable to political violence than they were in the past, precisely because of the multiplication of material and intangible exchanges (such as the ease of air travel, the existence of the World Wide Web, propaganda).

One of the most obvious limits of such a diaspora-based approach is the risk of considering a whole diaspora to be collectively responsible for crimes perpetrated by individuals. Such a generalization is detrimental. Diasporas themselves can be victims of illegal political or clandestine organizations that act against them by imposing a revolutionary tax or through organized crime. In the 1980s and 1990s, the Kurdistan Workers' Party (PKK) regularly hassled Kurdish entrepreneurs who lived in the EU. It is also highly probable that the Liberation Tigers of Tamil Eelam (LTTE) used to mobilize the Tamil diaspora around the world, and that many other violent political organizations operated in the same way.[7]

Jihadi Terrorism and the Diaspora

Jihadi terrorism is another problem. The jihadi doctrinal corpus relies heavily on a literalist theological approach that is far narrower than mainstream Islam. Jihadism is not unique in its influence on the diaspora. In the past, other terrorist movements and radical doctrines have acted as parasites on their diaspora. The negative symbiotic process between migrants and terrorists or violent political organizations is both ancient and systematic. Migratory flows can change according to structural factors such as the levels of development and conjuncture (the need for labor in potential host countries, changes in immigration laws, or economic and social conditions in countries of departure and arrival). This symbiosis does not change. There are several reasons:

—Some members of immigrant communities always feel legitimately concerned about what is happening in their country of origin.

—Via transnational networks and particularities of the host or home country's laws, operational militants or supporters of a violent political organization will be inclined to use their community of origin as a medium.

—Conflict-affected diasporas are victims of many activities related to terrorism, or even violent acts: physical intimidation to exert some control by coercion; logistical support; marriages of convenience; and others. Terrorists may pursue citizenship in a country that could provide them with extreme mobility, especially in the West. They may seek influence through propaganda. Sometimes they seek control and mobilization of supporters and diasporas by soliciting volunteers. The worst-case scenario is made possible when prepositioned operational cells clandestinely live among the host society.

Microfunding (via money laundering or petty crime) is one source of money for terrorist activity. Direct financial support and financial assistance provided by the diaspora are extremely variable. Many terrorist groups have never had enough militants or a solid demographic base from which to expect regular revenue. Such support is only possible for a violent organization that is fully integrated into a substantive social community, or better still, accepted as a legitimate political actor by this community. Revolutionary taxation can then prevail in the diaspora. In the 1980s, the PKK regularly carried out operations among Kurdish diasporas around the world, especially in the EU. According to Turkish sources, in the 1990s in "PKK land" (southeastern Turkey), this organization demanded that workers earning US$1,000 per month give at least $700 to the PKK.[8] After the first Gulf War, other Kurdish organizations continued to benefit from illegal oil trafficking (between 5 and 10 percent of each truck) during the embargo against Iraq.

Again, this financial and economic exploitation can be carried out using force. It has many advantages and gives the organization a sort of political control, or micro-sovereignty, over the population. In the wake of these practices, it seems obvious that a terrorist operational cell operating in a culturally or ethnically similar population presents far fewer difficulties than immersion in an exogenous population, where the language is foreign and cultural codes are unfamiliar.

Turkish Islamism, Radical and Violent Groups in Germany

An analysis of the recent past may be useful at this stage. Here I outline the impact of Turkish jihadi terrorism in Germany, the country with the biggest Turkish diaspora in Western Europe. Again, one must distinguish among this diaspora as a whole (its interest groups and organizations), the more radical groups, and the terrorist groups or individuals.

Approximately 3.5 million Muslims live in Germany. Their religion is shared by a broad range of people from divergent national and ethnic backgrounds. The Muslim presence in Germany dates back to the Turkish wars of the early twentieth century.[9] Most Muslims entered Germany via the state-controlled labor migration of the 1960s. This was exclusively concerned with the urban working class. Beginning in 1961, blue-collar "guest workers" were brought in mainly from Turkey, Morocco (1963), Tunisia (1965), and Yugoslavia (1968). Three-quarters of the German-born Muslims today are descendants of the guest workers from Turkey. They number around 2 million, the largest population of foreign residents in Germany. They are followed closely in number by former citizens of Yugoslavia. In 1973, when the migration of guest workers came to a halt, many migrants decided to settle in Germany with their families.

In the early 1970s, many Muslim organizations were founded on the local level using a legally recognized form, the *eingetragener Verein* ("e.V.," or self-organized association).[10] These were closely linked to the residence of guest workers, who yearned for a common place to practice their religion. Soon they formed supraregional umbrella organizations that have shaped the present scenario of a rich, multifaceted Muslim landscape of Islamic associations in Germany. The members remain closely tied to their roots through organizations in their home countries. The two major organizations on a federal level are the Turkish-dominated Islamrat e.V. and the Arab-dominated Zentralrat der Muslime in Deutschland e.V. These often compete with each other to represent Muslims in Germany.

The spectrum of Islamists within Germany ranges from social organizations that engage only in political and cultural activities to violent movements that seek to achieve their political ends with force.

The Islamist activities in Germany are not directed only at Muslims. A wide range of strategies, activities, and social institutions are designed to enhance their sphere of influence in Germany. Among the most common practices are:

—advocating Islamist positions in the social sphere

—focusing on Muslim target groups to maintain and enforce an "Islamic identity"

—segregating young Muslims and Germans

—lobbying for the acceptance by German agencies and institutions of an official/legal status for a person practicing Islam

—promoting interests of Islamist organizations through cooperation with nonextremist Muslim umbrella organisations

Turkish Islamist organizations have long been the strongest Muslim groups in Germany. The "Islamic Community Milli Görüs" (IGMG) wields the largest influence. It is also active in the Netherlands, Austria, and France.[11] The IGMG seeks to diminish the laicist state order in Turkey. It intends to reintroduce a social system—"a just order"—that is based on the IGMG's interpretations of the Koran and Shari'a (the religious law of Islam). Its activities in Germany are that of a political-cultural organization working to maintain, develop, and enhance the Muslim identity. The principle behind its concept of "Muslim identity" is to limit the integration of Muslims into German society. Young Muslims are the specific target group of their welfare and educational work.

Young mothers receive particular attention because they play an influential role in children's education. The IGMG offers a wide range of leisure and educational activities such as holiday camps, computer training, assistance with homework, and sports clubs as a way of tying them to the ideology and interests of the organization. The purpose of these cultural and social activities is to keep young Muslims separated from outside influences.

The Caliphate State, a Turkish organization banned in December 2001, is probably the most sensitive example of a Turkish radical, and sometimes violent, organization. First known as the Union of Islamic Associations and Communities (ICCB), it was founded in 1984 by a Turk, Cemaleddin Kaplan, in Cologne. In March 1994 he appointed himself the "Emir of the Faithful and Caliph of the Muslims." The ICCB soon changed its name and members now refer to it as the Caliphate State (Hilafet Devleti). After the death of Cemaleddin Kaplan, his son, Metin Kaplan, took over the organization.[12] At its peak, it had about 1,100 adherents and was of enormous importance to Islamism in Germany. Both the earlier ICCB and the Caliphate State strive for the dissolution of the laicist system in Turkey and its replacement through an Islamic order. However, the Caliphate State, though in the decline, was much further along in its objectives and strategies. The ultimate goal of the association was the world supremacy of Islam under the leadership of the Caliph. It also strongly rejected the compatibility of democracy with the Muslim faith:

> Islam is both a religion and a state, both divine worship and politics! Islam does not recognize the laicist regime! Islam never will be compatible with democracy! In short, the democratic regime, intrinsically, in essence and in the last analysis is contrary to Islam.[13]

This ideological orientation allowed for agitation against Western laicism and the Turkish government, thus hindering the integration of Muslims into (German) democratic society. In 1983 the draft of an Islamist "kaplanci" constitution was presented that stipulated Shari'a as the only order for law and society. Non-Muslims would be political and juridical second-class citizens.[14] In addition, strong anti-Semitic utterances drew public attention.[15]

Beginning in 1988, the association drew more public attention owing to the aggressive statements by Kaplan. The attitude and views of the Caliphate State are publicized in the union organ *Ümmet-I-Muhammed* (Mohammed's Community). Its propaganda was also disseminated through its TV program, "Hakk TV" (True Islamic Television), transmitted outside Germany.

The eventual split in the organization came in 1996 with the self-appointment of the "Anti-Caliph," Halil Ibrahim Sofu. The internal conflict resulted in an exodus of its members and increased the isolation of Muslims in Germany.[16]

Sofu received death threats after *fatwas* were issued against him by Kaplan. On May 8, 1997, Sofu was shot dead by unidentified persons in Berlin. On November 15, 2000, Kaplan was sentenced by the Higher Regional Court of Appeal in Düsseldorf to a prison term of four years. He was found guilty of public inciting criminal acts by calling for the assassination of his adversary. It is suspected that the premeditated murder was executed by Kaplan's adherents, who fought as volunteers in Afghanistan and Bosnia.[17] On December 8, 2001, the German minister of the interior passed a decree banning the organization from December 12, 2001, onward.[18] The ban also covers the Caliphate State's subsidiary organizations and led to the confiscation of all its properties. On October 10, 2004, the German police managed to arrest Mohammed Metin Kaplan at an Internet café in Cologne, drove him straight to an airport in nearby Düsseldorf, and deported him back to Turkey. In June 2005 he was sentenced to life imprisonment in Turkey.

Members of the Caliphate State attempted to blow up the Atatürk Mausoleum in Ankara and a mosque in Istanbul in 1998. That was followed by twenty-five arrests, among them many followers of Kaplan who had arrived from Germany. More arrests and imprisonments took place in the autumn of 2001 in Germany.[19]

On September 6, 2002, the German police arrested a couple who plotted an attack on the U.S. military bases in Heidelberg on the anniversary of the September 11, 2001, terror attacks.[20] German police raided their apartment in Walldorf, near Heidelberg, and found 130 kilograms of explosive chemicals and five pipe bombs, along with a picture of Osama bin Laden, Islamist literature, and books on the assembling of bombs. There were indications that the German-born Turkish citizen and his American fiancée both detested Jews. The woman worked in a supermarket on a U.S. military base located in Heidelberg. The couple appeared to be acting alone.

In Germany this attack received great attention because it represented the first intended attack with Islamist motivation against the military on German soil. What was more alarming was that it was planned by independent perpetrators with no links to an Islamist network. The Kaplan case shows how "glocal" by nature (a mix of global and local agendas and factors) many radical and potentially violent organizations can be. On one side, they try to exert control on diasporas for the aforementioned reasons; on the other side, their agenda is very often related to the country of origin.

Having said that, a security analysis such as this would be both incomplete and biased if it did not take into account more positive and balancing initiatives, such as the moderating influence that an Islamist party may have on radical terrorism. The Islamist Adalet ve Kalkınma Partisi (AKP), for example, was democratically elected to power in Turkey. Other organizations can also contribute decisively to preventing radicalization and terrorism. The Turkish imam Fethullah Gülen's organization, for instance, manages 600 schools around the world and seems to promote a mainstream moderate Islam that can counterbalance any radicalization.[21]

It is hard to see terrorism, or more accurately, a possible terrorist threat, coming from radical Turkish networks as the main fear. This sort of violence is essentially very intense, but the Turkish state appears to be able to act decisively against it. No terrorist attack plotted by Turkish radical groups seems to have succeeded in the EU until now, although some powerful Turkish organizations are presently operating in the EU, in diasporas. They exert influence—cultural and religious—that can sometimes be perceived as contrary to Western values, democratic ideals, or successful integration. For these reasons, until now, the Turkish radical groups have been mostly regarded as more of a political and social problem than a substantial security challenge. The threat of terrorism is not often invoked by opponents of Islam or European far-right groups. Demographic issues, the "Islamization of Europe," and arguments over low-cost workers are used much more to rally anti-Turkish opinion. Other challenges are far more sensitive and large scale than terrorism, especially should Turkey become a member of the EU. The reality of the EU having shared boundaries with the Caucasus, Iraq, Iran, and Syria deserves to be carefully examined, particularly with regard to the EU military and diplomatic means, or "no-means." Turkish organized crime is already active inside the EU. Full membership would probably facilitate many activities, from trafficking to money laundering. More broadly, such an enlargement (which will likely be slow to come) would have major social, economic, and demographic consequences that are not analyzed here.

Notes

1. Brent Hayes Edwards, "The Uses of Diaspora," *Social Text* 19, no. 1 (2001): 45–73.
2. Pnina Werbner, "Introduction: The Materiality of Diaspora—Between Aesthetic and 'Real' Politics," *Diaspora* 9, no. 1 (2000): 5–20.
3. William Safran, "Diasporas in Modern Societies: Myths of Homeland and Return," *Diaspora* 1, no. 1 (1991): 83–99.
4. Stuart Hall, "Cultural Identity and Diaspora," in *Identity: Community, Culture, Difference*, edited by J. Rutherford, pp. 222–37 (London: Lawrence and Wishart, 1990).
5. Robin Cohen, *Global Diasporas: An Introduction* (Seattle: University of Washington Press, 1997).

6. Khachig Tölölyan, "Rethinking Diaspora(s): Stateless Power in the Transnational Moment," *Diaspora* 5, no. 1 (1996): 3–36.

7. Gabriel Sheffer, "Diasporas and Terrorism," in *The Roots of Terrorism*, edited by Louise Richardson, pp. 117–29 (New York, Routledge, 2006).

8. *Milliyet*, November 4, 1993.

9. For a historical description see Thomas Lemmen, "Muslime in Deutschland—Eine Herausforderung für Kirche und Gesellschaft," Ph.D. dissertation, Sankt Augustin, 1999, pp. 10–25.

10. The *eingetragener Verein* is much more limited in its rights and opportunities than a public corporation. See Thomas Lemmen, "Muslime in Deutschland," pp. 228–31.

11. See, for instance, the website of the Communauté Islamique du Milli Görüs de la Région Lyonnaise (www.milligorus.fr/index.php).

12. Werner Schiffauer, *Die Gottesmänner—Türkische Islamisten in Deutschland, eine Studie zur Herstellung religiöser Evidenz* (Frankfurt: Suhrkamp Verlag, 2000).

13. Metin Kaplan, *Ümmet-i Muhammed,* February 17, 2000, p. 10.

14. Karl Binswanger and Fathi Spahioglu, *Türkisch-islamische Vereine als Faktor deutsch-türkischer Koexistenz* (Munich: Benediktbeuren, 1988), p. 106.

15. See, for example, *Ümmet-i Muhammed*, February 17 and 24, 2000, and June 22, 2000.

16. In 1985 the association had about 10,000 adherents. By 1995 the number had decreased to 2,900. Today the prohibited organization has about 1,100 members.

17. In 1997 a delegation of the "Caliphate State" organization visited the Islamist terrorist Osama bin Laden. See *Focus*, no. 40 (October 1, 2001): 65.

18. Under the antiterror legislation introduced after the terror attacks of September 11, Germany loosened legal protection for religious groups. This paved the way for the outlawing of foreign-based groups. The German government banned in the meantime three Islamist groups: the "Caliphate State" in December 2001, the Al-Aqsa organization in August 2002, and Hisb-ut-Tahrir in January 2003.

19. Douglas Frantz, "Terror Plan Born in Germany and Aimed at Turkey Gets New Scrutiny," *New York Times*, February 5, 2002, p. 12.

20. Fox News, September 6, 2003.

21. See the website of Fethullah Gülen (http://en.fgulen.com/).

UMBERTO MELOTTI

9 Immigration and Security in Europe: A Look at the Italian Case

Between immigration and security there are many links, principally between immigration and crime, terrorism, and urban conflict. But other links, which partly interact with these, concern crime and terrorism and crime and urban conflict.

Links between immigration and crime exist in every country, but they are particularly strong in Italy, owing to shortcomings in policing and law enforcement, inefficiencies and delays in the judicial system, and the longstanding underestimation of the problem by many politicians. Moreover, in Italy immigration is largely due to push factors in the countries of origin rather than to pull factors in the countries of destination. In Italy, immigrants have difficulty finding regular jobs (also because of the high levels of domestic unemployment and labor on the black market), and many of them, in particular those entering the country illegally, encounter powerful criminal organizations, which are no longer only Italian.

The links between immigration and terrorism became headline news after the terrorist attacks in the United States on September 11, 2001. In Europe, Islamist organizations claimed responsibility for terrorist attacks in two of Europe's most important capitals, Madrid, in 2004, and London, in 2005. Another serious attack was foiled in 2008 in Paris, which had already been targeted in the previous decade by the Islamic Salvation Front, an organization that, according to the local authorities, was responsible for more than 100,000 victims in Algeria alone.

Italy has not yet experienced any equally serious attacks from such quarters, but various attempts have either failed or been foiled. Rome in particular, which is both the capital of Italy and the center of the Catholic Church, has been seriously threatened, especially after a lecture by Pope Benedict XVI in Regensburg, Germany, on September 12, 2006, in which he harshly criticized Mohammed's ideas on violence and holy war.

There had been serious terrorist attempts in Italy even before that. Rome's Fiumicino Airport was targeted twice by Palestinian groups: the first attack, against a Pan American airliner, left thirty-two dead and fifteen injured in December 1973; the second, against the El Al and TWA airline check-in desks, killed thirteen and injured seventy-seven in December 1985, while a simultaneous attack at the Vienna airport killed seven and injured forty. A few months earlier, in September 1985, another Palestinian group had hijacked an Italian cruise ship, the *Achille Lauro*, killing an American passenger of Jewish background and provoking the most serious postwar diplomatic crisis between the United States and Italy, when, after having struck a deal with the Palestinian organizations for the release of the hostages, the Italian government prevented the American military from arresting the perpetrators of the crime when they were forced to land in Sicily.

We must also recall the 1981 attempt on the life of Pope John Paul II in St. Peter's Square. Its perpetrator was Turkish, though some aspects have never been fully explained, particularly the role played by certain Eastern European agencies. More recently, Islamist-inspired attacks have been thwarted in Naples, Bologna, Vicenza, Perugia, Milan, and, more than once, Rome.

The links between immigration and urban conflict, which have been present since the mid-1950s in the United Kingdom, the late 1970s in France, and the early 1990s in Germany, flared up in 2005 with the widespread revolt in the French *banlieues*, the poor and peripheral suburbs of the largest towns, which had long been seen as the "new internal security frontiers."[1] Similar unrest has also occurred in other countries, including Italy, where concern about a possible "*banlieue* risk" has been raised repeatedly. In 2005, on the eve of standing again to serve as prime minister for the center-left coalition, Romano Prodi immediately raised the issue. Giuseppe Pisanu, minister of the interior in the then center-right government, said in 2005 that "even though Italy has no real *banlieues*, there may well be grief in the future." Giuliano Amato, minister of the interior in the following center-left government, recognized in 2006 the existence in Italy of "embryonic *banlieues*." And Roberto Maroni, minister of the interior in the present center-right government, confirmed this diagnosis in 2010, after a specific survey carried out for his department.

In this chapter I look at all three main links in broad terms, with a focus on the Italian case. I concentrate on the first and third links, because many aspects of the events relating to terrorism have still to be assessed, and their connections with immigration have not been fully proved, even though a number of

Islamic centers in Italy, as elsewhere, have been engaged in propaganda, recruitment, and logistical support to terrorists.

Immigration and Crime

The issues in Italy are still little known abroad and even at home have not been properly analyzed, partly because of an overriding misplaced "political correctness." This has led to widespread ideological "denialism," which not only flies in the face of ordinary everyday experience but also contradicts statistical data.

Some Background Data on Immigration and Crime in Italy

For a long time now, data have shown a sharp rise in crimes committed by immigrants, in both absolute and relative terms.[2] These data obviously have to be handled cautiously, because they are affected to a certain extent by various types of bias, owing to the level and the forms of social control and the intervention in their collection and processing by specific groups and individuals. The crimes committed by immigrants clearly account for an increasingly large proportion of crime in Italy, where, precisely because of the immigrants' substantial contribution, crime rose steadily, at least until 2007.[3] Whereas crimes committed by Italians have been slowly declining in number, during the ten-year period 1993–2002 the percentage of crimes committed by foreign nationals more than doubled, from 3.2 percent to 6.8 percent, even though in that period three major immigration amnesties created a large increase in the number of legal immigrants, on which the crime rate is calculated.

The most accurate indicator should be the number of convictions recorded, but that statistic does not provide a clear picture of the crimes committed over the course of the year in which judgments are handed down. Other indicators must therefore be used, such as the number of reported crimes and the number of people taken into custody.

There has been a constant rise in the share of foreign nationals reported in these situations, from 7.5 percent in 1992 to 18.7 percent in 2000, and 23.6 percent in 2005. According to information reported in 2009 by Italy's National Institute of Statistics (Istat), in 2001, 89,390 foreign nationals were reported to the authorities out of 513,736, or 17.4 percent; in 2002, 102,675 out of 541,507, or 19 percent; in 2003, 116,392 out of 536,237, or 21.7 percent; in 2004, 110,712 out of 529,184, or 20.9 percent; and, in 2005, 130,131 out of 550,773, or 23.6 percent, as already stated. Similarly, the Ministry of the Interior assembles data on persons reported to the judicial authorities and persons arrested or detained.[4] In 2006, reports regarding foreign nationals totaled 283,316 out of 801,823, or 35.3 percent; in 2007, 304,483 out of 860,982, or

35.4 percent; in 2008, 301,960 out of 889,793, or 33.9 percent. To better understand these figures, it should be recalled that on December 31, 2008, according to Istat, the legal immigrant population in Italy totaled 3,891,295, which was only 6.5 percent of the total population, and, according to the most reliable estimates, there were fewer than 1 million undocumented immigrants, a further 1.5 percent of the population. Then there is the fact that the number of *individuals* reported is far fewer than the number of *crimes* reported (2,415,023 in 2005; 2,771,430 in 2006; 2,933,146 in 2007; and 2,694,811 in 2008, according to the Ministry of the Interior), because four-fifths of the crimes are committed by unknown persons, and this makes it impossible to distinguish between nationals and non-nationals. In addition to the number of crimes reported, there is the "dark number" of unreported crimes, whose perpetrators are undoubtedly members of both groups.

The percentage of foreign nationals reported as committing certain serious crimes is particularly high. In 2005 (the last year for which Istat data are available at this writing) foreign nationals were accused of more than four-fifths of reported crimes connected with enslavement and human trafficking (81.7 percent), about one-half of crimes relating to prostitution (inducement, abetting, and exploitation), about one-third of other fairly serious crimes (theft 39.5 percent; disturbing the peace 37.1 percent; resisting arrest 34.8 percent; production and trafficking of drugs 34.0 percent; actual or attempted robbery 33.2 percent; sexual violence 28.1 percent), and almost one-sixth of actual or attempted homicides (15.5 percent).[5] According to the Ministry of the Interior, in 2007 foreigners accounted for 49 percent of thefts, 39 percent of rapes, 36 percent of homicides and armed robberies, and 27 percent of deliberate injuries. The number of foreign nationals detained in custody has also risen considerably (owing in part to their lesser ability to mount a legal defense), indirectly confirming the sharp rise in immigrant crime. Between 1990 and 1995, the number of foreign nationals held in custody more than doubled, from 4,017 out of 26,150 (15.4 percent) to 8,628 out of 47,344 (18.2 percent); between 1996 and 2000 the figure almost doubled, to 15,582 out of 54,039 (28.8 percent), an increase of more than 10 percentage points; and between 2001 and 2005 it rose still further to 19,836 out of 59,523 (33.3 percent), an increase of 4.5 percentage points. On July 31, 2006, the date of the last remission of criminal penalties, the total stood at 20,088 out of 60,710 (33.1 percent). After that pardon, which within the space of one year entailed the release of 26,570 prisoners (16,730 nationals and 10,200 non-nationals: about 44 percent of the total prison population), the percentage of imprisoned foreign nationals began rising again. On December 31, 2006, the foreigners in prison numbered 13,152 out of 39,005 (33.7 percent); on December 31, 2007, they were

18,252 out of 48,693 (37.5 percent). On December 31, 2008, they were 21,562 out of 58,127 (37.1 percent), despite the fact that a Decree Law approved on May 23 that year had made it easier to repatriate foreign nationals. On December 31, 2009, the percentage remained unchanged, but their actual number rose further, to 24,112 out of 64,910, and on December 31, 2010, their number arrived at 24,954 out of 67,961 (36,7 percent). Whereas in 1995 one prisoner in six was a foreign national, by 2005 the figure stood at one in three, and that fraction has since further increased. In 2009 Justice Minister Angelino Alfano said: "Italian prisons are adequate to house Italian prisoners, but with the influx of these foreign nationals we have superseded their statutory, and also their tolerable, capacity."[6]

Note should also be taken of the recent sharp increase in the number of crimes that cause considerable social alarm, such as robberies in isolated homes, sometimes accompanied by brutal beatings, leaving the victims injured and dead, and the rape of young boys and girls and old women, who are often also deliberately murdered or accidentally killed. Considering the frequency of such crimes (Milan averages four rapes a month), according to a well-known psychologist, "we can actually talk about serial crimes" and "we should not be afraid to be afraid."[7]

Rapes, in particular, are committed occasionally but not by chance. A psychotherapist who has studied them has written that "poor immigrants, whom no woman wants, and who cannot afford to pay prostitutes, live in particularly stressful situations, in cities where they are bombarded by sexual messages and references. Consequently their inhibitions yield under the pressure of desire compressed by abstinence."[8] In addition, rapes are sometimes viewed by their perpetrators as payback for violence committed in the past against women in their own countries. One Eritrean rapist she interviewed made that quite clear, when he said: "Your ancestors raped our women. If the situation is reversed from time to time, I don't think it is fair to make a tragedy out of it." These horrific words reveal a culture, in the anthropological sense of the term, in which women are viewed as objects to be used for transactions or for proxy vendettas.

But that same mentality can also be found in "honor crimes" committed within entrenched misogynous groups, which include many of those from the Islamic countries,[9] and in the female genital mutilations imposed in some of these groups and in others.[10]

Unsustainable Denialism

An old proverb says that "an ass remains an ass even when it shakes its ears to say no." This seems to be confirmed by the fallacious arguments used in some quarters to back up an obstinate "denialism," an attitude that still seems to be widespread, despite the statistical evidence. There are even monothematic denialists. These include the scholars who, when gang warfare between immigrant groups (particularly young Latin Americans) was rife, leaving people dead and wounded, saw fit to publish papers reducing them to the level of play groups engaged in harmless "rituals" or even denying their very existence, speaking about the "gang bogey."

But the statistics are undeniable, and cannot be manipulated by, for example, excluding offenses committed by illegal immigrants and foreign "travelers" from the crime figures, almost as if these groups were wholly extraneous to the immigration universe, or falsely arguing that "the propensity of documented immigrants to commit crimes is only slightly above that of the Italian population as a whole,"[11] whereas their actual crime rate is 25 percent higher.

Among the most determined denialists are those who hold that it is unlawful to analyze deviancy and crime among immigrants on the grounds that "merely planning research of that kind is tantamount to authorizing implicit prejudice against the population being surveyed" or even that "addressing the issue in terms of security legitimizes racism."[12] Such scholars have thereby demonstrated that they are no better than those left-wing politicians who, disregarding all evidence to the contrary, continued for years to deny the existence of any security problems posed by immigration, and consequently refused to adopt the necessary measures, if in government—or to challenge them, if in opposition. The current president of the republic and former communist militant, Giorgio Napolitano, is a case in point: when he was minister of the interior, and therefore had at his disposal all the data on the situation, he categorically denied the possibility of any "equation" between immigration and crime, forgetting that the equation is not some generic equivalence (which no one had ever even suggested) but an equivalence subject to various coefficients, some extremely complex, known and unknown, to be identified and studied.[13] The same words were repeated by another former communist, Livia Turco, who, as minister of social solidarity, signed off on the 1998 Immigration Act jointly with Napolitano.[14] Similarly, the speaker of the lower house at the time, Luciano Violante, another former communist, did not shrink from stating that merely associating these two things was "foolish."[15] Curiously, a politician from the opposite end of the political spectrum, the former neo-Fascist Gianfranco Fini, who became speaker of the lower house in 2008, made the same mistake in 2009.

There have been a few, but important, exceptions. In particular I would recall the opinions expressed by the center-left mayors of a number of Italian cities. Exactly for this position, Bologna's mayor, Sergio Cofferati, the charismatic former leader of Italy's largest trade union confederation, CGIL, was attacked with such vehemence by some important leaders of his majority coalition that he decided not to stand for reelection.

One scholar, Marzio Barbagli, has with appreciable intellectual honesty acknowledged his previous "ideological blindness," a blindness that unfortunately continues to afflict many people.[16] Above all, the ever-present newcomers to the subject not only persist in their dogged ideological denialism, but tend to attribute the concerns about security exclusively to "unfounded alarmist campaigns" by the media. This is what all the speakers did at a CGIL conference in Rome in March 2009: instead of addressing the problem critically, they skirted the issue by blaming it on the press. I would therefore like to conclude my comments on this subject by expressing the hope that they will not suffer the same fate as Alessandro Manzoni's character in the novel *The Betrothed,* who, obstinately denying that the plague existed, died of it, blaming his doom on the stars.

Immigration and Urban Unrest

Several years have passed since the great unrest in the *banlieues* in Paris and many other French cities: a collective action primarily by young immigrants, and children and grandchildren of immigrants, mostly from the former French African colonies. These clashes attracted the attention of both politicians and scholars.

The French Events

The revolt in 2005, which lasted almost a month, was triggered by a serious incident to which the young people living in the *banlieues* reacted furiously. On October 27, 2005, at Clichy-sous-Bois, in Seine-Saint Denis (the department with the highest percentage of immigrants, many of whom were young and unemployed), three foreign-born teenagers, believing that they were being chased by the police, entered a power substation, where two of them were electrocuted and the third suffered serious burns. News of the event spread like wildfire, giving rise to extensive rioting throughout the country. Enormous damage ensued, some 10,000 vehicles were burned or destroyed, and properties were torched and looted, leaving hundreds injured and one person dead. More than 3,000 people were stopped by the police, who made over 500 arrests, and the aftermath was long, with a curfew (the first imposed in France since the end of the Algerian War in 1962) that remained in force until the new year.

Politicians and scholars have interpreted these events in many different ways. France's president at the time, Jacques Chirac, attributed the unrest to the young immigrants' "identity crisis."[17] The then minister of the interior, Nicolas Sarkozy, blamed it on uncivilized behavior by "scum" (*racaille*), as he had already defined the young troublemakers of the outskirts.[18] The French-Jewish philosopher Alain Finkielkraut attributed the violence to hatred of the West fomented by Islamic preaching.[19] Conversely, Europe's best-known Islamic intellectual, Tariq Ramadan, said that it was the result of discrimination against all the young people living in the *banlieues*, regardless of their race, religion, and culture.[20] In contrast, the Marxist theorist Étienne Balibar said that a mix of race and class discrimination led to "violent stigmatization" and "daily police checks" that allegedly targeted immigrants of African origin.[21] The historian Hélène Carrère d'Encausse blamed it on immigrants' large families (which, according to her, were also the result of polygamy) and the consequent life of many youths on the streets, in contact with criminal activities.[22] The sociologist Alain Touraine saw the riots as the consequence of failed social integration, and his well-known pupil, Michel Wieviorka, cited the young immigrants' total loss of hope.[23] A sociologist of Algerian extraction, Sami Naïr, who had been an adviser on immigration to former president François Mitterrand, similarly spoke of "despair [that was] transformed into street violence."[24] In contrast, the anthropologist Marc Augé stressed the desire of the young street gang members to appear—through spectacular acts of violence—on television screens, the new fragmented and wide-ranging virtual centers of the nonplaces of their lives.[25] And there were also those who saw it as a "generational issue," an "urban question," a problem due to the alleged "non-assimilability" of the new immigrants, and even "a crisis of urban civilization." The German sociologist Ulrich Beck iconoclastically described it as the "revolt of the superfluous," for those young people would be not only unemployed or underemployed, but unemployable in any advanced society.[26] Some spoke of the establishment in the country of a "parallel society" living out of the pale of the republic's values and laws, even though, according to others, those young people were battling not against the republic, but to win respect for their constitutional rights. Last, Toni Negri, the former leader of a violent extreme-left Italian organization, Autonomia Operaia, who lived in Paris in golden exile and later became the bard of the revolt of the "multitudes," saw the "Muslims in the *banlieues*," together with the black and Hispanic activists, aggressive feminists, and Somali pirates, as "heroes of destruction" in the struggle against the global empire.[27]

Considered in isolation, none of these interpretations is satisfactory. Account must simultaneously be taken of many of the above-mentioned factors, and others as well, including those that came to light the following March, when students protested against a law that made it easier to hire and fire young workers—although the main actors of this movement were neither foreign nationals nor *banlieue* residents. In any event, the revolt in the *banlieues* was the unexpected non-peaceful outcome of the "peaceful invasion of the outside proletariat" that had been sympathetically analyzed by many scholars (though, for the recent migratory phases, "underproletariat" would have been a more accurate term).

These events were not limited to Paris, or even to France alone, which had experienced similar clashes in the past, albeit on a smaller scale: in 1979, 1981, 1983, and 1990 in Lyon, in 1991 in Paris, in the following years in Rouen, Strasbourg, Toulouse, Lille, Bordeaux, and other towns and cities, large and small. In the United Kingdom, there have been riots by "ethnic minorities" at various times in the London suburbs, in the inner cities of Manchester (1981, 1982), Liverpool (1981, 1985, 2001), and Birmingham (1985, 2005), and in several other places, such as Bradford (1976, 1981, 1995, 2001, 2002, 2010), Bristol (1980, 1990–92), Brixton (1981, 1985, 1991), Oxford (1991–92), Oldham, Leeds, and Burnley (2001), Windsor (2006), and Brighton (2009). In Germany, too, there have been serious clashes between nationals and non-nationals, which were due much more to the xenophobia of the former than to the anger of the latter. After the German reunification in particular, attacks against immigrants increased, with heavy casualties, and they still occur from time to time.[28]

The Case of Italy

Italy has not yet experienced any immigration-related urban unrest on a comparable scale, even though it has experienced serious urban unrest of a different kind, such as the July 2001 riots in Genoa at the time of the G8. In this case a crucial role was played by violent groups of foreign nationals, who were not, however, immigrants.

Various factors explain why Italy has had fewer such incidents. In particular,

—immigration is a relatively recent phenomenon, therefore, until recently, there have been fewer second-generation immigrants;

—immigrants account for a smaller percentage of the population (in 2008 they accounted for only 8 percent of Italy's population);

—immigrants belong to many different ethnic groups, while other countries have large concentrations of immigrants from specific areas (from the Maghreb in France, the Indian subcontinent in the United Kingdom, Turkey in Germany), although this situation is now changing more or less everywhere;

—women made up a large percentage of immigrants—around 50 percent, although they are very unevenly distributed among the different ethnic groups;

—a large percentage of immigrants are present for political reasons, though very few qualify for refugee status;

—Italian towns have few neighborhoods resembling the French *banlieues* or British inner-city areas;

—immigrants are more widely scattered throughout the country, and even in different areas of towns and cities;

—many local councils, mainly in the north and center, have gained experience managing earlier internal migrations; and

—the prevailing political culture (particularly in Catholic and left-wing circles) emphasizes "solidarity" over legality and security.

Even so, there have been cases of urban unrest directly linked to immigration. Roughly speaking, we might identify the following types of reactions:

Public reaction to the lack of security and social and environmental degradation caused by, or attributed to, immigrants. In some neighborhoods in large cities ad hoc committees have been set up to plan and manage demonstrations.

Public reaction to ethnic ghettos in some agricultural districts in central and southern Italy. It should be noted that these districts are functionally integrated into the neighboring metropolitan areas, and their conflicts are not much different from urban ones: it is not competition for farming jobs causing the tension, but rather reaction to the anomalous concentrations of immigrants, environmental degradation, lack of services, and a sense of insecurity. And, more than anywhere else, it is in these areas that criminal organizations are operating, attempting to control certain activities, such as illegal labor, drug trafficking, and prostitution. Such organizations were behind the murder of six African immigrants at Castelvolturno in the province of Caserta, which gave rise to an angry and violent reaction on the part of the immigrant community in September 2008 and the wounding of two immigrants at Rosarno, in the province of Reggio Calabria, leading to a riot that left thirty-seven people injured in January 2010.

Public reaction to illegal immigrant settlements (Roma camps, shantytowns, and ethnic ghettos of various kinds). Some Roma camps have been firebombed, and explosive gifts have been given to their children. These clashes worsened when Romania joined the European Union in January 2007 and the number of Roma migrating from that country to Italy rapidly increased.

Reactions of immigrants on being evicted from certain squatter camps or illegally occupied buildings. Some of the most violent clashes have been backed by activists from "antagonistic" organizations, which usually exploit these opportunities to attack the local authorities, including left-wing ones, accusing them of placing legality above solidarity.

Reactions by immigrants to measures they perceive as vexatious or discriminatory. In Milan, young people rioted in the local "Chinatown," waving the red flags of the People's Republic of China. The Chinese consul intervened to oppose the Milan city council's attempt to enforce the regulations governing the use of public highways and trade on April 12, 2007. This was the first open conflict in a large Italian city between an ethnic community and the local authorities.

Reactions by immigrants to the high-handedness of Italian criminal organizations. In particular, in 2007 Chinese traders rebelled in the Forcella district of Naples against the payment of protection money demanded by the Camorra.

Ethnic clashes between different groups of immigrants. Conflicts of this kind have occurred in Rome, on the occupied premises of Pantanella, and more recently in the Via Anelli district in Padua. It was here in July 2006, after a night of guerrilla warfare between Moroccans and Nigerians involved in drug trafficking and other illegal activities, that the center-left mayor erected a steel barrier eighty-four meters long and three meters high to isolate the area.

Fighting between gangs of young immigrants or immigrants' children. The first serious incidents occurred in 2005 in Genoa and Milan between the Ecuadorian and Peruvian communities, but clashes soon spread to other towns and now involve many other ethnic groups.

Protests by immigrants in support of specific demands. In Rome in September 2007, immigrants occupied the central post office, protesting the delays in issuing residence permits, and in Naples in July 2008, a group of immigrants took over the cathedral and clashed with the police after their eviction from a tenement building.

"Cultural" clashes against the opening of places of worship and religious schools for Muslims. There were public demonstrations against the construction of large mosques in Genoa, Bologna, Milan, and Colle Val d'Elsa in the province of Siena, the opening of a Muslim school in Milan, and the inauguration of a training course for imams in Brescia.

However, the event that most closely recalls the incidents in the French *banlieues* was the reaction to the killing in Milan of a 19-year-old man from Burkina Faso in September 2008. Early one morning, near the central station, the young man was hit on the head with a metal bar by a street vendor from whom he had stolen a few packets of candy. Violent riots followed, with acts of vandalism and stand-up fights with the police.

Such conflicts are becoming increasingly frequent, violent, and widespread. The bell of Saint-Denis has also tolled for Italians.

The Impact on Migration Policy

The new demand for security and the need to combat crime, terrorism, and urban unrest have greatly influenced migration policies in the European countries.

One year before 9/11, in 2000, the European Commission for the first time set out its guidelines for immigration policy (which until a few years earlier was the exclusive competence of each member state). In its "communication" (a kind of soft law) it called for "social integration in respect for cultural diversity."[29]

Today these may seem rather banal words. But then, the main European receiving countries practiced quite different policies. One only needs to recall that France was still committed to the cultural assimilation of immigrants, according to its old republican model of integration, which had been strongly reconfirmed at the beginning of the 1990s, while Germany, mainly for the new immigrants from Eastern Europe, had resumed its old *Gastarbeiter* (guest-worker) policy, which made no provision for their integration.[30]

At first, all the member states accepted the proposal of the European Commission, but after 9/11 the climate changed rapidly and, almost everywhere, security concerns prevailed.

In France, where some nonconformist intellectuals had begun to propose a "French-style multiculturalism" (a sort of compromise between the republican model and the claims of the immigrant communities), the concerns about security led to other solutions. In October 2003 tougher measures were enacted against illegal immigration and its consequences, and in February 2004 women were prohibited from wearing the Islamic veil in public buildings. Later, in his 2007 presidential campaign, Nicolas Sarkozy insisted on the need to "clean up" the *banlieues*, and in 2010, after his election, he began to dismantle the illegal Roma camps.

In 2000 in Germany the new Red-Green government coalition officially recognized the immigrant-receiving character of the country, which the previous governments had obstinately denied for fifty years, and enacted a new citizenship law limiting the dominance of *jus sanguinis* (the policy that children's citizenship is determined by their parents'), which was so deeply rooted in German political culture. The same government coalition subsequently approved a socially very advanced immigration law in March 2002, in spite of fierce resistance from the two Christian parties. But this law was struck down by the federal court, and two years later, by agreement with the opposition, it was replaced by another law that met the new security requirements. More recently, in October 2010, Chancellor Angela Merkel declared that the attempts to build a multicultural society in Germany had "utterly failed" and that immigrants willing to settle in the country must adapt, learn German as quickly as possible, and assimilate into the society.

In the United Kingdom, there was wide-ranging acceptance of multiculturalism. Prince Charles, who on acceding to the throne would also take on the role of *defensor fidei*, publicly declared that he would perform it not in favor of the Church of England alone, but as the defender of all the faiths in the country. But subsequently, in November 2002, an asylum, immigration, and nationality law sought to curb the arrival of asylum-seekers and unskilled migrants and required the biometric identification of all newcomers. Two years later, in 2004, Queen Elizabeth herself, explicitly referring to the "time of global uncertainty with an increased threat from international terrorism and organized crime," announced that Prime Minister Tony Blair's Labour government would reintroduce the obligation to carry identity cards, which had lapsed after the Second World War. Another sign of this climate was the publication of a provocative report by an influential New Labour think tank, which, "in the wake of the 11 September attacks and the riots of Summer 2001," openly called for "reclaiming Britishness."[31]

An increasingly evident tendency to contain immigration emerged some years later, in response to Islamist terrorism. In July 2005 some British-born Asian young people perpetrated deadly suicide attacks in London, which caused fifty-two deaths and left approximately 700 injured; some days later, other young men from the same background tried to emulate them. In August 2006 twenty-four young men of Pakistani origin were arrested as they prepared suicide attacks against airlines bound for the United States. In June 2007 two car bomb attacks, jointly planned by young British citizens of Asian origin and foreign nationals, who seemingly had been fully integrated into British society, were foiled in central London, and another attack, partially botched, was carried out against the Glasgow airport.

Moreover, in the aftermath of the 2005 attacks, an opinion poll revealed that 88 percent of the Muslims living in the United Kingdom, including those born there, did not feel British, and later opinion polls showed that one Muslim in four sympathized with terrorists, 40 percent of young British Muslims wanted to live under Koranic law, and one-third of Muslim students at British universities believed that it was right to kill in the name of Allah.[32] These findings drew severe criticism of the British multicultural model, which was blamed for fostering the formation of nothing short of a "Londonistan," in a country with two and a half million Muslims and 2,000 mosques. In any event, it was here that many of those "robots of death" had grown up, aspiring to sacrifice their lives in order to strike the hated West.

It should not be forgotten that ethnically defined gangs of youths bent on violence have continued to proliferate in British cities. At this writing in 2011, there are about 170 gangs of this kind in London, with at least 5,000 members, some very young, and their fighting has caused the deaths of many dozens of teens. In Liverpool one of the most recent victims was only eleven years old, and the six youths arrested for the crime were aged fourteen to nineteen, all of them living in one of those underproletarian estates bursting at the seams with weapons and drugs, and housing a fluctuating population of immigrants with poor and nondescript social relations.

These events have led the present Conservative/Liberal Democrat coalition to further curtail immigration, and to push through a new law for this purpose. In February 2011, at a security conference in Munich, Prime Minister David Cameron himself attacked the "failed policy" of multiculturalism, blaming it for Islamist extremism. He called for "a lot less of passive tolerance and much more active, muscular liberalism" where equal rights, the rule of law, freedom of speech, and democracy are promoted to create a stronger national identity.

In Italy, the immigration law enacted in 2002 (known as the "Bossi-Fini law," after its two main sponsors) responded to similar concerns, just one year after the 9/11 attacks. But that law was accompanied, contradictorily, by the largest general immigration amnesty ever implemented in Europe (700,000 immigrants were legalized), mainly to appease the Catholic Church. Even though the law had been bitterly criticized by the left, which even accused it of being racist, it was not repealed but merely adjusted by the next center-left government (2006–08). This law, however, had not questioned the principle of social integration in respect for cultural diversity, which in Italy had already been sanctioned in 1986 (long before the aforementioned European Commission's "communication") in the first Italian immigration law. But in 2008, after winning the general election once again, the center-right enacted a package of security measures, specifically "addressing widespread unlawful activities linked to illegal immigration and organized crime."

In Spain, too, migration policy has focused mainly on restricting illegal entry. This policy was tightened up after the attacks on three Madrid train stations on March 11, 2004, by local cells of Islamic extremists of Moroccan origin—the deadliest peacetime attacks in Spain's history (192 dead and 2,057 injured). However, the restrictive measures were accompanied in 2005 by a massive regularization of undocumented immigrants (almost 700,000 applications), which some EU authorities have bitterly criticized as being too loose. The subsequent severe financial and economic crisis, which created high unemployment (16 percent of Spanish nationals and 28 percent of foreigners in 2009 were unemployed), induced the government to control the situation more closely. The policy of the Socialist leader José Luis Zapatero (who won the general election three days after the 2004 Madrid attacks and again in 2008, a few months before the crisis broke) seems to be specifically designed to contain immigrant arrivals; it offers voluntary repatriation incentives on the one hand, while maintaining social cohesion and fostering social integration on the other.

Attempts are being made all over Europe to achieve security through policies combining a mix of immigration containment, terrorism prevention, counterterrorism, common crime prevention, and social measures aimed at integration and multiculturalism. Perhaps there is no alternative to this recipe, but nothing guarantees that it will work successfully. Unfortunately, the attitudes of some of its essential partners are anything but reassuring.

Notes

1. See Adil Jazouli, *Banlieues: les nouvelles frontières intérieures. Rapport de synthèse* (Paris: Banlieuescopies, 1992).

2. For an initial summary see Caritas/Migrantes, *Immigrazione. Dossier Statistico 2008. XVIII Rapporto* (Rome: Idos, 2008), which provides the 2001–05 data, and for a broader historical series, earlier reports by the same organization, which cannot be suspected of any bias against immigrants because of its clearly pro-immigration and xenophile orientation. Moreover, there are the reports published yearly by the Fondazione Ismu (Milan: Franco Angeli) since 2003, and in particular the 2008 report, which openly acknowledged that "this problem can no longer be played down," as its own reports had done before 2002, even going so far as to claim that Italy was "one of the safest countries in Europe and the world." See Salvatore Palidda, "La devianza," in *Ottavo rapporto sulle migrazioni 2002*, edited by Fondazione Ismu (Milan: Franco Angeli, 2003), p. 177. The same tendency to play down the problem also emerged in the reports published by a commission set up by the center-left governments in power at that time. See Commissione per le politiche di integrazione degli immigrati in Italia, *Primo rapporto sull'integrazione degli immigrati* (Bologna: Il Mulino, 2000) and *Secondo rapporto sull'integrazione degli immigrati* (Bologna: Il Mulino, 2001).

3. In 2008, owing to new measures against illegal immigration and organized crime enacted by Decree Law 92 (May 23) and Law 125 (July 24), the crime rate fell by 8 percent from its 2007 level.

4. Ministero dell'Interno, *Rapporto sulla criminalità in Italia*, Rome, 2007. These figures do not tally with Istat's. Among other things, it should be noted that they refer to reported crimes, and not to reported individuals, and one individual may have been reported for several crimes.

5. See Franco Pittau, "Stranieri e criminalità: i dati di un quinquennio," in Caritas/Migrantes, *Immigrazione. Dossier Statistico 2008*, p. 214.

6. See *Il Secolo XIX*, August 27, 2009, p. 3.

7. Silvia Vegetti Finzi, "Il crimine seriale e le reazioni," *Corriere della Sera*, May 25, 2009, p. 20.

8. Marina Valcarenghi, *"Ho paura di me." Il comportamento sessuale violento* (Milan: Bruno Mondadori, 2009), p. 169.

9. According to the United Nations Population Fund, at least 5,000, and perhaps 10,000, "honor crimes" are committed every year in the world, mostly in Islamic countries. Immigration has once again spread them to places from which they had almost disappeared.

10. Genital mutilations affect 140 million women worldwide and 40,000 in Italy (a record in Europe).

11. Istat, *Rapporto annuale: la situazione del Paese nel 2008* (Rome, 2009). This statement, which was also published in a previous report (*Rapporto sulla criminalità in Italia*, 2007), was first given to the press on June 20, 2007, when it was presented by Giuliano Amato, then minister of the interior.

12. Alessandro Dal Lago, *Non-persone. L'esclusione dei migranti in una società globale* (Milan: Feltrinelli, 1999), p. 12. Also see his interview in *Micromega-online*, May 14, 2009.

13. *La Repubblica*, October 25, 1996, p. 25.

14. *Roma Caritas*, 1999, 6, p. 12. For her later partial self-criticism, see "Sugli immigrati sbagliavo" (interview), *Corriere della Sera*, February 21, 2009, p. 3.

15. See *Corriere della Sera*, January 20, 1999, p. 10.

16. Marzio Barbagli, "Immigrati e reati, io di sinistra non volevo vedere" (interview), *Corriere della Sera*, February 18, 2009, p. 18. Barbagli has addressed this argument in three books: *Immigrazione e criminalità in Italia* (Bologna: Il Mulino, 1998), *Immigrazione e reati in Italia* (Bologna: Il Mulino, 2002) and *Immigrazione e sicurezza in Italia* (Bologna: Il Mulino, 2008).

17. In his first TV speech on the revolt, November 14, 2005.

18. He used this word on October 25, 2010, in Argenteuil, Val-d'Oise, to describe the youths who had met him with insults and stones.

19. In an interview with the Israeli newspaper *Ha'aretz*, November 17, 2005.

20. In an interview with the German weekly *Der Spiegel*, November 14, 2005.

21. In an interview with the Italian newspaper *Il Manifesto*, November 22, 2005. Also see Etienne Balibar, "Uprising in the Banlieues," *Constellations* 14, no. 1 (2007): 47–71.

22. In an interview with a Russian TV network. See *Liberation*, November 14, 2005. This statement was repeated by Minister of Labor Gérard Larcher (*Le Monde*, November 16, 2005) and by the chairman of the UMP Party group at the National Assembly, Bernard Accoyer (in a TV interview).

23. Alain Touraine, interviews with the Italian newspapers *La Repubblica*, November 3, 2005, and *Il Giornale*, November 7, 2005. Michel Wieviorka, personal communication, 2006.

24. See Sami Naïr, "Las llamas francesas," *El Pais*, November 12, 2005.

25. Marc Augé, *Non-places: Introduction to an Anthropology of Supermodernity*, trans. John Howe (London: Verso, 1995).

26. See Ulrich Beck, "Die Revolte der Überflüssigen," *Süddeutsche Zeitung*, November 15, 2005.

27. See Michael Hardt and Toni Negri, *Commonwealth* (Cambridge, Mass.: Belknap Press of Harvard University Press, 2009).

28. See Umberto Melotti, *Le "banlieues". Immigrazione e conflitti urbani in Europa* (Rome: Meltemi, 2007).

29. European Commission, *Communication to the Council and the European Parliament on a Community Immigration Policy*, Brussels, COM (2000) 757 final, November 22, 2000.

30. As for France, see Haut Conseil à l'Intégration, *Pour un modèle français d'intégration. Rapport au Premier Ministre* (Paris: La Documentation Française, 1991); as for Germany, see Hedwig Rudolph, "The New *Gastarbeiter* System in Germany," *New Community* 2 (1996): 287–300.

31. Foreign Policy Centre, *Reclaiming Britishness*, edited by Mark Leonard and Phoebe Griffith (London, 2002). The book included an essay by David Blunkett, then the home secretary.

32. See *Daily Telegraph*, July 23, 2005; and *Sunday Telegraph*, February 20, 2006, and July 26, 2008.

PART THREE

Energy Policies: Between Environmental and Power Politics

ALESSANDRO ORTIS

10 The Challenge of the European Union's Energy Policy and Regulation

Energy policy and regulation are closely intertwined. This chapter briefly outlines the energy issues of major concern in the global arena, energy supply and climate change. It then examines these issues from a European perspective in relation to EU energy policy and the single energy market, the internal and external frontiers, the energy supply bridges to Europe, and energy innovation. It concludes with a discussion of the role of regulation and regulators of energy policy within and outside Europe.

Security of the Energy Supply

Energy security has been an issue of major international concern over much of the past decade as oil production in the countries of the Organization for Economic Cooperation and Development (OECD) reached a long-expected plateau and began its irrevocable decline; oil demand in the less-developed countries (LDCs) began surging at sustained rates, and OPEC (the Organization of Petroleum Exporting Countries) attempted a delicate balancing act, restraining increases in supply to achieve the highest possible margins "while allowing for suitable economic growth."

Most observers agree that speculation in the oil sector and secondary markets was the major driver of the price escalation. In a period of weakening fundamentals, experienced during 2007–08, it was difficult to ignore the effects of the rapid increase in so-called speculative contracts on future oil prices entered into by hedge funds and exchange-traded funds: their number increased from around 200,000 in 2004 to over 1.4 million immediately before the plunge in oil prices in 2008.

Though the global financial and economic crisis was not spurred by energy, it was closely connected to it. The short-lived cycle of crude oil prices in 2007 and 2008, marked by a tripling in prices in eighteen months and followed by an abrupt fall to values below the initial levels over the following six months, could not originate from supply-and-demand fundamentals, though these indeed provided support to the price increases. The turning point in July 2008 coincided with the dollar appreciation against the euro and the beginning of the worldwide meltdown of financial markets. Between July and December 2008 the Dow Jones Industrial Average and the price of West Texas Intermediate crude oil dropped together in almost perfect synchrony.

Following the decline in oil demand in the OECD and other developed economies, and increases in production capacity (mostly in Saudi Arabia), OPEC spare capacity at this writing in 2011 is back to a level of around 5 million barrels per day. But this situation is likely to be short-lived as the world economy takes off again in the following year or two. Primary energy consumption is already back on course in the developing countries, where it increased by 4.7 percent in 2009 over 2008, compared to an average decline of 5.3 percent in developed countries in the same period.

The International Energy Agency has warned that oil supply could soon face difficulties in keeping abreast of increasing demand, leading to further increases in oil prices (independent of speculation) and potentially stifling renewed economic growth. The major concern is oil, which still meets 35 percent of the world's energy demand in final-use markets, principally the transport sector, where substitution with other energy sources is difficult or slow. But energy hunger in the developing countries, driven by strong population growth and economic development, is so great as to lead to tight markets for other energy sources.

The major issue of energy supply security is the achievement of stable energy prices at levels that are high enough to stimulate expansion in production capacity but not so high as to depress demand. In the free-trade market economies it may be impossible to avoid economic cycles. In the long run these cycles are even beneficial for efficiency improvements and innovation, but every effort should be made to safeguard against violent fluctuations.

The experience of 2008–10 provides ample evidence that energy price security cannot be attained except through improving regulation and monitoring financial and energy markets. The objective is to consolidate the key pillars of providing liquidity and enhancing competition at the same time that market integrity is ensured by preventing abuses.[1] For example, one way to limit price volatility and encourage long-term investment in oil supplies to the European market would be to establish a regulated trading platform with the following key requisites: trading of only physical barrels with delivery in Europe; limitation of trading to key operators who meet certain standards for long- and very-long-term standard contracts; and transactions guaranteed by a reliable European counterpart, such as the European Investment Bank. Such a system would guarantee against price volatility and ensure reasonable returns on long-term investments, ultimately contributing to a more suitable level of spare capacity. Similar solutions could of course be devised for other world regions.

Energy and Climate Change

The continuing unabated increase in greenhouse gas emissions and the expiration of the Kyoto Protocol seem to be the energy-related environmental issues of most concern for governments around the world. Carbon dioxide emissions from the burning of fossil fuels have increased by 37 percent worldwide over the past two decades. However, this is a composite figure resulting from a 9 percent decline in the European Union, a 9 percent increase in the OECD as a whole, a 40 percent decrease in the countries of the former USSR, and a massive 135 percent increase in the developing countries.

In its "reference scenario" the *World Energy Outlook* (WEO) forecasts an increase in carbon dioxide emissions to 40.2 billion tons by 2030, a 40 percent increase from 2009 levels.[2] Some 97 percent of the increase would come from today's developing countries, with the African continent contributing about 3 percent of the increase, Latin America 6 percent, the Middle East 10 percent, and Asia 78 percent. In the WEO low-carbon scenario, stabilization of atmospheric greenhouse gas concentration at 450 ppm (parts per million) requires a 35 percent reduction in fossil-related emissions to 26.4 billion tons in 2030, at about the same level as in 2004. At this concentration the Intergovernmental Panel on Climate Change (IPCC) estimates there is a 50 percent chance of achieving an average global temperature increase of less than two degrees Celsius, which still does not guarantee against a rise in sea level, increases in the frequency of extreme climatic events, the disappearance of fauna and flora, and other consequences.

Given these critical conditions, what stands out the most is the insistence of the EU on carrying out its lone battle against climate change. The 20 percent cut in emissions from 1990 levels by 2020, together with a 20 percent renewable energy target, decided in 2008, gave a clear signal to the rest of the world that the EU was doing things in earnest and ready to take the action required to lead the world in achieving sustainable development. However, the EU Commission sees the 20 percent target by 2020 just as a warm-up to put emissions onto the right path. In December 2008 the European Council confirmed "the European Union's commitment to increasing this reduction to 30 percent, within the framework of an ambitious and comprehensive global agreement in Copenhagen on climate change for the period after 2012, on condition that the other developed countries undertake to achieve comparable emission reductions and that the economically more advanced developing countries make a contribution commensurate with their respective responsibilities and capabilities." This goal does not seem to have been in any way upset by the failure of the Copenhagen summit. In its most recent communication on the topic, the European Commission goes on to say that all developed countries will need to make an additional effort, including cuts of 80–95 percent by 2050.[3]

All in all, it has to be acknowledged that the unilateral commitments made by the EU have been ineffective. Within the context of globalization, these efforts may even to some extent have favored the process of delocalizing production to countries that still have poor or inadequate environmental policies, such as China, India, and other Asian countries. A precise evaluation of the impact is inevitably complex and beyond the scope of this chapter, but a rough calculation gives an idea of the magnitude of the effect. For example, in China, which has been the world's top emitter since 2008, with emissions greater than those of all countries of the EU combined and increasing at a rate of close to 10 percent per year, domestic consumption of goods and services accounts for just over one-third of gross domestic product. The bulk of production and the related carbon emissions are induced by European and American consumption of products, many of which might have been produced more efficiently and in a more environmentally friendly way in Europe and the United States.

Therefore, it would be preferable to aim for arrangements set up within the framework of the World Trade Organization (WTO), rather than for agreements based on Kyoto-type protocols, requiring excruciating multilateral negotiations. Arrangements at the WTO level should focus on the CO_2 content of the products being traded and purely on this basis introduce border taxes and market adjustment mechanisms, while guaranteeing against protectionist intentions through appropriate checks and constraints, as well as other WTO requirements.

Energy Policies of the EU

Energy policy was not included among the supranational competences originally assigned to the European Community in the Treaty of Rome, and responsibility in this sector continued for many years to be shared between the EU and its member states. The concept of introducing a mandatory and comprehensive European energy policy was accepted only at the meeting of the European Council of 2005 in London.

A Union-wide energy policy is perhaps difficult to imagine considering the great diversity between the member states, characterized by import dependence; the role played by the different primary energy sources; the size, structure, and governance of the energy systems and energy sector industries; and the role of energy in the national economies.

Security of the gas supply is one of the key issues. Natural gas provides more than one-quarter of all primary energy supplies to the EU. More than one-fifth of the electricity consumed is generated from gas. Imports account for 63 percent of consumption. In volume terms, gas imports have doubled since 1990 and are expected to increase by another third over the next two decades. The gas dispute between Russia and Ukraine in the winter of 2007 and two years later in January 2009 confirmed many of the weaknesses of existing legislation.[4] New legislation is under discussion that would allow public authorities at the national and EU levels to anticipate, avoid, and respond to a gas supply disruption that seriously affects one or more member states. A key innovation is the application of the N-1 rule, which sets off emergency measures when a dominant gas installation (import pipeline, regasification terminal, or production facility) in a given country is out of operation. Needless to say, the successful management of gas supply disruptions involving the EU as a whole depends to a large extent on the existence of adequate infrastructures with interconnections between member states, allowing also a reverse flow of gas, while the vast majority of existing supply lines are planned for securing gas to national markets.

The EU energy policy action with the greatest consequence by far is the formal adoption by the European Parliament in April 2009 of the so-called climate and energy package, consisting of different pieces of complementary legislation:[5]

—a directive setting binding national targets for increasing the share of renewable energy sources in the energy mix

—a directive creating a legal framework for the safe and environmentally sound use of carbon capture and storage technologies

—a directive revising the EU Emissions Trading System (EU ETS), accompanied by an "effort-sharing" decision setting binding national targets for emissions from sectors not covered by the EU ETS

Though dealing more with climate than with energy, the directives in many ways determine the direction of future EU energy development. Taken together, they amount to achieving three conditions by 2020: a 20 percent reduction in primary energy use, compared with projected levels, to be achieved through improvements in energy efficiency; a 20 percent share of renewable resources in final energy consumption; and a 20 percent reduction in greenhouse gas emissions from 1990 levels.

The EU Single Energy Market

The Internal Energy Market (IEM) was originally conceived as a single EU-wide space where energy producers and consumers could undertake transactions without distinctions as to nationality, activity, size, or any other characteristic. Without commercial obstacles of any kind, competition between suppliers in a market consisting of over 450 million people would lead to increasing efficiency and to declining costs and prices, thus favoring Europe's competitiveness. Legislation liberalizing the EU electricity and gas markets, adopted in 1996–98 and in 2003, was focused on opening up the markets by identifying producers and consumers qualified to enter into energy transactions with complete freedom of choice.[6] It aimed at preventing discrimination by separating energy transmission and other monopolistic activities from supply and other economic pursuits open to competition. More generally, it set a general framework for energy regulation at the member state level.

Considering the very different starting points and energy sector structures of the member states, as well as the short time frame during which the IEM was expected to pan out, it was no great surprise that the results of the inquiry on the status of electricity and gas markets, issued by the EU Commission in January 2007, led to somewhat disappointing results. It found too much market concentration in most national markets. If anything, this concentration had increased through aggressive merger-and-acquisition activity by the incumbents. Market concentration still reflected the old market structure, characterized by national or regional monopolies (usually vertically integrated companies) that controlled electricity prices in the wholesale market and blocked new entrants. In the gas sector, incumbents tended to control imports and/or domestic production. Lack of liquidity, insufficient transparency of market information, and small balancing zones favored the incumbents and inhibited successful new entries, even at the lower level of trading and retail sales. Customers too frequently remained tied to previous suppliers through long-term downstream contracts and through regulated prices. The level of unbundling between network and supply interests was found to be inadequate to support efficient market functioning and provide investment incentives. Above all, there was little or no integration between member state markets.

The situation has not changed significantly since 2007. All in all, the EU is still very far away from the concept of a single energy market. The Union still operates with many separate national energy markets and few signs of integration. The member states have very different degrees of liberalization, forms of unbundling, and rules of competition. Lack of investment in interconnectors leads to costly congestion and hinders cross-border operations. In essence, though transactions do take place in the broader EU space, they still represent only a small fraction of the total market, despite fairly strong price differences between countries.

The third liberalization package, first presented by the Commission at the end of 2007, has important new features that promise to more fully liberalize the EU electricity and gas markets in the coming years. The two directives and three regulations provide ever more rigorous rules and procedures for harmonizing the rules governing cross-border exchanges, access to networks and network codes, congestion management, consumer rights, provision of information, penalties for infringements, new interconnections, charges for network use, and international compensation.[7] They establish European networks of transmission system operators to promote cross-border trade in electricity and gas and coordinate technical standards for network operation and development.

The central provision of the directives, around which there was considerable wrangling, regards the unbundling of supply from network operation. The directives identify three distinct options based on *ownership unbundling*, the solution preferred by the Commission; the establishment of an *independent system operator*; regulatory supervision by an *independent transmission operator (ITO)*. Unbundling between the network and supply businesses is a key issue. Member states that have not already opted for ownership unbundling show a clear inclination toward the ITO model, which allows the vertically integrated company to continue making key investment decisions, even if under regulatory supervision. It remains to be seen from 2012 and beyond (the deadline for the implementation of unbundling) whether this setup is effective in providing the network capacity required by the market without discrimination.

A final achievement of the third package would be the establishment of an Agency for the Cooperation of Energy Regulators (ACER), with the objective of overcoming the lack of coherence in the powers and remits of national energy regulators, one of the biggest hurdles in creating a functioning EU energy market. The third liberalization package would aim to resolve this problem by

—harmonizing and strengthening the powers and duties of national regulators so that they are able to issue binding decisions on companies and impose penalties on those that fail to comply

—ensuring that all national regulators are truly independent of industry interests and government intervention, with authority over their own budgets and the application of strict rules for management appointments

—mandating all national regulators with a binding requirement to cooperate with each other.

The third package promises in principle to resolve many of the problems in the functioning of the IEM.

The Enlargement Process and the External Frontiers

The accession of ten new member states to the EU in 2004 and the addition of two more three years later introduced new complications in the convergence toward a single energy market. Despite the inherent problems, soon thereafter the EU launched the process of enlargement in the energy sector, reaching out to the seven states and territories of the Balkans: Albania, Bosnia and Herzegovina, Croatia, the former Yugoslav Republic of Macedonia, Montenegro, Serbia, and the United Nations Interim Administration Mission in Kosovo.[8] The Energy Community Treaty, aiming at the future creation of an internal market in electricity and natural gas extended to thirty-four countries, was established in May 2006.[9]

The treaty, which entered into force on July 1, 2006, and has a ten-year duration with the possibility of extension, has objectives that fit closely with the concept of the European energy space: to create a stable legal and market framework capable of attracting investment in order to ensure a stable and continuous energy supply; to create a single regulatory space for trade in network energy; to enhance security of supply and develop cross-border relations; to improve energy efficiency and the environmental impacts of network energy and develop renewable energy sources; and to develop network energy market competition.

An important issue for the security of Europe's energy supply is the EU-Russia relationship. Russia is the largest oil, gas, and coal exporter to the EU, while the EU is by far the largest trade partner of the Russian Federation. Given the strong mutual interdependence and the common interest in its further development, in 2000 the EU and Russia launched the EU-Russia Energy Dialogue with the objective of providing "reliability, security and predictability of energy relations of the free market in the long term and to increase confidence and transparency between both sides."[10] Confidence building at all levels is a major achievement of the dialogue, helping to overcome the 2009 gas crisis and reach an agreement on the EU-Russia "early warning mechanism" to ensure rapid communication and prevent further supply interruptions in the field of gas, oil, or electricity.

The energy partnership aims at improving investment opportunities in the energy sector in order to ensure continued energy production, to secure and expand transport infrastructure, and to reduce the environmental impact. The partnership also targets the promotion of energy efficiency and energy savings and of environmentally friendly technologies and energy resources on the way to a low-carbon economy. Finally, it encourages the opening up of energy markets. Despite progress in many areas, it is on this last point that the dialogue appears to be held back; Russia has refused to ratify the Energy Charter Treaty and specifically to agree on the transit protocol. In a speech to the European Parliament, unveiling new proposals to be included in what was to become the third package, the president of the EU Commission, José Manuel Barroso, said that a "genuine single European energy market will continue to be open to our partners around the world, as long as they play by the same rules as our companies. In other words, we will protect competition in our newly-liberalized market." He went on to say that "to protect the openness of our market, to protect the benefits that unbundling will bring, we need to place tough conditions on ownership of assets by non- EU companies to make sure that we all play by the same rules."[11]

The reciprocity clause was inserted into the text of the third package in response to fears that ownership unbundling of integrated energy firms' production assets from their transmission assets would lead to the indiscriminate acquisition of EU energy grids by third countries. Under the reciprocity clause, all non-EU countries will be required to comply with the same unbundling requirements as EU companies before they are certified to operate in the EU market.[12] Moreover, member states must refuse certification if it is deemed to "put at risk the security of energy supply of the member state and the Community." The EU Commission has final supervision over the acquisition of control over a Community transmission system or transmission system operator. The reciprocity clause does not preclude foreign acquisition of controlling rights, but it does give scope for member states and the Commission to decide whether to let a third-country company enter the EU market, acknowledging that member states have the right to national legal controls to protect legitimate public security interests.

Bridges to the European Union

Energy resources within 2,000 kilometers of the EU's borders hold over 70 percent of the world's proven oil and gas resources. However, there are practically no common borders between the EU member states and the resource-endowed countries. Energy has to cross seas by ship or by pipeline or flow overland across one or more transit countries. The bridges to Europe, their security and costs, vary significantly between oil and gas and by exporting region.

Oil transport from the Middle East and North Africa is less critical since relatively short pipeline connections to seaports that do not cross third countries are almost always possible. However, the passage to Europe by sea depends on unpredictable conditions in the Strait of Hormuz and the Suez Canal. Bringing Caspian oil to Europe holds other problems since two or more transit countries, and even inland seas, need to be crossed.

Pipeline transport to the EU borders accounts for just 8 percent of total oil imports but 84 percent of total gas imports to the EU. While interruptions in oil exports from producing countries are usually not exceedingly difficult to resolve by substituting oil supplies from the global market, replacement of a major import source of natural gas has strong infrastructure limitations related to maximum pipeline and liquefied natural gas (LNG) terminal capacities. As a consequence, building secure bridges to Europe is much more critical for natural gas than for oil. Currently over 40 percent of pipeline imports of natural gas are pumped through Belarus and Ukraine, transit routes that have proved to be not entirely reliable in terms of continuity of supplies. Another 25 percent come through undersea routes, which are in principle subject to more complicated repair procedures and longer downtime in the event of breakdown or sabotage. In the interest of supply security, some measure of redundancy in pipeline routes is therefore welcome, even at the expense of lower capacity utilization and thus higher transport costs for consumers.

Numerous pipeline bridges to Europe are currently under planning or construction, aiming at increasing the security of supplies. When finally completed around 2015, two major projects are expected to supply together over 110 billion cubic meters of Russian gas, equivalent to the quantity that currently transits to the EU through Belarus and Ukraine. There is also the North Stream pipeline, emerging from the Baltic Sea in Germany, and the South Stream pipeline, crossing the Black Sea and surfacing in Bulgaria.

While the North and South Streams are conceived to supply Russian gas to Europe avoiding transit countries, another three projects, also planned to come on line early in this decade, aim at increasing supplies sourced from the Caspian and the Middle East. The Turkey-Greece-Italy Interconnector (TGI) will have a nominal capacity of 8 to 10 billion cubic meters; the Trans Adriatic Pipeline (TAP) expects to double this capacity (depending on the demand) and is aimed mainly at supplying Italy through Greece and Albania. The Nabucco pipeline, the largest of the three projects with a planned throughput of 31 billion cubic meters of gas, targets Turkey, Bulgaria, Romania, Hungary, Austria, and the Czech Republic. These projects are very similar in three basic aspects: none have as yet certain sources of gas; they all pass through a number of transit countries; they rely on Turkey as the bridge to Europe.

If, as seems likely, the North and South Stream projects will largely supplant Russian gas exports through Belarus and Ukraine, then these three projects taken together will barely be sufficient to meet import demand over the decade 2010–20. Their maximum combined capacity is 61 billion cubic meters, while total import demand (even under the EU's 2020 objectives) could be as great as 250 billion cubic meters of gas or more, considering the decline in domestic production. New pipelines from North Africa, for example the Galsi project from Algeria, another (Mediterranean) bridge to Europe, could help to bridge the gap, as could LNG projects from other producing countries.

Energy Innovation

Energy innovation is the most subtle frontier. Energy systems are highly dynamic. As they develop, preexisting energy resources are used differently and old technologies are replaced by new ones. At the basis of this change is energy research, development, and demonstration. But energy R,D&D alone does not guarantee innovation; this is a societal process that requires implementing the whole body of actions needed to undertake scientific and applied research, to incorporate and diffuse technological change throughout society. The EU has for many years sponsored broad technology innovation programs as part of a major policy to modernize its energy system and bring it up to best practice anywhere in the world.

The "knowledge triangle" (research, education, and innovation) is a core factor in European efforts to meet the ambitious goals of the Lisbon strategy to become the "most dynamic and competitive knowledge-based economy in the world." EU energy R&D funding began to take shape in the 1980s with the launching of the Framework Programs for Research and Technology Development. Over time, EU research funding has become much more intricate and sophisticated than the traditional top-down topic-oriented allocation of funding.

The Seventh Framework Program (FP7), running from 2007 to 2013, bundles all research-related EU initiatives together under a common roof and plays a crucial role in expressly addressing Europe's employment needs, competitiveness, and quality of life. Other important sources of funding technology innovation are the Competitiveness and Innovation Framework Program (CIP) and the Structural and Cohesion Funds for regional convergence and competitiveness.

A key role in the coordination of research programs and policies of a transnational nature is played by the European Research Area (ERA), established in

2000 with the objective of preventing research fragmentation and providing access to a Europe-wide open space for knowledge and technologies in which transnational synergies and complementarities are fully exploited. Other organizations are also intrinsically involved in guiding the EU research landscape, such as the European Research Council, the Joint Technology Initiatives, and the European Institute for Innovation and Technology. The EU's own research structures, including the European Organization for Nuclear Research (CERN), the European Atomic Energy Community (Euratom), and the Joint Research Centre (JRC), have also conducted research over the past five decades.

The broad objectives of FP7 have been grouped into four categories: cooperation, ideas, people, and capacities, each with its own specific program corresponding to the main areas of EU research policy and all working together to promote and encourage the creation of European poles of scientific excellence.

The CIP includes the Intelligent Energy Europe (IEE) program, geared specifically to the promotion of energy efficiency and renewable energy. The IEE program does not fund technical projects but rather acts as a catalyst for socioeconomic, market, regulatory, policy, and institutional changes, including international transfer of experience, promotion of best practices, education and training, institutional capacity building, information dissemination, and the creation of new standards and norms.

Overall funding of EU innovation programs over the period 2007–13 amounts to a little over €55 billion, of which FP7 accounts for about €50 billion. It is impossible at this time even to estimate the fraction of this budget allocated to energy-related R,D&D, while calls for proposals are still under way. The fraction of energy in the total FP budgets has declined over time to an estimated 12 percent in FP6 (2003–07), from about 50 percent in FP1 (1984–87), presumably reflecting the energy crisis of the early 1980s.[13] It is also interesting to note the increasing role of the EU in promoting Union-wide research, while the member states have been progressively reducing their publicly funded R&D commitment. Between FP1 and FP6, the R,D&D budgets increased almost fourfold at the same time that member-state financing from public sources decreased by over 60 percent. As a result, the share of EU financing in overall member-state and EU research funding almost doubled, from 17 percent in FP1 to around 30 percent in FP5 and FP6.

Energy Policy and Regulation

In principle, energy policy and regulation are quite distinct, the former essentially dealing with the choice of energy resources, security, technologies, and incentives or subsidies, the latter with market efficiency and the rules for energy distribution and utilization. But the border between the two is never well defined, and overlapping competences can be an issue.

Powers of the Regulator

The mandate and responsibilities of energy regulators vary broadly from one country to another, even within a relatively uniform administrative space, such as the EU, or even the provinces of one country. There are major differences in sectoral mandates, regulatory powers, autonomy, and independence from other bodies.

The electricity and natural gas sectors (both network-based) are the most common remit of energy regulators, but responsibilities can and frequently do stretch to oil, renewable energy, district heating, and even non-energy sectors such as water. Tariff formulation for "grid services" is the most diffuse regulatory power, but in too many cases tariff proposals have to be approved by ministries or other government bodies before they are enacted. Also, tariff-making and price-monitoring powers vary widely over different segments of the supply chain. Powers of separation of network from supply activities are almost always limited to the milder forms of unbundling (accounting and functional), although many regulators have the power to monitor compliance with the standards. Likewise, powers of sanctioning for infringement of the rules tend to be limited, particularly the extent of the penalties. Significant diversity is apparent also in the role of energy regulators in setting the standards for and guaranteeing quality of service, improving energy efficiency, and setting the rules for and overseeing market operations. Financial autonomy also varies widely, with some regulators being financed from public funds, others from levies on the regulated industries, and others from licenses.

One key issue is the role of the regulator in fostering the infrastructure investments necessary to guarantee security of supply. Network expansion, maintenance, and modernization rely on tariffs sufficient to cover the investment and operating costs. The regulator plays a critical role in defining tariffs and tariff incentives, which guarantee that the investments will be made when and where they are most needed. To this end, some regulators have the power to go even further by setting the investment planning rules and the standards for infrastructure adequacy, by approving investment plans, by monitoring the timely implementation of investments, and by sanctioning operators for non-compliance with the investment plan. Regulators can also influence investments in energy production through market organization and monitoring and by introducing specific rewards and penalties based on capacity payments, capacity auctions, balancing charges, and other factors.

International Cooperation between Energy Regulators

In the late 1990s, 15 energy sector regulators existed worldwide: in today's global world there are more than 300 that are more or less independent from other government bodies. Regulation by accountable institutions, independent of political, financial, and industry pressures, in cooperation with relevant competition authorities, plays an indispensable role in securing adequate energy volumes and price stability, by providing operators and consumers with efficient and competitive energy markets and with transparent, stable, and predictable rules, by promoting confidence in the functioning of markets, and by stimulating new investments. Achieving these goals in regional and global energy markets is impossible without international cooperation between energy regulators, as well as between governments. Important steps in this direction have been taken over the past decade with the establishment of regional and global associations of energy regulators. EU energy regulators are closely involved in four of these.

The Council of European Energy Regulators (CEER) was set up in March 2000 by ten EU energy regulatory authorities as a voluntary association with the objective of facilitating cooperation for the promotion of a single competitive, efficient, and sustainable internal market for gas and electricity in Europe. The CEER—which has since been extended to all twenty-seven regulatory authorities of the EU—acts as a platform for cooperation, information exchange, and assistance between national energy regulators and as their interface at the European level. It also cooperates with the European Commission and competition authorities to ensure consistent application of competition law to the energy industry. Since its beginning, the CEER has shared its regulatory experience worldwide through links with similar associations in the United States (National Association of Regulatory Utility Commissioners, NARUC) and in Central and Eastern Europe (Energy Regulators Regional Association, ERRA) and its membership in the International Energy Regulation Network (IERN). CEER has taken a central role in developing an effective and competitive electricity and gas market in the Energy Community of South East Europe as described above.

The European Regulators' Group for Electricity and Gas (ERGEG) was founded with the European Commission in 2003 as the EC's official advisory body on internal energy market issues. It is made up of the national energy regulatory authorities of all the EU member states. ERGEG advises and assists the Commission on its own initiative or upon request, in particular with respect to the preparation of draft implementing measures in the field of electricity and gas. In advising the Commission, ERGEG is required to consult stakeholders through written documents and public hearings at an early stage of preparation of new regulations and legislation following the four guiding principles of openness, transparency, consistency, and accountability. ERGEG has played an important role in initiating and managing the so-called Regional Initiatives (seven electricity and three gas market regions) as an intermediate step in the creation of a single competitive EU electricity and gas market, and is intimately involved in the electricity and gas forums held, respectively, in Florence and Madrid on a twice yearly basis.

The Euro-Mediterranean Energy Regulators Association (MEDREG) brings together twenty-two countries bordering the Mediterranean, of which eight are member states of the EU.[14] The principal aim of the association is to promote the achievement of a consistent, harmonious, and investment-friendly regulatory framework in the Mediterranean energy market. The actions of MEDREG, in collaboration with the European Commission, are seen as crucial to enable a permanent, stable, and strong cooperation among Mediterranean energy regulators, with a view to providing benefits to energy consumers of the Mediterranean region as a whole. The regional approach is the necessary starting point for cooperation on energy regulation, in the perspective of an integrated and efficient regional market that requires the modernization of existing infrastructure and the implementation of new grids, as well as the establishment of a legislative and regulatory framework for energy that is as harmonious, coherent, and as stable as possible.

The MEDREG member countries undertook a first project financed by the European Commission in 2008–09 to "support the development of a modern and efficient energy regulatory framework in the Mediterranean Partner Countries and strengthen their cooperation with EU energy regulators." A second financing extended the project for the two-year period 2010–12. The aim of the project is to facilitate information exchange between EU and partner country regulators by assisting the Mediterranean countries in establishing independent energy regulators, empowering those that already exist, and developing the technical capacities of their staff. An important part of the project is the training of the staff of the Mediterranean Regulatory Authorities at the Florence School of Regulation.

The International Confederation of Energy Regulators (ICER) provides a voluntary framework within which energy regulators around the globe can exchange information and diffuse best practices through structured contacts and common activities, with the ultimate objective of improving public and policymaker awareness and understanding of energy regulation and its role in addressing a wide spectrum of socioeconomic, environmental, and market issues.[15] Cooperation and coordination between energy regulators has been taking place at the regional level in different areas of the world for many years, but the ICER is the first association to bring together energy regulators from around the globe.[16]

The regulatory associations participating in ICER work together to promote dialogue and cooperation on regulatory issues that go beyond national and regional borders. In the three-year time frame to the World Forum on Energy Regulation in 2012 (WFER V) they are focusing on three key energy issues where energy regulation can play an important role: reliability and security of supply; climate change; and competitiveness and affordability of energy supplies. They will also be examining the issues of independence, powers, responsibilities, best practices, and the training of regulators toward these ends.

Although energy regulators deal mostly with natural gas and electricity, more rarely with oil, their actions are felt throughout the energy field because of the strong technological and economic interrelations across energy sources—for example, oil price indexation and fossil fuel inputs to power generation. Likewise, in many less-developed countries security of supply depends more on the availability of wood fuel than on modern energy resources.

Notes

1. G8+ Regulator's Statement, "Regulation, Energy Markets and New Investments: Their Contribution to Economic Recovery, Clean Energy Technology Deployment and Energy Security," Round Table of Energy Regulators, G8 Meeting of Energy Ministers, G8 Summit 2009, Rome, May 24, 2009.

2. International Energy Agency, *World Energy Outlook 2009* (Paris: IEA, 2010).

3. European Commission, "Analysis of Options to Move beyond 20 Percent Greenhouse Gas Emission Reductions and Assessing the Risk of Carbon Leakage," communication to the European Parliament, the European Council, the European Economic and Social Committee, and the Committee of the Regions, COM (2010) 265, May 26, 2010.

4. Council Directive 2004/67/EC of 26 April 2004, concerning measures to safeguard security of natural gas supply.

5. The legislation of greatest importance here is Directive 2009/28/EC of the European Parliament and of the Council of 23 April 2009, on the promotion of the use of energy from renewable sources and amending and subsequently repealing Directives 2001/77/EC and 2003/30/EC.

6. Directives 96/92/EC and 2003/54/EC on electricity and 98/30/EC and 2003/55/EC on natural gas.

7. The directives and regulations are as follows:

—Directive 2009/72/EC of the European Parliament and of the Council of 13 July 2009 concerning common rules for the internal market in electricity and repealing Directive 2003/54/EC.

—Directive 2009/73/EC of the European Parliament and of the Council of 13 July 2009 concerning common rules for the internal market in natural gas and repealing Directive 2003/55/EC.

—Regulation (EC) no. 713/2009 of the European Parliament and of the Council of 13 July 2009, establishing an Agency for the Cooperation of Energy Regulators.

—Regulation (EC) no. 714/2009 of the European Parliament and of the Council of 13 July 2009 on conditions for access to the network for cross-border exchanges in electricity and repealing Regulation (EC) no. 1228/2003.

—Regulation (EC) no. 715/2009 of the European Parliament and of the Council of 13 July 2009 on conditions for access to the natural gas transmission networks and repealing Regulation (EC) no. 1775/2005.

8. In December 2009 Moldova and Ukraine also entered into the treaty.

9. Council Decision 2006/500/EC of 29 May 2006.

10. EU-Russia Energy Dialogue, *9th Progress Report*, Paris 2008.

11. José Manuel Barroso, speech to the European Parliament, September 19, 2007.

12. Article 11, Certification in Relation to Third Countries, in both Directives 2009/72/EC and 2009/73/EC.

13. See "Analysis of Energy R&D Expenditures in the Energy Sector in the EU, the USA and Japan," in *Technology and Social Visions for Europe's Energy Future—a Europe-Wide Delphi Study* (EURENDEL), September 2004. The data reported in this analysis refer to EU 15 (the fifteen member states before enlargement in 2004).

14. The non-EU members of MEDREG are Albania, Algeria, Bosnia-Herzegovina, Croatia, Egypt, Jordan, Israel, Lebanon, Morocco, Montenegro, the Palestinian Authority, Syria, Tunisia, and Turkey. The EU member states are Cyprus, France, Greece, Italy, Malta, Portugal, Slovenia, and Spain.

15. ICER was established at the World Energy Forum on Energy Regulation IV, held in Athens in October 2009, following the commitment of the G8+ energy regulators to increase cooperation.

16. ICER currently includes eleven regional associations covering 128 countries.

MASSIMO GAIANI

11 Translating Energy Strategy into Policy with EU Enlargement

There is a wide consensus that the European Union's fifth enlargement, the one that brought in an additional ten member states in 2004, and another two in 2007, has made Europe not only bigger but also stronger, more dynamic, and culturally wider, bringing huge economic benefits to everyone.

Does this very positive judgment also apply to the energy sector? In this sector, the outcome of the enlargement is more questionable. None of the new member countries produces significant energy, and the EU energy balance did not improve after the fifth enlargement.

In the long negotiation that preceded the accession of the new states in 2004, energy received attention mainly for two reasons: the new member countries had to shut down a number of nuclear plants that did not meet international security standards and they needed to liberalize their internal energy sector markets.

Enlargement had almost no impact on the energy security of either the EU or the acceding countries, since it has not reduced the EU's dependence on an external supply. Furthermore, in a moment of tight markets, the liberalization of the new member countries' energy sectors made them more vulnerable.

Their full integration into the EU energy system is far from complete and still requires huge investments. For instance, the minister of energy of Lithuania, Arvydas Sekmokas, in 2010 called the Baltic states an *energy island* because of their isolation from EU countries and their reliance on energy from the east. The same situation exists in the other countries of Central Europe and the Western Balkans, which are still dependent on Russia for their energy supply. The 2009 gas crisis in Ukraine is clear evidence of this dependency.

It is also true that, in comparison with other policies, a European energy policy is relatively new and has been developed only in the past decade. It was not in place when the enlargement began to take shape. Since then Europe has tried to set up a new energy strategy aiming to ensure safe, secure, sustainable, and affordable energy for all through the following instruments: completion of an internal energy market, energy savings, and a low-carbon economy.

The Lisbon Treaty offers a solid legal basis for achieving those goals, with its inclusion of a section on energy. It assigns to EU policy not only the objective of ensuring the proper functionality of the energy market (as part of the internal market) but also the security of the energy supply, the promotion of energy efficiency, and the development of renewable forms of energy and interconnected energy networks.

Even if the member states are still free to determine their energy resources, energy mix, and energy supply, the growing role of the EU in action on climate change does not give member states a free hand on these issues. The responsibility of the EU in this field is set to increase further, and a new energy strategy for Europe 2011–20 is expected to be adopted in 2011.

The new strategy will reaffirm the overall goal to ensure safe, secure, sustainable, and affordable energy. In particular it will set specific objectives for:

—completion of the internal energy market

—improvement of energy infrastructures (regional network initiatives, projects in the framework of the European economic recovery plan)

—the development of new technologies to increase energy produced by renewable sources, to boost energy efficiency and to increase nuclear safety

—a strong external dimension in order to increase the EU influence on regional and global energy markets and protect the security of energy supplies for all its members

The stock-taking document that anticipates the new European energy strategy for the years 2011–20 addresses the need for a strong and coordinated external energy policy. It appears that a possible way to ensure solidarity and mutual support in the event of import disruption could be the further integration of energy markets with neighboring producers and legally binding agreements to transit third countries.

Therefore there is good reason to consider energy as one of the key factors in the current enlargement process. If we really want to improve energy security there is a better instrument than the integration process.

In other words, in the current EU enlargement process, energy policy does not play as large a role as it deserves, and the need for further integration of energy markets with neighboring producer and transit countries does not seem to be duly respected.

The question that we should ask ourselves is: does Europe fully consider its energy security and the goals of its energy strategy in examining countries' applications for EU membership?

For the Western Balkans the answer is yes, since the Energy Community Treaty provides a framework for implementing the relevant *acquis communautaire* (to create an integrated energy market, to enhance the security of supply, to strengthen competition, to improve respect of the environment, to exploit economies of scale, and to attract investments). Moreover, the Renewable Energy Directive states that "green energy" produced in the area is to be considered equivalent to that produced in the EU. Still, the Western Balkans have limited weight in the energy equation.

The real issue is Turkey and its heavy weight in energy terms because of its geostrategic position. And for Turkey the answer to our question is not as clear.

Although some official documents of the Commission recognize the key role that Turkey plays in regional security, energy supply, and dialogue between countries, energy plays only a very minor role in the decision to extend EU membership to Turkey. The focus seems to be on other issues—the rule of law, internal constitutional and judicial reforms, human rights, and, of course, the Cyprus problem.

It almost seems that, when examining the Turkish case, Europe is not looking after its own interests. The underlying message being sent is that Europe is a club with certain rules, and unless you accept all of them, you won't be eligible for membership even if we desperately need you. And there is no doubt that Turkey's membership would bring Europe to the borders of the most important area of oil and gas production.

So much for membership. What about the role that energy plays in the external action of Europe?

In this case as well, Europe does not consider its own interest when defining its relations with its neighbors. In the short term, the most relevant issue is the relationship with Russia, Europe's main energy supplier. Within the EU there are different views on this subject. Some member states acknowledge the importance of Russia; others seem to be guided by other factors.

There are other examples of the tendency of Europe to neglect its interests in the energy sector when devising the enlargement and external action strategies. But Turkey and Russia are certainly the two most prominent cases, and they suffice to prove the point that energy is one of the most relevant EU policies.

This is even more true if we consider that energy and climate change are closely intertwined and that climate change has been a European priority since at least 2007. Despite that, Europe has not been capable of translating this internal strategy into its external projections, either through the enlargement process or in its relations with third countries. There are several explanations for this apparent incoherence: the decisionmaking process of the EU on enlargement, which allows a single member state to paralyze the EU initiative; the difficulty making external action coherent with internal policy; and the inability of the EU to play a leading political role, at least in the European neighborhood, by using all the instruments at its disposal to look after its strategic interests.

In the case of Turkey, the fear of including a big country with a mostly Muslim population has, for the time being, outweighed Europe's strategic interests; as for Russia, memories of the past combined with the worries of a predominant Russian role in the energy sector have prevented EU member states, and the EU as a whole, from upgrading their bilateral relations with Russia.

All of these arguments testify to the importance of energy policy. But because of its peculiar nature—its need to take account of a large number of member states with their own strategic interests, a decisionmaking process that still requires unanimity in certain areas—Europe, despite its economic weight, has not translated its energy policy into power politics, perhaps because Europe is not a political power, at least in the traditional sense.

PART FOUR

The New Frontiers of Economic Development for Europe

MAURIZIO CARBONE

12 Development Policy in a Changing Europe: More Donors, New Challenges

Development policy has been one of the most dynamic policy areas in the European Union since the turn of the twenty-first century. On the one hand, the emphasis has been on poverty eradication and on making foreign aid more efficient. On the other hand, the incorporation of new issues such as security, migration, and trade liberalization into the development agenda has reflected the EU's priorities. And new in the 2000s is the attempt to promote a common European vision of international development, with the understanding that a single voice enhances the EU's visibility and impact in international debates as well as in its relations with countries and regions. Under the leadership of the European Commission, in March 2002 and in April 2005 the EU's member states jointly committed to boosting their volume of aid. Moreover, the 2005 European Consensus on Development, together with the ambitious agenda on aid effectiveness and on policy coherence for development, provided a policy platform setting out common objectives and principles of development cooperation for both the EU and its member states.[1]

Another important change in the 2000s, which has not received adequate attention in the literature, has concerned the expansion of the frontiers of Europe and its potential impact on the relations between the EU and the developing world. This chapter addresses this gap, by looking not only at the 10+2 enlargement rounds of 2004 and 2007 toward the Central and Eastern European countries (CEECs), but also at the next wave toward countries in Southeastern and Northern Europe. The expectation is that any new member state would embrace the development *acquis*. The case of the enlargement round of the mid-2000s points to how difficult that prospect was in that none of the acceding countries had a consolidated tradition in this field. A similar scenario—though the cases of Turkey and Iceland are somehow different—presents itself before the next enlargement rounds. In addition to the consequences of enlargement, this chapter looks at the implications of the Treaty of Lisbon and the European External Action Service (EEAS) for development policy. In spite of widespread fears about its potential subordination to foreign policy, the autonomy of development policy was preserved and even reinforced.

The Impact of the 10+2 Enlargement Round

There are a number of potential explanations for the evolution of development policy in the European Union, particularly in the fields of international relations and EU studies. Those who take an intergovernmentalist approach have emphasized the preferences of two former colonial powers (France and the United Kingdom) and the changing membership of the EU as among the most important factors.[2] Undeniably, every time the EU has become bigger, development policy has undergone some transformations. A good way to capture these changes is to look at the debate between regionalists and globalists. Regionalists—that is, France, Belgium, and less openly Italy—emphasized the strategic links between Europe and its former colonies. Globalists—that is, Germany and the Netherlands—placed more emphasis on poverty eradication. If with the Treaty of Rome the regionalists prevailed and development assistance mainly concentrated in francophone Africa, with subsequent enlargements the pendulum swung back and forth. With the first enlargement of 1973, the United Kingdom sought to protect the members of the British Commonwealth, not only in Africa but also in the Caribbean and Pacific, as well as Asia. With the southern enlargement of the 1980s, there was an intensification of relations with Mediterranean and Latin American countries. With the northern enlargement of 1995, development became a multifaceted concept, including democracy, human rights, gender issues, and environmental issues. The repercussions of the eastern enlargement of the 2000s could not be easily predicted, not least because these countries lacked a consolidated tradition in the field.[3]

During the cold war, most of the countries in Central and Eastern Europe were members of the Council of Mutual Economic Assistance (CMEA). Their foreign aid program was characterized by a strong ideological orientation, concentrating on political allies and friendly countries that were pursuing socialist goals. Measuring CMEA aid was not easy owing to the lack of verifiable data. The three countries that allegedly provided larger amounts of aid were East Germany, Czechoslovakia, and Bulgaria. When the Berlin Wall fell, the CEECs discontinued their aid programs and became recipients of foreign aid. In view of their accession to the EU, and having partially overcome their transitional crisis, they (re)launched their development policies, thus facing the unique situation of being recipients of aid while simultaneously preparing to become donors. Before accession, their aid level was very small and allocation was mainly motivated by geographic proximity, with a preference for the former Soviet Union and the Balkans. In terms of quality of aid, most of these countries made extensive use of project aid (instead of program aid or budget support) and of tied aid, with the view to gaining public and business support in their efforts to boost the volume of aid.[4] Unsurprisingly, in the accession negotiations little attention was placed on development policy. In general, it seemed that the EU had "development on the accession agenda, but considering the many essential political topics and policies that were discussed during accession negotiations, one cannot expect development to receive disproportional amounts of attention."[5] The final report produced by the European Commission in 2002, nevertheless, concluded that all candidate countries—with the exception of Bulgaria and Romania—had aligned their policies with the *acquis* in the field of external relations.[6]

Although only a few years have passed since the CEECs joined the EU, it is possible to make an initial assessment of the impact of enlargement on development policy, which may contribute to better understanding the next enlargement wave.[7] All CEECs have increased their volume of foreign aid, and some have more than doubled it, despite the financial crisis that began in 2008. Yet they failed to meet the target to which they had committed in April 2005 (that of allocating 0.17 percent of their gross national income [GNI] by 2010 to international development), although Lithuania and Slovenia were not far off.[8] A number of CEECs have adapted their overall development frameworks and have significantly invested in institutional capacity—the Czech Republic, Estonia, and Slovakia have produced very detailed documents—but the lack of coordination between ministries involved in development has compromised the effectiveness of aid. Poverty eradication, however, has not yet become the main priority; only Hungary has unequivocally committed itself to poverty eradication, while Estonia and Poland have listed poverty eradication as one of their objectives.[9] Moreover, an analysis of aid flows has confirmed that countries in the Western Balkans, Eastern Europe, and Central Asia, all middle-income countries, have been the top (and in some cases the only) recipients; Poland, the Czech Republic, and Bulgaria have, however, started targeting sub-Saharan African countries.

The role of the EU in triggering these changes has raised some controversies. Drawing on the Europeanization literature, Simon Lightfoot argues that the European Union has significantly contributed to the reemergence of development policy in the CEECs. In this sense, "EU pressure forced the new states to formally and publicly commit themselves to increasing their quantity of ODA," though "as soon as political priorities changed in light of the current economic situation, aid budgets were cut dramatically." Moreover, "EU influence has produced a situation whereby all new member states have been forced to create administrative and legal structures for development both at home and Brussels."[10] Ondřej Horký, by contrast, maintains that the impact of the EU is less clear-cut, because it would not be possible to disentangle EU norms from a broader consensus on international development to which the EU itself contributes: "the EU and its member states operate in a multilevel environment and form a multilevel policy network themselves; this complicates attribution."[11] In particular, a number of CEECs have been influenced by norms acquired in their interaction with the Development Assistance Committee (DAC), United Nations Development Program (UNDP), and other bilateral donor agencies. Moreover, at least in the case of the Visegrad countries, Balázs Szent-Iványi and Andrád Tétényi noted a degree of path dependence from the legacy of their communist past, and this effect was deemed more significant than the EU development *acquis*.[12]

The other side of this debate concerns the impact of the CEECs on EU development policy. In general, the expected (partial) shift in the geographic scope of EU aid has not materialized. However, when Slovenia and the Czech Republic held the rotating presidency, they sought to place more emphasis on the eastern dimension of the EU. In the first semester of 2008, Slovenia made the Western Balkans one of its priorities and launched the Black Sea Synergy initiative, which set out activities in an area that had previously been overlooked. In reaction to Sarkozy's idea of a Union for the Mediterranean, Poland and Sweden proposed the "Eastern Partnership," which was actually launched under the Czech presidency in 2009. More generally, the CEECs have tried to emphasize that, having benefited from EU aid and as countries in transition, they could play a unique role in supporting efforts to deliver aid more efficiently and to foster a better understanding of the problems faced by developing countries. The European Transition Compendium (ETC), a compendium of the experiences, good practices, and expertise of new member states in the field of political and economic transition, as well as the management of external aid, was compiled by the European Commission and supported by the Czech presidency. Meanwhile, in the second Barroso Commission (2009–14), the post of development commissioner was assigned to the Latvian Andris Piebalgs, who came from a member state with relatively little experience in development cooperation, but he had a great deal of experience in EU politics and impressed everybody in his audition before the European Parliament.

The Treaty of Lisbon and the Development *Acquis*

The development *acquis*, to which candidate countries are bound, is composed of both primary law, particularly the articles included in the treaties devoted to this field, and secondary law, which includes development-related regulations as well as a large body of soft law instruments. The Treaty of Maastricht introduced a legal framework for development, including three new principles: complementarity, coordination, and coherence (the so-called 3Cs). In a nutshell, complementarity implies that development policy is a shared competence and that the program managed by the European Commission should complement those of the member states. Coordination implies that member states and the European Commission should consult on their aid programs, with a view to speaking with a single voice in international forums; the European Commission may take initiatives to promote such coordination. Coherence implies that the EU should take the development objectives into account in any of its policies that is likely to affect developing countries.

With the Treaty of Lisbon, not only was development cooperation kept as an autonomous policy in a separate section, but "sustainable development" and "poverty eradication" were even included among the EU's overall objectives in its external action. The creation of the new post of high representative (HR) for foreign affairs and security policy—who chairs the new Foreign Affairs Council and at the same time is the vice president of the European Commission—aimed to improve coherence between the intergovernmental and the supranational dimensions of EU external relations. The HR will receive support from the EEAS, made up of officials coming from the member states, the Council Secretariat, and the European Commission. In line with several resolutions adopted by the Council since the early 2000s, poverty eradication was elevated to the central goal of EU development policy.[13] The reference to the three Cs was left largely untouched. Development cooperation will continue to be an area of shared competence, but while previously EU development policy had to complement national development policies, now the two must "complement and reinforce each other."[14] Finally, the Treaty of Lisbon introduced the legal basis for the provision of humanitarian aid. In particular, it established that humanitarian aid operations must be conducted in conformity with the international principles of impartiality, neutrality, and nondiscrimination, and that the operations of the Union and the member states must "complement and reinforce each other."[15]

In addition to primary law, a significant amount of secondary legislation has been adopted over the years in the field of development policy, such as regulations covering the various financial instruments, sustainable development, and food aid, among others. Although they are nonbinding, a large body of soft law instruments, which include resolutions, declarations, and policy statements adopted by the Council, may be even more important.[16] A central place is for the European Consensus on Development—signed by the presidents of the European Commission, Parliament, and Council in December 2005—which for the first time in fifty years provided a policy platform setting out common objectives and principles of development cooperation for both the EU and its member states. The European Consensus reaffirmed that the primary objective of development policy is the eradication of poverty and that the EU promotes broad values (respect for human dignity, freedom, democracy, equality, the rule of law, and human rights) as well as development-related goals (ownership, participation, gender equality) in its relations with the developing world. It also stressed that the EU promotes effective multilateralism and is committed to delivering more and better aid and to achieving greater policy coherence for development.[17]

As mentioned earlier, the Treaty of Lisbon brought a number of significant changes to the EU's external relations. The vagueness of some provisions generated mixed feelings among development scholars and practitioners. Some were satisfied that development cooperation had been kept in a separate section. Moreover, further deconcentration, with new responsibilities devolved to the EU delegations, was expected to have a positive effect on the implementation of programs, though it was anticipated that the heads of the development cooperation sections would have to fight for relevance and resources. Others, in contrast, warned against a potential sidelining of development, with funding being instrumentalized to pursue foreign policy objectives.[18] Observers taking a foreign policy perspective claimed that it would be nonsense for a development policy to be completely autonomous from foreign and security policy; the Lisbon Treaty itself was an attempt to create "a more coherent, effective and visible Union on the international scene."[19]

One of the most contentious issues is related to the structure and functions of the EEAS, particularly the division of labor between the EEAS and the European Commission in the field of development policy. Following a proposal presented by High Representative Catherine Ashton in March 2010 and intense negotiations with the European Parliament, a compromise was struck in June 2010: all the "geographic desks" dealing with individual countries would become part of the EEAS, but the substantive aspects of development would remain with the European Commission. Moreover, any proposal regarding developing countries "shall be prepared jointly by the relevant services in the EEAS and in the Commission under the responsibility of the Commissioner in charge of development policy and then jointly submitted with the High Representative for decision by the Commission."[20] These provisions strengthened the role of the development commissioner, who de facto had the final say on all development strategies, including for countries in Latin America and Asia. In the event of disagreement between the development commissioner and the high representative, the College of Commissioners would have to make the final decision. Interestingly, Ashton admitted that "it is right and proper that development policy operates differently from diplomacy, crisis management and humanitarian aid."[21] The consequence of all these decisions, however, was that the Directorate General (DG) for Development lost some of its staff, but it gained more importance as EuropeAid became accountable to it rather than to the successor of DG for External Relations (the EEAS). For this, the decision to merge DG Development and EuropeAid, announced in November 2010, was not surprising.

New Forces in Development Policy

The entry into force of the Treaty of Lisbon gave new momentum to the EU's enlargement agenda. With the next wave, the frontiers of Europe are meant to stretch from Turkey to Iceland, passing through the Western Balkans. Croatia, Iceland, Montenegro, Macedonia, and Turkey have been granted the title of "candidates," while Albania, Bosnia and Herzegovina, Serbia, and Kosovo are "potential candidates." At the end of 2010, accession negotiations with the five candidates showed that not all of them were ready to join the EU in the short term. Negotiations with Croatia entered their final phase, and now Croatia is expected to join the EU in 2012. Similarly, Iceland fulfilled most of the accession criteria. Negotiations with Turkey advanced, albeit slowly. Macedonia sufficiently fulfilled the political criteria, but its dispute with Greece over its name prevented the formal opening of the negotiations. Finally, Montenegro received the status of candidate country in December 2010.[22] The case of development cooperation policy confirms that these five countries form a heterogeneous group: on one side are Iceland and Turkey; on the opposite side are Macedonia and Montenegro; in the middle is Croatia.

Iceland has an established tradition in development policy that goes back to the early 1970s. The emphasis at that time was on foreign aid as moral duty with the view to bridging the gap between rich and poor; policymakers also committed to going beyond the 0.7 percent target. In the 1980s and early 1990s, the pursuit of political and economic benefits became a more prominent objective. Unlike other Nordic donors, Iceland privileged bilateralism over multilateralism, and this was in line with a foreign policy in which the United States occupied a special place. In the mid-1990s a stronger internationalist approach emerged, and this shift was a consequence of changes in the political elites and of external pressure. Iceland became more active in the Nordic group of countries, which often adopt common positions on international development; this unity allows them to set agendas in international conferences and international organizations. Since the early 2000s a greater percentage of resources has been allocated to promoting the development-security nexus. An important role is played by the Icelandic Crisis Response Unit (ICRU), which has made peace building and post-conflict reconstruction a central component of Iceland's contribution to international development.[23]

Turkey, at the end of the 2000s, was both a recipient of development assistance and an emerging donor. Since the implementation of the Marshall Plan, it has received significant resources from the United States, Japan, and Germany, as well as multilateral donors, most notably the UNDP. In the mid-1980s, it started allocating small amounts of development assistance, which increased with the dissolution of the Soviet Union. Initially the emphasis was mainly on its neighborhood, with the aim to help newly independent states in their transition toward democracy and a market economy; cultural ties with Turkish-speaking countries also played an important role. Gradually Turkey started to target poorer countries, especially in sub-Saharan Africa, but at the same time foreign aid followed broader foreign policy priorities. In line with its "zero problem with the neighbors" policy, it promoted political cooperation and economic integration in its proximity, but it also become increasingly involved in post-conflict situations, most notably in Afghanistan, Iraq, Georgia, and the Middle East. In this sense, Turkish governments have combined two objectives while engaging in international development. On the one hand, they have pursued commercial interests, with the aim to find new markets for Turkish products. On the other hand, they have sought to promote the view of Turkey as a "responsible player" that cares not only about the stability of its region but also about sub-Saharan Africa, and more generally about poverty eradication.[24]

The other three candidate countries have limited, if any, tradition in development policy. Croatia began a slow transformation from recipient to donor country only at the end of the 2000s. Resources for development cooperation were earmarked for the first time in the 2008 national budget. A department for development cooperation and a development strategy were respectively set up and published in 2008 and in 2009. By contrast, Macedonia and Montenegro have been significant recipients of foreign aid since the disintegration of Yugoslavia, but by the end of 2010 had not yet set up a development policy.

The fact that the five candidate countries form a heterogeneous group is reflected in the pre-accession reports published by the European Commission.

Development cooperation policy has been included in chapter 32 with trade policy, under the heading "external relations." The accession negotiations, at least up to the end of 2010, showed that neither the European Union nor the candidate countries attached any importance to this field. In particular, according to an EU official, "in principle, candidate countries have to align their development policy to the one of the EU; but this has not been a stumbling block in the accession negotiations."[25] This is hardly surprising: candidate countries, especially in the Balkans, needed to address more pressing economic and political problems; moreover, because of the different traditions of development policy in the five candidate countries, the European Commission found it difficult to adopt a common approach, unlike in the early 2000s.[26]

The reports published in November 2010, however, showed remarkable differences between countries. In the case of Turkey, the level of alignment was considered "satisfactory."[27] For Iceland, the only preoccupation was how to ensure that volume of aid would not "decline further."[28] For Croatia, "some progress" was noted, but "further efforts" were required "to complete the legal framework in this area and to reinforce the administrative capacity."[29] Much more critical were the assessments for Macedonia, for which institutional capacity was considered "[not] yet sufficient to enable the country to participate fully . . . in the fields of development policy and humanitarian aid,"[30] and for Montenegro, which had not yet been involved in any donor activities and had "no legislation on development policy and no relevant administrative structure in place."[31]

The first challenge that the candidate countries (and likely any future member state in the Balkans) face concerns volume of aid. Interestingly, in the case of the 10+2 enlargement round, the view inside the European Commission was that it would be unreasonable to expect the acceding countries to meet the EU targets in the short term.[32] As of December 2010, Croatia had a very small foreign aid program, whereas Montenegro and Macedonia had yet to allocate resources for developing countries. By contrast, Iceland and Turkey were broadly in line with the EU's commitments. Iceland pledged to achieve 0.35 percent by 2009, and in 2008 it reached 0.47 percent despite the economic crisis. Turkey saw its percentage of aid over GNI fluctuate for most of the 2000s, from 0.04 percent in 2003, to 0.18 percent in 2006, to 0.11 percent in 2008.[33] Nevertheless, it should be noted that because the new members must contribute to the general EU budget, part of which is devoted to external relations activities, their volume of aid would inevitably increase. A different issue is the contribution to the European Development Fund (EDF), used for African, Caribbean, and Pacific (ACP) countries, which is replenished by voluntary contributions from member states every five years. But, as argued by a Commission official, "the EDF has not been an issue as member states have to deal with it only after accession."[34]

A second challenge concerns institutional capacity. The situation is more serious for Macedonia and Montenegro, where there is a more general problem, connected to the lack of political will and the absence of a development constituency. It would in fact be difficult for politicians to justify the provision of external assistance when their countries still face major economic problems. Moreover, the absence of a vibrant civil society does not help to raise the salience of development policy in public debates. In 2006 Croatia established the Department for International Development Cooperation within its Ministry of Foreign Affairs for the formulation and implementation of development policy. Moreover, it adopted a "law on development cooperation and external humanitarian assistance" and a "national strategy for development cooperation for 2009–2014" in December 2008 and February 2009, respectively. In Turkey, the Turkish International Cooperation and Development Agency (TIKA), created in 1992, has become a global aid agency, with about 200 employees working both in the headquarters and in field offices in numerous countries of Central Asia and Africa. NGOs have been involved in the implementation of development programs, and since the mid-2000s have become key actors in raising awareness on development issues.[35] In Iceland, the Icelandic International Development Agency (ICEIDA), established in 1995, has operated as an autonomous agency attached to the Ministry of Foreign Affairs. A new development act came into force in October 2008, which established a comprehensive framework for both bilateral and multilateral development.[36] In addition to adjusting their administrative systems, the candidate countries are expected to set in place arrangements that enable them to participate in decisionmaking bodies at the EU level and in other development forums.

A third challenge is connected to the geography and scope of aid. Four of the candidate countries (all except Iceland) have ties with countries that, traditionally, are not among the poorest countries in the world. In the case of Turkey, historically large percentages of aid have been allocated to countries in Central Asia, the Caucasus, and the Balkans. Since the late 2000s, a much more prominent role in Turkey's external relations has been occupied by Africa, where activities have concentrated on infrastructures, cultural activities, and productive sectors, including agriculture.[37] In the case of Croatia, the focus for 2009–14 is on its neighborhood, primarily Bosnia-Herzegovina, though the government has indicated its intention to strengthen relations with African countries. In the case of Iceland, no geographic area has been favored; in the past the focus was mainly on fisheries projects, but recently attention has been placed on social and energy sectors.[38] All candidate countries (including Iceland) have used a project-based approach, rather than program aid or budget support. Turkey, however, seemed ready to provide aid not only via projects but also through sector-wide approaches.

Conclusion

This chapter has shown that the two major changes in the 2000s that were perceived as a threat to the status of development policy within the European Union—the 10+2 enlargement round and the adoption (and implementation) of the Treaty of Lisbon—did not have the expected consequences. The new member states slowly adapted their development policy to the new environment, and the feared redirection of aid toward countries that had not been among the largest recipients of EU development assistance did not materialize. In light of this, and considering that some of the candidate countries have already aligned their development policy with EU principles and rules, it seems unlikely that the implications of future enlargement rounds for the EU's development policy will be significant. In line with this, the Lisbon Treaty represents an important step forward for development cooperation by making poverty eradication the central aim of development policy, strengthening the principles of policy coherence, and requiring that member states' and the EU's development policies complement and reinforce each other.

During the first decade of the new century a number of events opened a new phase in the relations between the European Union and the developing world. In fact, these changes have had an impact on the nature of EU development policy, the role of the EU in the international arena, and the international development agenda. First, significant emphasis has been placed on efficiency and coherence in external relations over participation and ownership, thus altering the nature of the relations between the EU and the developing world. Second, the will to project a "European vision of development" through the European Consensus on Development and the new agenda on aid effectiveness is not only an attempt to make aid work better but is also consistent with the EU's overall agenda in external relations—that is, to establish itself as a global power. Finally, not only is the EU the largest aid donor in the world, but a number of policies that have a direct impact on developing countries (such as trade, agriculture, fisheries) are negotiated and decided in Brussels. With the policy coherence for development agenda, the European Union achieved less than it had anticipated, but it still became evident that the attitudes of member states and the European institutions had changed, and they seemed eager to act in a more coordinated and coherent fashion.

Notes

1. For a review of EU development policy, see Maurizio Carbone, "The EU and the Developing World: Partnership, Poverty, Politicisation," in *International Relations and the European Union,* edited by Christopher Hill and Michael Smith (Oxford: Oxford University Press, 2011), pp. 324–48. See also Amelia Hadfield, "Janus Advances? An Analysis of EC Development Policy and the 2005 Amended Cotonou Partnership Agreement," *European Foreign Affairs Review* 12, no. 1 (2007): 39–66; Maurizio Carbone, *The European Union and International Development: The Politics of Foreign Aid* (London: Routledge, 2007); Patrick Holden, *In Search of Structural Power: EU Aid Policy as a Global Political Instrument* (Farnham, Surrey, UK: Ashgate, 2009); Maurizio Carbone, ed., *Policy Coherence and EU Development Policy* (London: Routledge, 2009).

2. For a review of these theories and approaches, see Maurizio Carbone, "Development Policy: The EU as a Bilateral and Multilateral Donor," in *The European Union and Global Governance: A Handbook,* edited by Jens-Uwe Wunderlich and David Bailey (London: Routledge, 2011).

3. For an analysis of the impact of different enlargements, see Maurizio Carbone, "Development," in *European Union Enlargement,* edited by Neil Nugent (Basingstoke, UK: Palgrave, 2004), pp. 242–52; Mirjam van Reisen, "The Enlarged European Union and the Developing World: What Future?" in *EU Development Policy in a Changing World: Challenges for the 21st Century*, edited by Andrew Mold (Amsterdam: Amsterdam University Press, 2007), pp. 29-65; Simon Lightfoot, "Enlargement and the Challenge of EU Development Policy," *Perspectives on European Politics and Society* 9, no. 2 (2008): 128–42.

4. See Kunibert Raffer and H. W. Singer, *The Foreign Aid Business: Economic Assistance and Development Co-operation* (Cheltenham, UK: E. Elgar, 1996); Michael Dauderstädt, *EU Eastern Enlargement and Development Cooperation* (Bonn: Friedrich Ebert Stiftung, 2002); Léna Krichewsky, *Development Policy in the Accession Countries* (Vienna: Trialog, 2003).

5. Simon Lightfoot, "The Europeanization of International Development Policies: The Case of Central and Eastern European States," *Europe-Asia Studies* 62, no. 2 (2010): 334.

6. Carbone, "Development."

7. Lightfoot, "The Europeanization of International Development Policies"; Martin Vittek and Simon Lightfoot, "The Europeanization of Slovak Development Cooperation?" *Contemporary European Studies* 4, no. 1 (2009): 21–37.

8. The average for the EU-12 countries was 0.11 percent. The best performers, in addition to Malta (0.19 percent) and Cyprus (0.17 percent), were Lithuania (0.15 percent) and Slovenia (0.15 percent), whereas the worst performers were Bulgaria (0.05 percent), Romania (0.08 percent), and Slovakia (0.08 percent). See European Commission, "Financing for Development—Annual Progress Report 2010: Getting Back on Track to Reach the EU 2015 Target on ODA Spending?" SEC (2010) 420, April 21, 2010.

9. Lightfoot, "The Europeanization of International Development Policies."

10. Ibid., pp. 339, 342.

11. Ondřej Horký, "The Europeanisation of Development Policy: Acceptance, Accommodation and Resistance of the Czech Republic," Discussion Paper 18/2010 (Bonn: Deutsches Institut für Entwicklungspolitik / German Development Institute, 2010), p. 8.

12. Balázs Szent-Iványi and Andrád Tétényi, "Transition and Foreign Aid Policies in the Visegrád Countries: A Path Dependent Approach," *Transition Studies Review* 15 (2008): 573–87.

13. In the Treaty of Maastricht, it was stated that the aim of development policy was the sustainable economic and social development of the developing countries, and more particularly the most disadvantaged among them; their smooth and gradual integration into the world economy; the campaign against poverty in the developing countries; and the promotion of democracy, the rule of law, and respect for fundamental rights and freedoms.

14. The Lisbon Treaty had some potential implications for relations between the EU and the ACP (African, Caribbean, and Pacific) countries. In fact, the reference to the intergovernmental nature of EU-ACP relations was deleted, which seemed to confirm the trend toward the normalization of relations between the EU and the developing world. Moreover, the "Declaration on the European Development Fund," which stipulated that the EDF is outside the budget, was removed. This, nevertheless, did not mean that the EDF would be budgetized.

15. The treaty also mentioned the establishment of a European Voluntary Humanitarian Aid Corps. In response to this, NGOs expressed some concern about the possible deployment of inexperienced young Europeans to developing countries.

16. Elisa Morgera and Gracia Marín Durán, "Enlargement and EU Development Policy: An Environmental Perspective," *RECIEL* 13, no. 2 (2004): 152–63. An inventory of development-related regulations was prepared before the 10+2 enlargement round, and can be found in European Commission, *The Implications of Enlargement for Development Policy*, report prepared by Development Strategies/IDC, September 2003. It has not been updated since then. Interestingly, in a meeting in February 2010 with CONCORD, the umbrella organization of European NGOs, Commissioner Andris Piebalgs proposed to build an EU development *acquis*.

17. Carbone, "The EU and the Developing World."

18. Eleonora Koeb, "A More Political EU External Action: Implications of the Treaty of Lisbon for the EU's Relations with Developing Countries," *InBrief* no. 21 (Maastricht: ECDPM, June 2008); Mark Furness, "The European External Action Service: A New Institutional Framework for EU Development Cooperation," Discussion Paper 15/2010 (Bonn: German Development Institute, 2010).

19. Simon Duke and S. Blockmans, "The Lisbon Treaty Stipulations on Development Cooperation and the Council Decision of 25 March 2010 (Draft) Establishing the Organisation and Functioning of the European External Action Service," EIPA Working Paper 2010/W/01 (Maastricht: EIPA, 2010), p. 13.

20. Meanwhile, a coalition of NGOs in April 2010 had issued a paper arguing that the proposal on the EEAS was in breach of EU law. They claimed that the Lisbon

Treaty mentioned only the CFSP (Common Foreign and Security Policy) and that therefore the EEAS was not applicable to development policy. This legal claim was raised at a later stage in the process, but NGOs still sought to make their case with the European Parliament, which historically has been more receptive to their requests.

21. *European Voice*, July 15, 2010.

22. European Commission, "Enlargement Strategy and Main Challenges 2010–2011," Brussels, COM (2010) 660, November 9, 2010. For a concise overview of the EU's enlargement policy, see Ulrich Sedelmeier, "Enlargement: From Rules for Accession to a Policy Towards Europe," in *Policy-Making in the European Union*, edited by Helen Wallace, Mark A. Pollack, and Alasdair R. Young (Oxford University Press, 2010), pp. 401–29.

23. Kristín Loftsdóttir and Helga Björnsdóttir, "The 'Jeep-Gangsters' from Iceland: Local Development Assistance in a Global Perspective," *Critique of Anthropology* 30, no. 1 (2010): 23–39; Hilmar Þór Hilmarsson, "How Can Small States Like Iceland Work Effectively with International Financial Institutions?" *Nordicum-Mediterraneum* 5, no. 1 (2010) (http://nome.unak.is/); Ministry for Foreign Affairs, "*Iceland's Policy on Development Co-Operation 2005–2009*, September 2005.

24. Hakan Fidan and Rahman Nurdun, "Turkey's Role in the Global Assistance Community: The Case of TIKA (Turkish International Cooperation and Development Agency," *Journal of Southern Europe and the Balkans* 10, no. 1 (2008): 93–111; Musa Kulaklıkaya and Rahman Nurdun, "Turkey as a New Player in Development Cooperation," *Insight Turkey* 12, no. 4 (2010): 131–45; Mehmet Özkan and Birol Akgün, "Turkey's Opening to Africa," *Journal of Modern African Studies* 48, no. 4 (2010): 525–46.

25. Personal communication with an official in the European Commission, January 2011.

26. In the case of the 10+2 enlargement rounds, DG Development commissioned a report that served as the basis for subsequent discussions. European Commission, *The Implications of Enlargement for Development Policy*.

27. European Commission, "Turkey 2010 Progress Report," SEC (2010) 1327, November 9, 2010, p. 95. It should be noted that the chapter on external relations was suspended in December 2006, together with seven other chapters.

28. European Commission, "Iceland 2010 Progress Report," SEC (2010) 1328, November 9, 2010, p. 39.

29. European Commission, "Croatia 2010 Progress Report," SEC (2010) 1326, November 9, 2010, p. 63.

30. European Commission, "The Former Yugoslav Republic of Macedonia 2010 Progress Report," SEC (2010) 1332, November 9, 2010, p. 74. The section on development policy mentioned that a unit for humanitarian and development aid with two employees had been established within the Ministry of Foreign Affairs.

31. European Commission, "Commission Opinion on Montenegro's Application for Membership of the European Union," SEC (2010) 1334 final, November 9, 2010, p. 119.

32. Carbone, "Development."

33. These figures are extracted from the annual reviews published by the Development Assistance Committee, which contain a section on both Iceland and Turkey.

For the latest report, see OECD, *Development Co-operation Report 2010* (Paris: OECD, 2010).

34. Personal communication with an official in the European Commission, December 2010.

35. Fidan and Nurdun, "Turkey's Role in the Global Assistance Community"; Kulaklıkaya and Nurdun, "Turkey as a New Player in Development Cooperation."

36. Hilmarsson, "How Can Small States Like Iceland Work Effectively?"

37. Özkan and Akgün, "Turkey's Opening to Africa."

38. Hilmarsson, "How Can Small States Like Iceland Work Effectively?"

LUCA EINAUDI

13

The Euro Crisis and the New Economic Governance

After three years of financial crisis, a great recession, and a year of turmoil over sovereign debt in Europe, in 2011 the euro area faces its largest challenge since its creation. It is now trying to establish a new basis for the future. The optimism of mid-2009 about the beneficial effect of the euro in protecting its members from sudden destabilizing currency fluctuations has been replaced by doubts about the viability of the project and the search for a new equilibrium. In mid-2009, when the global financial crisis was showing signs of abating and the recession began to relent, the consensus in Europe was that the euro had sheltered its member states from even worse outcomes, preventing major disruptive devaluation within the area. An authoritative assessment of ten years of euro history concluded then that "in the midst of the greatest financial crisis of the last 70 years, the world's only transnational major currency has delivered price stability to the people of the Euro area, retained its value in international markets and proven capable of weathering the storm. . . . While a few increasingly shrill and lonely naysayers remain, the Euro has amply demonstrated its sustainability."[1]

Assessed from the viewpoint of early 2011, such words seem to belong to a different era. The years 2010 and 2011 have been characterized by crises: the Greek debt crisis and the creation of the European Financial Stability Mechanism, followed by the Irish crisis and fear of further contagion and debt restructuring by some countries. These events have led to a dramatic reversal of some of the principles on which the euro was conceived (the prohibition for member states to bail out other national governments or for the European Central Bank (ECB) to buy their public debt or to monetize it). The IMF has returned to Europe, and now five EU members are receiving IMF loans and follow austerity programs dictated by the IMF, the European Commission, and the ECB (Romania, Hungary, and Latvia in 2008, Greece and Ireland in 2010, and Portugal in 2011, of which Hungary has dropped out of the program).

Beginning in the spring of 2010 many experts forecast a Greek default, a more or less rapid demise of the euro or its reduction to a core membership. They saw this as a consequence of a lack of fiscal discipline and of imbalances in trade, productivity, and growth caused by an excessively large and unruly monetary union. Euroskeptics remain much stronger in the United States and the United Kingdom than in the euro area itself, where governments still believe that the euro will prosper thanks to institutional reforms and restored discipline. After a long period of uncertainty and internal contrasts, the EU has again mustered its energies, achieving a level of cooperation and solidarity in supporting ailing members unmatched outside unified sovereign states. In May 2010 the EU managed to construct a mechanism to protect its weakest members from immediate risk of default, through bilateral loans to Greece and the creation of a mechanism available to other euro members, used by Ireland in November. As this book went to press, the euro area, through a continuous flow of reforms, is redrawing its institutional framework. It is improving policy coordination to strengthen the stability and growth pact and reinforce budgetary discipline, to contain real macroeconomic imbalances and restart growth (the "Euro plus pact" and "Europe 2020"). It is also creating a permanent crisis management instrument (the "European Stability Mechanism," or ESM). It is also struggling with the issue of whether it is still possible to prevent insolvency in Greece and how to manage some sort of default if the worst comes.

What many commentators from outside the euro area failed to grasp is that the euro is a major political project, part of a long-term strategy to adapt Europe to globalization. It is a project to which political leaders are highly committed, to the point of accepting significant sacrifices and policy shifts in order to preserve it and protect Europe from an accelerated loss of its economic and political role in the world. It is not just a currency issue, and therefore it is much more stable and capable of weathering crises than a superficial external view might suggest. The construction of the euro is a long-term process, arguably almost as old as the idea of a united Europe.[2] It was extensively discussed before its implementation; it relied on a set of rules and institutions that proved to be insufficient and partially inadequate upon implementation, although many had argued for its missing pieces more than a decade earlier.[3] As in previous experience with monetary unions, there is an ongoing debate on how to adapt the rules and improve governance while the game is being played. Such debates are difficult and controversial because they impose harsh sacrifices; they are distributed unequally between different countries, and they can impinge on national sovereignty.

The challenge for the EU is now to reinforce fiscal rules without creating a recessive bias in its policy framework. It is to reinforce coordination of fiscal policies despite a generalized refusal by national governments to devolve fiscal policy to the European level. In this process it is essential to maintain effective support for member states facing liquidity crises, sufficiently credible with bond markets to block the run on public debt of "peripheral" countries. This will have to happen under difficult circumstances, without either exhausting the willingness of the taxpayers and governments of Northern Europe to maintain support, or transforming readjustment of public finances into massive self-defeating recessions.

This chapter addresses the way euro rules were initially conceived, how they developed and proved to be inadequate, and how the process of reinventing them is proceeding. It argues that a complex revision of rules will last for some time, with a difficult balancing act between the conflicting needs for fiscal prudence and for growth, made more complex by fears of multiple sovereign defaults. However, the latter seem to be exaggerated in the European context.

The Original Framework for the Euro

The euro was launched as a political and economic project after a thorough debate, including the Werner report in 1970, the Delors report in 1989, and the Maastricht Treaty in 1992, and was concluded with the launch of the single currency in eleven countries in 1999, with substantial rules and institutions. The original governance of the euro area dealt with issues on the basis of economic theory and past experience. Monetary issue was tightly controlled through a common central bank (the ECB) with the single mandate to fight inflation, and not to support growth, following the model of the German Bundesbank. Orderly public finances were defended through limits to public debt (no more than 60 percent of GDP) and to deficits (maximum 3 percent), introduced as requirements to join the single currency. They were made permanent by the Stability and Growth Pact, requested by Germany to ensure that the euro would be as stable as the deutsche mark. Financial penalties were to be imposed on states that ran deficits persistently above the 3 percent threshold, after an excessive deficit review procedure voted by the European Council. To discourage moral hazard and inflationary risks, the EU treaty prohibited monetization of fiscal deficits, the ECB was barred from acquiring government bonds of member states, and assistance in paying other countries' debts was banned (by the "no bailout" clause). An intense exchange of information, through national statistical institutes, central banks, and governments, was also mandated by the treaty to ensure that the rules were respected. To block speculation, membership in the euro was defined as irreversible, and no rules were established to allow a voluntary exit or an expulsion from the economic and monetary union (EMU).

The euro was meant to advance both the political and the economic integration of Europe, completing the single market, reducing transaction costs, and securing fair competition, by eliminating the possibility of devaluations in the area and reducing exchange fluctuation risks. The project was also intended to reinforce the international role of Europe by creating a common currency capable of competing with the dollar. For Southern Europeans the euro represented a challenge to end a model of trade competitiveness based on periodic devaluations and to move toward more sustainable public finances. Some federalists hoped that the euro would lead toward further political integration by increasing economic integration, following the old functionalist approach of the French federalist Jean Monnet. In the early 1990s the French and the Italians also intended to bind Germany more closely to the European project, to prevent a shift of German priorities eastward after reunification and to forestall nationalist feeling.

How the Euro Really Worked

The difficulties that emerged in 2010 in the midst of the debt crisis should not hide the fact that the euro had reached a substantial number of its objectives since its launch in 1999. Interest rates between euro members declined and converged thanks to the euro, contributing substantially to the reduction of government deficits and preventing an explosive path of debt in several countries. In the case of Italy, the cancellation of an interest rate differential with Germany (over 4 percent in the five years preceding EMU) facilitated a reduction of debt from 122 percent of GDP in 1994 to 103 percent in 2007. Italian deficits before the convergence toward the euro were above 10 percent of GDP per year and declined to 3 percent between 1999 and 2008. A similar decline was experienced by Spain but not by Greece. The euro had produced greater convergence in public finances and in GDP growth, but had not totally canceled such differences, also because it did not affect preexisting levels of government debt. Furthermore, the euro prevented uncontrolled devaluations during the global crisis of 2008–09, helping to contain protectionist pressures. This should be compared with the massive devaluations of the Italian lira, the British pound, and the Spanish peseta in 1992–95.

Despite those previous successes, the 2010 crisis revealed some major weaknesses in the rules that made some of those mechanisms ineffective. The Stability and Growth Pact did not prevent the growth of public debt to dangerous levels. The debt limit was always interpreted "politically," meaning that it was initially sufficient to see it declining, even if it remained above 60 percent. The Stability Pact did not produce the expected results because its rules were not followed strictly from the beginning; budgets were not kept close to balance in good times and then exploded during the crisis. The excessive deficit procedure never led to a fine. Governments were reluctant to inflict anything more than verbal admonishments on each other. Greece did not respect the 3 percent deficit ceiling in any year, and even the strongest and supposedly more rigorous members, France and Germany, breached the limit on several occasions. A first revision of the Stability Pact was agreed on in 2005, following German and French requests to delay the readjustment of their own budget deficits. The new pact linked the decision to start a review procedure of countries with excessive deficits, based on parameters such as behavior of cyclically adjusted budgets, level of debt, duration of slow growth, and the possibility that the deficit was related to productivity-enhancing measures. The weakening of the Stability Pact and persistent low growth in the euro area contributed to an increase in public debt, while low interest rates stimulated a credit boom and rising private debt (especially in the United Kingdom, Spain, and Ireland) and unsustainable increases in home prices, creating a time bomb that was outside the watch of the Stability Pact.

In 2008–09 European governments also decided to suspend the effects of the pact to respond to the great recession through macroeconomic stimulus programs and to allow automatic stabilizers to play out in full to prevent a fall in demand during the recession. In any case, the decline in GDP in 2009 was substantially larger than the 2 percent level that activates the escape clause from sanctions for excessive deficit. The financial crisis of 2008–09 also imposed such high costs for the rescue of the financial system on some governments that public debt exploded despite previous fiscal prudence, placing almost all EU-15 governments above the 60 percent limit. The exchange of information proved incomplete, not only because Greece repeatedly provided false data, but also because attention was focused on too few issues and indicators. Too much emphasis was put on public deficits and too little on competitiveness and debt, both public and private (families as well as private financial and nonfinancial firms).

The rules of the pact itself would have been insufficient, given that countries such as Ireland and Spain were apparently the best performers until 2007, with persistent budgetary surpluses and low and rapidly declining debt-to-GDP ratios. Their structural deficit was in fact hidden by the effects of debt—fueling a housing bubble and a banking boom; the crisis in 2008 produced an explosion of those countries' deficits and debts, with the rapid transformation of private debt into public debt. Spanish debt increased from 36 percent to 63 percent between 2007 and 2010, and Irish debt rose from 25 percent to 94 percent. Given their budget surpluses, it would have been politically impossible to counsel Spain or Ireland before 2008 to tighten their public finances, or even to argue about their high current account deficits or high private debt. Neither the governments nor the public of those countries, who viewed themselves as highly successful, would have accepted such criticism, especially when other countries were chronically in budget deficit.

The absence of devaluations inside the EMU increases imbalances (in trade and current accounts) if productivity and competitiveness diverge substantially over the long term between member states. Without devaluations to compensate for them, persistent differentials in inflation, productivity, and wage growth have accumulated over time in parts of Southern Europe in the first ten years of the euro. Those countries with large balance-of-payments deficits now face readjustment mechanisms similar to those of the gold standard, requiring relative wage and price reductions.[4]

The no-bailout clause proved unsustainable under intense strain because of the threats of a member state's bankruptcy and of contagion leading to a new financial crisis, and the risk of the euro's dissolution. In fact, the no-bailout clause was suspended in 2010 because governments were too interconnected to fail, much as big banks were in 2008. The Greek debt crisis started producing contagion effects in April–May 2010, including sudden hikes in interest rates in some countries considered at risk to various degrees and a decline in interest rates in Germany and other sovereign issuers considered to be safe havens. The Greek debt crisis shattered interest rate convergence within the EMU and forced continuous rule changes (the end of the "no-bailout" clause, the creation of the European Financial Stability Facility, ECB bond acquisition programs, increased Eurostat monitoring, the beginning of the reform of the Stability Pact).

Bond markets brutally recreated interest rate differentials existing before the euro, suddenly realizing that sovereign default was a possibility, even in the euro area, and that different debts could not be priced independently of the specific conditions of the nation issuing it. After a blind underestimation of risk, bond markets moved to a common conviction that Greece would ultimately default, even after the EU introduced an effective support mechanism.

Markets overreacted, created contagion in a newly constructed category, the PIGS (Portugal, Ireland, Greece, and Spain), sometimes extending to Belgium and Italy, all countries with radically different combinations of problems and risk (bank crisis, public debt, private debt, lack of competitiveness, and current account deficit). The Delors report in 1989 had already shown full awareness of the inadequacy of market forces in constraining public deficits on a sustainable path: "the constraints imposed by market forces might either be too slow and weak or too sudden and disruptive."[5] IMF studies also showed the propensity of bond markets to overreact and overestimate default risks: "In our view, the risk of debt restructuring is currently significantly overestimated . . . considering data on sovereign bond spreads over the past decades, markets sounded false alarms in the vast majority of episodes."[6] In the past twenty-five years all the advanced countries that had to perform a fiscal readjustment of more than 7 percent did so without defaulting or restructuring their public debt. Default would not save countries from the necessary internal adjustment anyway, given that developed countries have a stock of public debt with a long maturity (for Italy the average maturity is over seven years) on which they pay the low interest rates obtained before the crisis. Therefore states would save rather little from a repudiation of part of their debt and a reduction of its interest rate. Lorenzo Bini Smaghi, the Italian member of the European Central Bank's executive board, has argued that markets "were wrong in the past in underpricing risk, are probably wrong at present in overpricing it, and will again be wrong in the future."[7]

Nevertheless, extraordinary measures had to be taken to avoid the self-realizing effect of expectations of rising interest rates on the sustainability of debt, which was threatening the euro itself (the euro declined from $1.50 to $1.20 during the most acute phase of the Greek crisis in the first half of 2010). If markets convinced themselves that ultimately a state would default, they would stop buying new bond issues and would try to sell existing ones as soon as the possibility arose, progressively closing access to credit and potentially causing a default of even the most solid government. Spain is targeted by markets despite a debt-to-GDP ratio that is still substantially below the European average, because of fear of possible unknown future banking losses. The EU filled a gap in the institutional setting needed to manage the Union, creating a mechanism to deal with crises and safeguard financial stability, introducing in April and May 2010 two mechanisms to provide coordinated bilateral loans to member states, later called the European Financial Stability Facility (EFSF). A further temporary relaxation of rules had to be decided to reduce the pressure on countries under attack. The ECB started acquiring some government debt to calm the markets, despite prohibition by the Treaty.

Figure 13-1. *Greek Budget Deficit: Announced and Actual Deficits, 1980–2010, and Austerity Program*

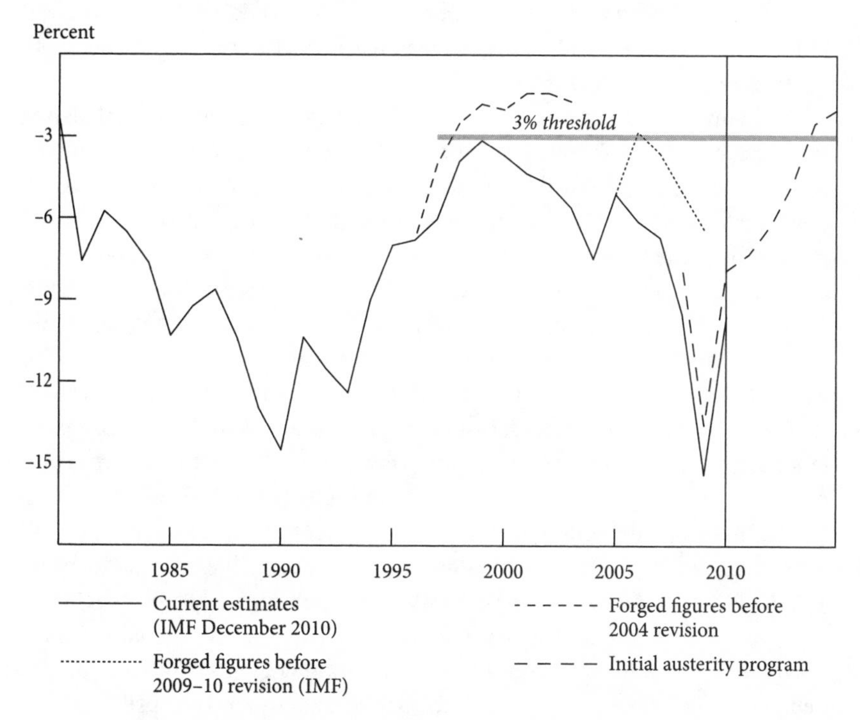

Source: Elaboration by the author on *Report by Eurostat on the Revision of the Greek Government Deficit and Debt Figures*, November 22, 2004; European Commission, *Report on Greek Government Deficit and Debt Statistics* (Brussels: European Commission, January 2010); International Monetary Fund, *IMF Country Report No. 10/372, Greece: Second Review under the Stand-By Arrangement—Staff Report*, December 2010.

The Greek and Irish Crises

The revelation of the real extent of the Greek deficit in late 2009—which instead of 6.4 percent was 12.7 percent of GDP, and finally revised to 15.4 percent at the end of 2010—coupled with the high and rapidly growing debt, triggered fears of default and attacks on the sustainability of monetary union. The newly elected government of George Papandreou had revised the fraudulent data provided by the previous conservative government. The Greek treasury had systematically transmitted forged figures to Eurostat through its national statistical institute from 2006 to 2009, repeating what it had done from 1997 to 2003 to fraudulently gain access to the EMU and to avoid sanctions for its excessive deficit. It had been caught and was required to correct its data and cut its deficit in 2004 but soon began operating in the same way (see figure 13-1). Until July 2010, Eurostat was not given the power to fully audit national accounts. Greece already had the second largest debt ratio in the EU in 2007 (105 percent of GDP), and it is expected to reach 158 percent by 2012 (according to IMF forecasts in December 2010).[8]

Germany requested severe punishment and austerity measures to rebalance the Greek budget. In several phases the Greek government cut public sector pay, froze spending, increased the retirement age and taxes, and agreed to crack down on tax evasion. The euro area governments then committed in February 2010 to help Greece with loans, if necessary. Various European support programs were announced with the intention to stabilize the situation, but initially with the clear hope and intent not to provide actual financing. Positive announcements were followed repeatedly by Germany's refusal to provide help, which destabilized expectations further, increasing the risk of default and facilitating financial speculation against Greek debt. Markets took German reluctance as an indication that no real support was coming. Interest rates rose as a consequence, from an average of 5 percent in 2009 to over 7 percent at the end of March 2010. On April 11, euro area governments agreed, as the last possible solution in emergency circumstances, to make available bilateral loans of €30 billion at market rates (an interest rate of approximately 5 percent). The IMF would complement this with another €15 billion. Continued German resistance to supporting Greece and the further downgrading of Greek public debt by rating agencies pushed rates to 13 percent at the end of April. German public opinion opposed a bailout, and the constitutional court was expected to block German participation in a bailout outside the EU treaty. The government of German chancellor Angela Merkel wanted to prove it would not act unless the euro and financial stability were under threat.

Ultimately the German behavior contributed heavily to the development of a full crisis and to multiplying the financial burden Germany ultimately had to bear to contain it. Fears of contagion also pushed up interest rates in Ireland and Portugal, and on a smaller scale in Spain and Italy (see figure 13-2). The EU and the IMF were forced to increase the support to Greece to €110 billion in three years,[9] and then to create a larger loan fund available to the whole euro area, for a total of €750 billion. The ECB agreed to buy the public debt of eurozone members on the secondary market. The new temporary mechanism, introduced for only three years, the European Financial Stability Facility was agreed by the EU on May 2010, aimed at preserving financial stability by providing financial assistance to eurozone states in difficulty.[10] An informal, ad hoc form of economic governance emerged, with euro area governments pushing, and obtaining, austerity measures from member countries with greater

Figure 13-2. *Debt Crisis and Policy Reactions*

Ten-year interest rates on government bonds (percent)

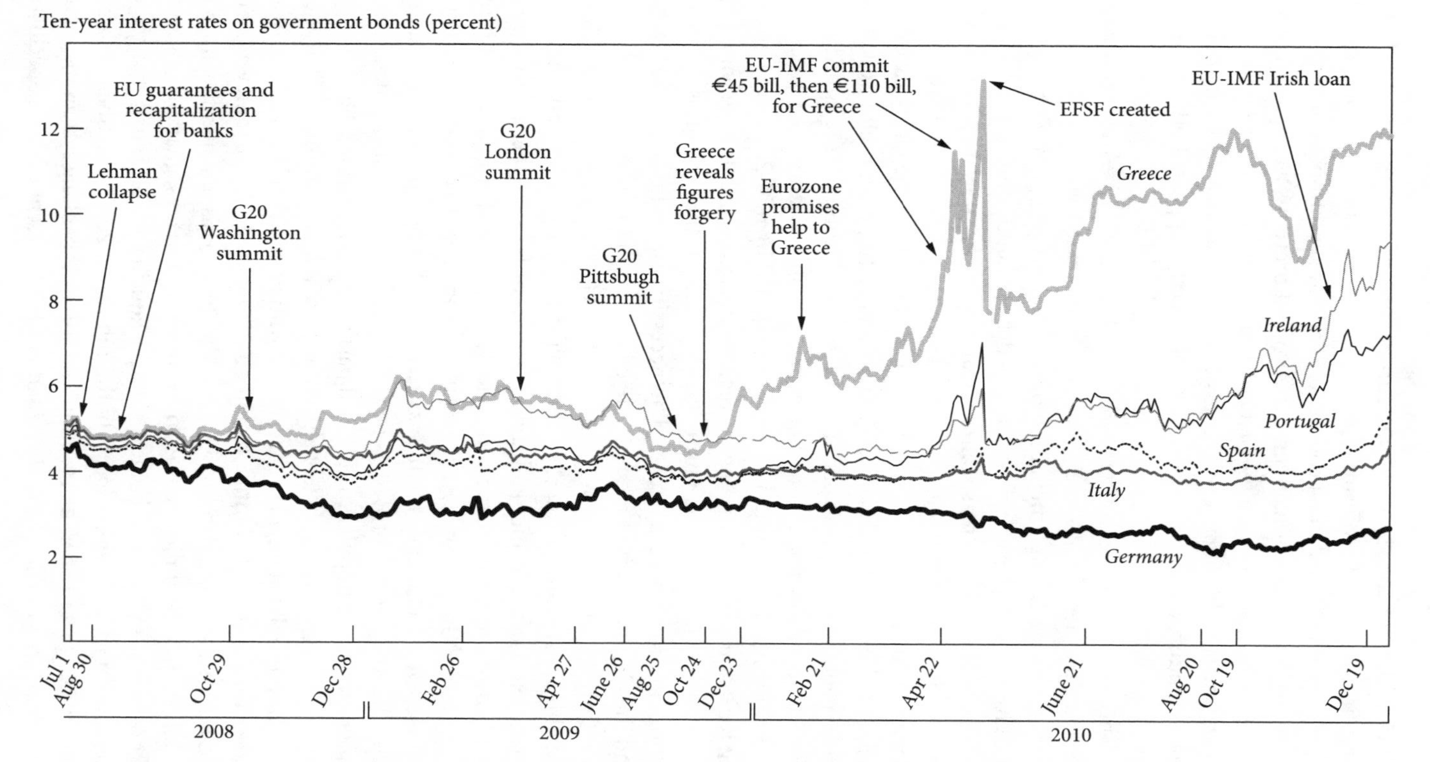

Source: Author's elaboration on Thomson Reuters data from the *Financial Times*, selected dates (July 1, 2008–December 31, 2010).

deficits. Despite concerns around Europe about Merkel's apparent lack of commitment to the European construction, the German government has ultimately agreed to substantial concessions, and at key turning points it always supported measures to maintain the euro and prevent sovereign defaults. In the end, German banks are the first creditors of peripheral European governments; they would suffer very large losses that the German government would have to endure anyway, even if it had not directly supported other European governments before.

The decisions made in May–June did not end the crisis. After a short-lived decline after the bailout, Greek interest rates increased again, to above 10 percent, despite early implementation of the austerity program. The conviction that Greece would have to restructure its debt at some point was reinforced by the size of Greek debt after stabilization and by further upward revisions of the data on debt and deficit. Furthermore, doubts lingered as to the extent of solidarity of Northern European governments and about the Greek capacity to resist the burden of austerity after an expected 10 percent fall in GDP over three years and widespread popular protest. Some economists regarded an exit from the euro, devaluation, and default as the only solution for Greece.

Such concerns became even more widespread by mid-2011 when persistent recession was undermining tax receipts in Greece and slowing willingness to accept further sacrifices pushed by Papandreou through massive privatization and further budget cuts. The necessity for additional EU-IMF help and the German request for a private contribution to the costs of the operation further convinced financial markets that Greece was going to default and possibly Ireland and Portugal as well, increasing ten-year interest rates above 18 percent for the former and above 11 percent for the other two. Germany scaled down again its request in June 2011 for fear that a perceived forced extension of Greek debt maturity would be considered a default by credit rating agencies. A new agreement was reached for further support, buying time, provided that Greece proved to be willing and able to continue its austerity program despite popular protest and parliamentary uncertainties.

The concerns over Irish debt already escalated in the autumn of 2010 after it was announced that Germany had agreed with France that bondholders would have to share the cost of future bailouts and that the Irish situation was spiraling out of control. Ireland had started the 2008 crisis apparently with good public finances, but the decision to rescue all of its banks, guaranteeing in full depositors as well as bondholders after the housing bubble burst, changed the situation at an astonishing speed. In the autumn of 2010 the Irish government announced that further intervention in favor of its banking system meant that the government deficit for 2010 would reach 32 percent of GDP. Speculation grew that there was no end to the costs of the Irish banking rescue, with rising bank losses and nationalizations due to a further decline in housing prices, and that ultimately bondholders would have to share in the cost of the bailout. An escalation similar to that which hit Greece a few months earlier took place again. Ireland finally bowed to the inevitable. When interest rates on ten-year bonds had climbed above 9 percent, it applied for help from the EU and the IMF, receiving a package of loans of €85 billion (see figure 13-2).

In April 2011 Portugal also was finally forced to apply for EU and IMF funds, despite a much lower debt and deficit than Greece and Ireland and the absence of a banking crisis. A €78 billion loan was agreed to in May, without reassuring financial markets.

Structural concerns remain about the sustainability of very high public debts in the euro area after a major crisis and markets expect some sort of default, and interest rates have increased for all countries more than they did during the Greek crisis. The wave of austerity plans decided in late spring 2010 was initially seen as a reassuring sign that the issue of fiscal sustainability was taken seriously. Soon, however, markets were caught by the doubt that harsh spending cuts and tax increases could precipitate a recession, which threatened to cancel the benefits of fiscal retrenchment and lead to even higher debt-to-GDP ratios or to a social rebellion.

The Argentine default of 2002 provided a dangerous precedent and traumatized bond markets for several reasons. It was a large-scale default that took place despite IMF assistance. It imposed very large losses on investors, because Argentine president Nestor Kirchner obtained an agreement that required Argentina to repay only 30 percent of its original debt. Furthermore, it proved that governments could get away with such ruthless treatment of markets. Thanks to a massive devaluation, and despite a deep recession and massive increases in unemployment and poverty, Argentina unexpectedly returned rather rapidly to fast economic growth and prosperity, without paying a large price for its heterodox policies. In some quarters, such events have increased the impression that devaluation and default can be a solution to Greek-style situations,[11] and therefore bondholders are more at risk than they thought they would be only a few months earlier. Default is not so advantageous, however, if the government debt is largely owned by nationals who could vote the government out and if interest rates on long-term debt already subscribed are not high. Reputation is also an important element, because default makes further loans much more difficult, and in the context of the single European market governments cannot afford to default on a debt owned by neighbors with whom economic, commercial, and political relations are very tight. A national default would further damage the banking system of creditor nations.

Figure 13-3. *Public Debt in Some Euro Countries, 1880–2015*

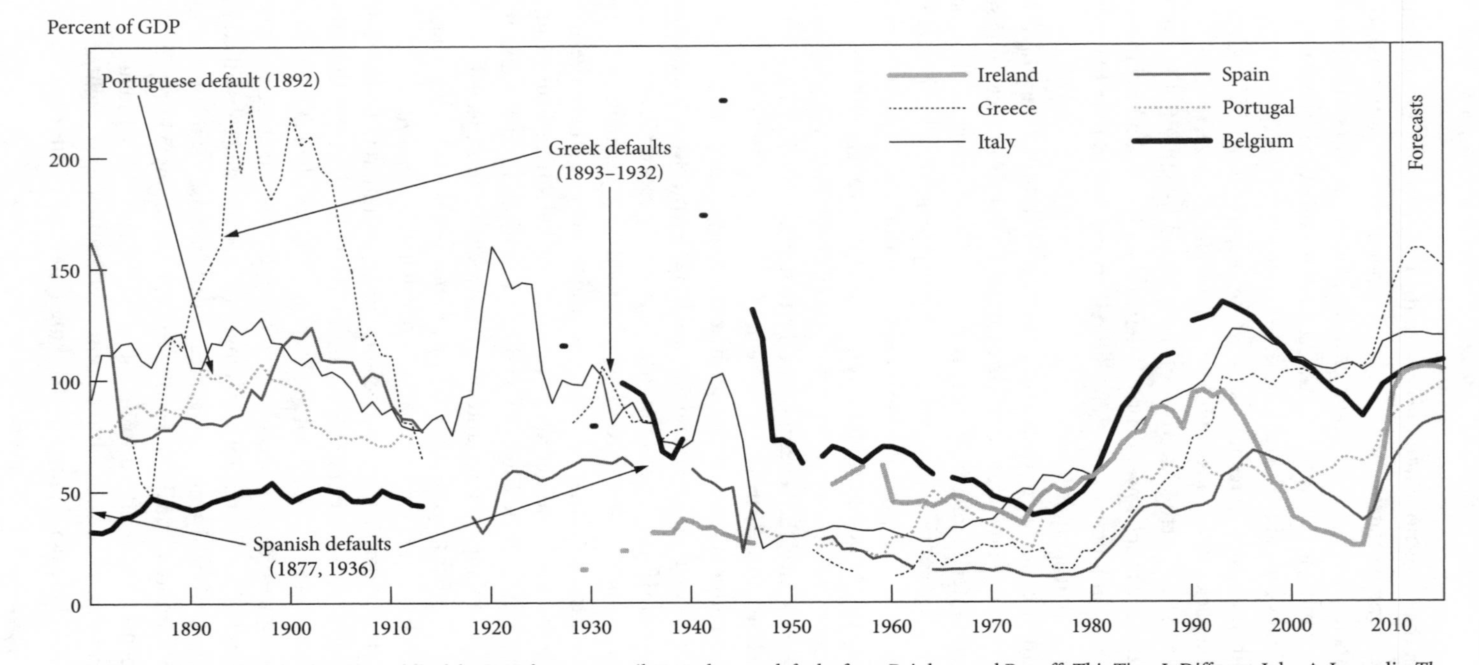

Sources: IMF historical database on public debt, IMF forecasts until 2015, data on defaults from Reinhart and Rogoff, *This Time Is Different*. John A. Levandis, *The Greek Foreign Debt and the Great Powers 1821–98* (Columbia University Press, 1944).

The lessons of history have been invoked repeatedly to argue that defaults are likely. Carmen Reinhart and Kenneth Rogoff have written that massive increases in government debt are the consequence of major financial and banking crises and that they are followed after a few years by clusters of sovereign default or rescheduling. They attribute thirteen defaults to Spain since 1476, six to Portugal since 1139, five to Greece since 1829, one to Italy since 1569, and none to Ireland.[12] Those figures, however frequently quoted, are misleading because they mix completely different economic and political regimes, and they overestimate the risk of default. Most Spanish defaults took place in the sixteenth and seventeenth centuries and were possible only because they involved the debt of an absolute monarch, who was able to deal with his lenders informally and could compensate them with other forms of income. Control by a parliament, which also represents the citizens owning government debt, is a major structural difference that reduces the likelihood of default in Europe today. Parliamentary democracies in Europe do not normally default. No defaults have taken place in Belgium, Italy, or Ireland since their independence, respectively, in 1831, 1861, and 1921, despite protracted periods of high public debt. This history demonstrates that it is possible to sustain high public debt for a long time, even if it is uncomfortable and reduces economic growth (see figure 13-3).

Managing the Union: How to Change the Rules during the Game

The Greek and Irish crises have highlighted again the difficulty of harmonizing national economic policies (especially fiscal ones), of effectively monitoring the implementation of commitments inside the Union, of changing the rules while the game is being played, and of sharing the costs of supportive intervention. A common response has been adopted, although the delay has increased the cost for all the governments concerned.

The extent of the crisis has forced all participants to reconsider their positions, at least in part. In February 2010 French president Nicolas Sarkozy reiterated his call of 2008 for stronger economic government of the euro area, including a formalization of the eurogroup at the leaders' level, with a permanent secretariat, in order to secure the supremacy of the political level over technicians. Merkel rejected that proposal, wishing to preserve in full the independence of the ECB against political pressure to accommodate larger deficits.[13] During a meeting on March 25, she managed to push through the idea of a less political revision of governance, reinforcing the Stability Pact to restore discipline through more effective sanctions, in exchange for German support for Greece. The European Council then created the Van Rompuy

Task Force composed of the twenty-seven EU finance ministers to rewrite the rules.[14] When the crisis worsened on May 7, the mandate was reinforced and accelerated. By June 17 a first set of proposals had been introduced to "reinforce the coordination of our economic policies," focusing on the level of debt and monitoring the evolution of competitiveness to avoid large imbalances.[15] This meant strengthening sanctions, focusing more attention on debt than in the past, presenting stability and convergence programs to the Commission, ensuring national budgetary rules and medium-term budgetary frameworks in line with the Stability Pact, and ensuring the quality of statistical data. Peer review of national budgets was also introduced: each government will present to the European Commission its broad estimates for growth, inflation, revenue, and expenditure levels in the spring, roughly six months before national budgets go through parliaments. A scoreboard will be developed to assess better competitiveness developments and imbalances and allow for early detection of unsustainable or dangerous trends.

As the summer went by and the Greek crisis seemed to abate, several member states began rejecting the harshest proposals advanced by Germany to enforce fiscal discipline. Member states rejected the German proposals to punish states that persistently flouted the rules, expelling them from the eurozone (but not from the EU), or withholding regional funding or voting rights in the European Council.

The German finance minister, Wolfgang Schäuble, also proposed a European Monetary Fund, as part of a structural European framework for crisis prevention, management, and resolution, in order to provide the means to enforce surveillance and to have a financial arm in the event of disequilibrium.[16] This was considered an excessively slow solution for dealing with immediate problems, and the responsibility for emergency intervention was given jointly to the IMF, the ECB, the European Commission, and the EFSF. Germany did not abandon its objective of a structural solution and proposed a resolution mechanism, adopted in principle by the European Council in December 2010.

Other proposals have been advanced to mutualize part of national debts, in order to reduce the market perception of risk and reduce interest rates. The Belgian prime minister, Yves Leterme, proposed that a European debt agency be established to manage eurozone government debt. The prime minister of Luxembourg and head of the eurogoup, Jean Claude Junker, together with the Italian economy minister, Giulio Tremonti, suggested a common issue of newly created eurobonds, covering up to 60 percent of each member state's GDP. Merkel and Sarkozy rejected this idea because it would increase lending costs for their countries; they would have to take responsibility for part of their neighbors' debt, and this would reduce those countries' incentives to fight deficits.

The European Commission proposed its own initiatives in September, similar but not identical to those later presented by the task force. They were stricter and gave the Commission itself a larger monitoring and decision-making power, to overcome national resistance to fiscal discipline.[17] The Van Rompuy Task Force, composed of the EU-27 finance ministers, presented its conclusions on October 21 and the European Council approved them, beginning a process of revisions and definition of secondary legislation that will continue for most of 2011.[18] The report reinforces the Stability Pact by calling for greater fiscal discipline to be pursued; it would also monitor the level of public debt more closely, along the existing deficit ceiling. It will not be sufficient anymore for a country to maintain its deficit at below 3 percent if its debt is not declining toward 60 percent of GDP at a satisfactory pace. Expenditure will have to grow at a slower pace than projected economic growth. It also calls for a wider preventive surveillance (enhanced reporting requirements), a wider set of financial sanctions that begin earlier and are easier to implement (interest-bearing deposits, which would then become non-interest-bearing and finally would be transformed into a fine in the event of unsatisfactory conclusion of the procedure). The Commission's recommendations on sanctions will be adopted unless they are blocked by a qualified majority. The conclusions of the task force leave the implementation details to negotiations to be concluded by the summer of 2011.

At the beginning of 2011 the options on the table are more restricted than they were in early 2010. The idea of reinforcing the euro by fully centralizing fiscal policy along with monetary policy to permit transfers to deficit countries, the federalist option, remains politically impossible, and no government supports it. Many observers insist that monetary union without budgetary and political union cannot work in the long run. Experience shows that this is true only in the very long term. Both the German states and the Swiss Confederation kept various monetary unions or separate currencies for several centuries before adopting a unified currency in the nineteenth century.

The process of redefining the Stability Pact to reinforce discipline through a more intense peer review, a wider examination of the sources of imbalance, and more effective and concrete sanctions is proceeding but is unlikely to resolve the issues by itself. The European budget semester, which allows the EU to oversee national budgets, has been adopted and is coming into force, but the risk of a generalized deflationary impulse in the EU is substantial if all countries whose debt is above 60 percent of GDP (almost all euro members now) undertake to reduce it rapidly at the same time. Governments still disagree on how automatic sanctions should be and how far the European Commission and the European Council will be allowed to go in dictating budgetary policy to member states. It will be important to have meaningful rules but not procyclical ones that would force retrenchment at a time when expansion is needed.

The decision of the European Council on December 16, 2010, to replace the temporary EFSF with a new permanent European Stability Mechanism (ESM) in 2013 is an important step in preventing the default of illiquid governments and managing orderly debt rescheduling where needed with the participation of private actors.[19] It is not, however, the solution to all problems, first because it will require a long treaty revision procedure, even if the simplified route is adopted.[20] Furthermore, markets are not convinced that the existing EFSF is large enough to cover all of the countries that might need it. Rising interest rates might precipitate before 2013 the situation in countries whose public finances would otherwise be sustainable. The fear of bondholders that they will take a "haircut" on their capital (lose part of their investment through a reduction of the nominal value of their bonds decided by the issuer) is closing several governments' access to capital markets, one after the other, and forcing the ECB to buy government bonds and the IMF and the EU to indirectly underwrite new ones. Through the financial crisis private debt has been replaced by public debt and is now being taken over by supranational financial institutions and EU governments. How long taxpayers and fiscally cautious governments will accept this situation is the unknown factor. So far the impression is that governments will ultimately keep doing everything necessary and will provide more resources in the event of new crises, even if at the last minute. If the private sector is required to endure part of the cost after 2013, it will be after a negotiation with private creditors on debt restructuring on a country-by-country basis.

Policies to restore growth are a necessary complement to the other institutional reforms. In the first decade of the 2000s, the gap in economic growth between Europe and emerging and developing countries grew above and beyond any precedent and expectations. The current German export-led model is not an adequate basis for economic growth for Europe and maintains imbalances, with current account surpluses in the "German area" (Germany, Netherlands, Belgium, and Austria) and deficits elsewhere. The EU as a whole cannot grow entirely through exports because of its size in the world economy. The same problem of global imbalances that the G20 is trying to tackle at the global level is reproduced at the European level by attempting to induce less asymmetrical adjustments between creditor and debtor countries, to compensate for deflationary impulses in deficit countries with increases in demand in surplus countries. To accelerate structural reforms to promote competitiveness and growth is a necessary complement, because without growth several fiscal readjustments will fail, as they did in the 1890s and the early 1930s. The EU cannot afford to return to the readjustment mechanisms of real imbalances of the gold standard, which enhanced recession and depression in the 1920s and 1930s.[21]

The European response to these concerns are the Euro plus pact, adopted in March 2011, and the simultaneous presentation of stability and converge programs and of the national reforms programs in the framework of the new European semester, to aim for growth in parallel with sustainable fiscal strategies. It is not clear though that the impact of structural reforms is going to be large enough to offset the impact of unavoidable fiscal readjustments.

The euro is an important factor in international economic and political stability and is likely to survive these hard times even if it will have to endure further financial instability and governance reform and might lose some of its smaller members unable to maintain competitiveness under a fixed exchange rate regime. The situation for the beneficiaries of the help of the EFSF is evolving: the continuation of a policy of loans is possible only if those states are really solvent and can pay them back, even in a distant future, without sinking their economies through excessive austerity. Other European countries such as Italy and Belgium stabilized after reaching debt to GDP ratios above 120 percent in the 1990s, so that Ireland and Portugal, whose debt is below that level, have good chances to avoid default. The Greek situation (debt close to 150 percent of GDP with persistent high deficit despite massive improvements) is more risky and has the potential to cause enormous disruption and further contagion. European efforts are ongoing to find a specific solution that will not undermine the European banking system nor force enormous hardships on the Greek population, but whatever the outcome, Greece will require many years to stabilize.

Notes

1. Fred Bergsten, "Preface," in *The Euro at Ten: The Next Global Currency?* edited by Jean Pisani-Ferry and Adam S. Posen (Washington: Bruegel Institute, 2009).

2. Luca Einaudi, "'The Generous Utopia of Yesterday Can Become the Practical Achievement of Tomorrow': 1,000 Years of Monetary Union in Europe," *National Institute Economic Review* (April 2000): 90–104.

3. Giancarlo Corsetti and Harold James, "Why Europe Needs Its Own IMF," *Financial Times*, March 8, 2010.

4. Barry Eichengreen and Peter Temin, "Fetters of Gold and Paper," mimeo, July 2010.

5. Committee for the Study of Economic and Monetary Union [Delors Committee], *Report on Economic and Monetary Union in the European Community* (Luxembourg: Office for Official Publications of the European Communities, 1989), p. 24.

6. Carlo Cottarelli, Lorenzo Forni, Jan Gottschalk, and Paolo Mauro, "Default in Today's Advanced Economies: Unnecessary, Undesirable, and Unlikely," IMF staff position note SPN/10/12, September 1, 2010.

7. See Tony Barber, "Saving the Euro: Tall Ambition, Flawed Foundations," *Financial Times*, October 11, 2010.

8. International Monetary Fund, *Country Report No. 10/372, Greece: Second Review under the Stand-By Arrangement—Staff Report*, December 2010.

9. IMF, "Executive Board Approves €30 Billion Stand-By Arrangement for Greece," Press Release No. 10/187, May 9, 2010.

10. One-third of the €750 billion was made available by the IMF and two-thirds by the EU, €60 billion of which were provided by the European financial stabilization mechanism, financed from the European Commission's budget, and €440 billion through the EFSF loan facility.

11. Several economists have argued for a joint decision to restructure public debt in crisis countries, especially by lengthening maturities and reducing interest rates. See, for example, Daniel Gros, "What Size Is the Fire Exit?" December 3, 2010 (www.project-syndicate.org); Nouriel Roubini, "After the Storm, a Survival Strategy for the Eurozone," December 16, 2010 (www.project-syndicate.org).

12. Carmen C. Reinhart and Kenneth Rogoff, *This Time Is Different: Eight Centuries of Financial Folly* (Princeton University Press, 2009), p. 99.

13. "Berlin impose sa vision à Paris sur un gouvernement économique," Reuters, June 14, 2010.

14. "Statement of the Heads of State or Government of the Euro Area," PCE 86/10, Brussels, May 7, 2010.

15. "European Council Conclusions," EUCO 13/10, Brussels, June 17, 2010.

16. Daniel Gros and Thomas Mayer, "How to Deal with Sovereign Default in Europe: Towards a Euro(pean) Monetary Fund," CEPS Policy Brief 202 (Brussels: Centre for European Policy Studies, February 2010).

17. European Commission, "Proposal for a Council Regulation on Speeding Up and Clarifying the Implementation of the Excessive Deficit Procedure," Brussels, COM (2010), 522 final 2010/0276 (CNS), September 29, 2010.

18. European Council, "Strengthening Economic Governance in the EU: Report of the Task Force to the European Council," Brussels, October 21, 2010 (www.consilium.europa.eu/uedocs/cms_data/docs/pressdata/en/ec/117236.pdf); European Council, "Revised Conclusions of the European Council (October 28–29, 2010)," Brussels, November 30, 2010 (www.consilium.europa.eu/uedocs/cms_data/docs/pressdata/en/ec/117496.pdf).

19. European Council, "Conclusions of the European Council (December 16–17, 2010)," Brussels, January 25, 2011 (www.consilium.europa.eu/uedocs/cms_data/docs/pressdata/en/ec/118578.pdf).

20. Formally it is a limited treaty change required by Germany to placate its constitutional court, modifying article 125 TFEU, the so-called "no bailout" clause, that slowed German support for the Greek rescue.

21. Eichengreen and Temin, "Fetters of Gold and Paper."

GIOVANNI B. ANDORNINO

14 European Union–China Relations in Light of Possible Future EU Enlargements

"Chinese top leaders spend at most a few hours a week thinking about foreign policy, and of that amount of time only a fraction is devoted to international players other than the United States or those located at China's borders."[1] This may appear to be a truism, but in a system where—despite a recent proliferation of the actors vying to influence Beijing's posture in world affairs—the opaque Politburo Standing Committee retains the ultimate decision-making power as the highest body of the Communist Party of China (CPC),[2] it is a rather consequential fact for Europe. The European Union, in short, cannot be described as preeminent in the strategic calculus of the Chinese leadership: the bilateral relationship is at best "aspirational," as David Kerr and Liu Fei have suggested.[3]

Facing an international environment fraught with perils for the stability of authoritarian regimes after the "Jasmine revolutions" in the Maghreb and the Middle East in 2011, and absorbed by a critical transition in the highest echelons of the party set for 2012, it hardly comes as a surprise that China's top leaders should stick to their pragmatic approach to foreign policy and to the EU in particular.[4] Such pragmatism indeed has an established tradition, dating back to Western Europe's inclusion in the "secondary intermediate zone" conceived by Beijing's diplomatic discourse to overcome the contradictory pressures deriving from the normalization of relations between the People's Republic of China (PRC) and France in 1964 and the cultural "agreements" with Western European countries in the early 1970s.[5] Subsequently, right at the end of the cold war, Europe was seen as instrumental in overcoming the most acute phase of China's isolation following the Tiananmen repression of June 1989. Later still, it emerged in Beijing's view as a key interlocutor in the context of an increasingly multipolar international system, eventually expected to constrain American power and hegemony.[6]

As for today—and for the short to medium term, at least—the PRC's objectives are neatly summarized in a "core interests" catalogue, much debated since the White House agreed to have this expression officially inscribed in the 2009 Joint Statement signed by President Barack Obama at the end of his official visit to China.[7] In the words of PRC state councilor Dai Bingguo, who also heads the National Security Work Leading Group of the CPC Central Committee, the leadership's fundamental concern is to "uphold [China's] basic systems and national security; and, secondly, the sovereignty and territorial integrity; and thirdly, economic and social sustained development."[8] Clearly, despite a perceivable pluralization of scholarly approaches in recent years,[9] the PRC's foreign policy remains eminently realist at its heart.

(An Enlarged) Europe's Impact on China's Interests

Given Europe's nature as a "type of entity with actor quality . . . experimenting with a new form of both unit and subsystem structure"[10]—or, to see it in a different light, an "unfinished" international actor, because its component members survive as nation-states[11]—the European Union necessarily adheres to a much less realist paradigm. The most obvious indicator is the scarce and declining emphasis on military power, both at the Union level and in member states. With national budgets under pressure after the 2008 financial crisis, European governments have markedly reduced spending on defense, prompting U.S. and NATO concerns that Europe may be focusing too much on humanitarian projects, leaving the United States to confront conflict situations almost solo.[12] This reflects more than fiscal preoccupations in European capitals: it is an indication of the consolidated perceptions of the broader security environment faced by a Union of stable democracies that have long subscribed to the liberal paradigm of nonviolent conflict resolution. According to SIPRI data, Western and Central Europe are precisely the regions in the world where military expenditure has grown the least, at a mere 7 percent since 2000, compared with 71 percent in East Asia. China itself remains the second largest spender on defense globally.[13] Clearly, the end of the cold war led to a significant desecuritization in Europe, whereas security dilemmas proliferate in China's neighborhood, starting with the always critical issues of North Korea and Taiwan.[14] Brussels' lack of strategic engagement with China's regional security dynamics and the perceived deficit of assets in European hands fundamentally diminish the Union's salience in Beijing's foreign policy calculus.

Judging from the reaction of a number of influential Chinese scholars, future enlargements per se are not likely to significantly modify the PRC's attitude in dealing with Brussels. Indeed, contrary to what might have been the case in the past, China today does not attach any particular relevance to the enlargement process of the Union.[15] In 1975, when EU relations with the PRC were established (later to be disciplined through the 1985 EU-China Trade and Cooperation Agreement), the Union's enlargements were perceived by Chinese observers as building blocks toward the emergence of a more robust European "pole" in world politics. Today, Beijing's evaluation of *shi* in the international environment—that is, the direction of the process of change that actors must recognize in order to operate properly[16]—still posits that "progress toward economic globalization and a multi-polar world is irreversible," so that the "international balance of power is changing, most notably through the economic strength and growing international status and influence of emerging powers and developing countries."[17] Europe, meanwhile, is considered by many Chinese observers as failing to evolve into a truly independent force in world affairs, sufficiently detached from U.S. strategic imperatives.

The most striking evidence of this, in Beijing's view, is Brussels' failure to lift the arms embargo that was established in 1989 on humanitarian grounds, following the violent repression of June 4. While some EU member states, including France, Spain, and Italy, have openly called for an end to a measure whose rationale is widely regarded as anachronistic, consensus is still lacking. Other countries, in fact, recall the blunt admonition that came from Washington in 2005, at a time when the issue appeared to be heading toward a solution: Assistant Secretary of State for Political and Military Affairs John Hillen warned that even a strengthened EU code of conduct on arms transfers would not be an adequate substitute for the EU's arms embargo of China, so lifting the embargo would "raise a major obstacle to future U.S. defense co-operation with Europe."[18] Beijing's choice to have the China National People's Congress pass an anti-secession law emphasizing its sovereignty over Taiwan in March 2005, coupled with a strong contrary vote of the European Parliament the following April, put any action on the embargo on hold. In 2010 the jailing of literary critic and pro-democracy activist Liu Xiaobo, that year's recipient of the Nobel Peace Prize, has added to the political complexity of tabling such a proposal at the European Council, despite the conciliatory approach favored by Catherine Ashton, the high representative for foreign affairs and security policy.

This specific quandary captures the reciprocal sense of frustration brewing on the two continents. The latest litmus test was the thirteenth EU-China Summit, held in Brussels on October 6, 2010, a few weeks after the celebration of the thirty-fifth anniversary of the establishment of diplomatic relations between the EU and China. From the Chinese perspective the summit confirmed both Europe's lack of resolve in distancing itself from American interests and the intractability of the European decision-making process, which has long allowed Beijing to exploit fissures between member states' China policies to its advantage,[19] but now shows its resistance to reaching consensus on some key decisions. The summit was so unproductive for the Chinese delegation—headed by Premier Wen Jiabao, a strong believer in EU-China relations—that the embargo, despite being little more than an issue of status, appears not even to have been raised, while Wen was forced to reject his European interlocutors' calls for a quicker appreciation of China's currency, the renminbi. Brussels' very public remarks on this issue were deemed a bow to Washington's desiderata, as European officials had usually been more nuanced than the United States in their criticism of the monetary policy of the People's Bank of China (the PRC's central bank). Several Chinese commentators have gone on to argue that Europe's alignment with Washington on this matter is economically unwise, sacrificing economic interests for tactical political gains in transatlantic relations.[20] Contextually, China's main bargaining goal, that of being granted "market economy" status, was frustrated by the opposition of several member states who rely on China's current status as a nonmarket economy to contain its competitive pressure.[21]

From the European standpoint, the summit was similarly disappointing, as it failed to constitute a significant step toward a more level playing field for European companies operating in China. Restrictive public procurement policies enacted by Beijing and aimed at offering preferential treatment to indigenous technologies, coupled with an increasingly sour business climate for foreign companies in China and the endurance of acute problems in intellectual property rights protection, are blamed for the EU's sizable trade deficit with the PRC: €128 billion in 2009. Nor does this contingency allow for much optimism about reducing the number of anti-dumping measures taken by the EU against products of Chinese origin, some 55 out of the 135 in place as of February 28, 2011, worth over €20 billion in lost trade, according to European Commission estimates.[22]

Even more striking was the absence of any explicit reference to human rights in the joint press communiqué at the end of the EU-China Summit, something that had never happened previously and a clear sign of irritation on the part of the Chinese delegation, considering that President Hu Jintao consented to weigh in rather candidly on the issue just a few months later during a state visit to Washington (January 18–21, 2011). The salience of the EU-China human rights dialogues in Brussels' perspective is greater than one might think considering it is just one of the more than fifty areas of specialized cooperation involving exchanges between Chinese and European officials. The main reason for this is political: the European Parliament has long been critical of China's human rights record, reflecting widespread public sentiment. The Pew Global Attitudes Project 2010 shows that in none of Europe's major countries does a majority of respondents harbor a favorable view of China, with critically low rates in Germany (30 percent), but also in Turkey (20 percent),[23] by far the most strategically important of the five candidate countries officially sanctioned by the EU commissioner for enlargement. Similar, if more analytical, findings are to be found in the Transatlantic Trends survey 2010, where a picture emerges of a European (including Turkish) public that is far more diffident toward China than its U.S. counterpart: on average, across twelve European countries, including all of the major ones, 61 percent of interviewed individuals stated that they do not believe that Europe and China share enough common values to be able to cooperate on international problems, against 27 percent who think they do.[24]

The approach of the European Parliament best illustrates the complex combination of interests and values affecting the EU policy-making process. On February 5, 2009, the Parliament adopted in plenary session a resolution on trade and economic relations with China, by a vote of 491 to 76, with twelve abstentions. This resolution—following a proposal contained in a report tabled by the Committee on International Trade—specifically linked the economic dimension of EU-China relations with active engagement over values. The European Parliament considered that trade relations with China should be based on the principles of reciprocity and fair competition, according to the common values of the EU and China and in adherence with WTO rules, while taking into account sustainable development, respect for environmental limits, and contributions to global goals in the response to climate change. However, "the development of trade relations with China must go hand in hand with the development of a genuine, fruitful and effective political dialogue, which should also cover human rights."[25] The matter becomes of prime political relevance as the European Parliament, whose consent on a wide range of international agreements negotiated by the Union is required under the new Lisbon Treaty, goes on to recommend "greater transparency in the negotiation of the Partnership and Cooperation Agreement (PCA)" between the European Union and China. It is unlikely to approve an agreement lacking certain "standard provisions," which include human rights. The PCA is intended to supersede the Trade and Economic Cooperation Agreement (TECA) signed in 1985, but its drafting has not yet been completed, despite having been announced at the 2006 EU-China Summit in Helsinki.[26]

As a longstanding matter of principle—grounded in China's experience as an informal colony and fragmented state in the nineteenth and early twentieth centuries, and embedded in the "five principles of peaceful coexistence" originally put forward by PRC premier Zhou Enlai in December 1953 and to this day a fundamental anchor of China's foreign policy narrative—the PRC cannot accept any link between trade and human rights. Mutual respect for each other's sovereignty and territorial integrity is a critical prerequisite for any bilateral relation in Beijing's eyes.

Here lies the fundamental contradiction between the European Union's approach to foreign policy as a postmodern polity—accepting, inter alia, that the protection of human rights may be tactically problematic but strategically beneficial for the long-term stability of international order[27]—and China's stance. While it is true that the success of the PRC as an authoritarian regime may not be described as a refutation of the liberal vision, given that it has depended on access to the international liberal order in the first place,[28] China's reincarnation from an ideologically charged totalitarian Maoist republic into a rather more stable experiment of "state-led capitalism"[29] and "consultative Leninism"[30] has not rendered it less impervious to the engagement of European values. To the contrary, under the tenure of the Hu Jintao–Wen Jiabao leadership, political reform appears to have largely stalled, both at the local level and with regard to the internal workings of the CPC, with "Western-style" democracy repeatedly denounced as ill-suited for China's purposes. In the words of PRC president and CPC general secretary Hu Jintao, China "must maintain the features and advantages of the socialist political system and define institutions, standards and procedures for socialist democracy to provide political and legal guarantees of lasting stability for the Party and the country. . . . The system of socialist core values represents the essence of socialist ideology. We must consolidate the guiding position of Marxism, persistently arm the whole Party with and educate the people in the latest achievements in adapting Marxism to Chinese conditions."[31]

The complexity of this contradiction emerges fully if one takes a closer look at the two main components of the authoritative force—that is, a form of power qualified by the legitimacy of "leading by example"—that gives substance to the EU's foreign policy. As has persuasively been argued by, among others, François Duchêne, Hanns Maull, and Ian Manners, Europe is at once a civilian power and a normative one. The very nature of the enlargement process is that of a civilizational approach to international affairs, one that has to do with the "domestication" of international politics, by bringing "to international politics the sense of common responsibility and structures of contractual politics," as Duchêne would say.[32] Today this is most evident with regard to the Western Balkans, where accession perspectives have worked as a powerful stabilizing force. Croatia is now the candidate country that will accede in 2012.[33] Iceland may be next. However, despite the success of the enlargement process (and of the related neighborhood policies) in rendering the EU an anchor of stability and, therefore, a net supplier of international order,[34] the risk to Brussels of excessive reliance upon this approach is that of cultivating a predominantly regional strategy while the Union grows into a global actor, and is called upon to play such role.[35] If we are to interpret a civilian power as an actor who accepts the necessity of cooperation with other actors in pursuing international objectives; utilizes nonmilitary, primarily economic means to secure its goals; respects and enforces international values and norms as defined by international institutions and treaties; and acts through diplomacy, economic means, and international institutions,[36] then China's form of "preventive revisionism" and its resistance to assuming a more "generous" leadership role in global governance are going to constitute the main stumbling blocks the EU is likely to encounter in the coming years.[37]

In the age of power diffusion—a far more complex scenario than a mere condition of power transfer would posit—the world will need to come to terms with the G-zero horizon discussed by Ian Bremmer and Nouriel Roubini, in which "no single country or bloc of countries has the political and economic leverage or the will to drive a truly international agenda."[38] In such a context, the "thinner" approach to international order—that of enforcing existing international norms—will be hard enough to pursue. Far more complicated will be any attempt by Europe to promote a "denser" option, requiring a shoring-up of international order by means of new, shared norms and governance tools that may help address the gap between the growing demands made on politics by a multitude of relevant actors and interests (and the common good of mankind) and the capacities of politics to steer events in the desired direction.[39] Europe is equipped to rise to this challenge, given its record in civilizing politics within itself and promoting democracy and good governance among partner countries in its vicinity. This normative project, however, will not fit the global dimension; nor will it suit several key interlocutors, starting with China, with whom the EU launched a "strategic partnership" in 2003, only to see it develop slowly and uneasily.

While such a partnership does exist, as was demonstrated by China's intervention in support of the euro in 2010 with the acquisition of important quantities of public debt issued by weaker members of the eurozone such as Greece, Portugal, and Spain, its nature appears to be eminently tactical. Beijing has tangible economic interests at stake in the Union, its main trading partner: under pressure to diversify the denomination of its vast liquid assets, mostly held in dollars, Chinese leaders can ill afford to see their European alternative implode financially. A tactical convergence of interests, however, cannot energize a truly strategic partnership. Such a goal will remain declamatory until a solution is found for the ontological incompatibility between the EU normative agenda and China's core interest in regime stability. The call for "strategic patience" featuring in the debate among member states and the emerging European External Action Service may buy some time, but does not on its own facilitate progress toward addressing this fundamental contradiction. Meanwhile, Europe's choice to relinquish voting powers for the sake of a more balanced representation of emerging countries in global institutions will be politically gratuitous,[40] leaving Brussels unable to capitalize on such actions to pursue a coherent push for a more effective multilateralism from the moral high ground of those who lead by example.[41]

Notes

1. Interview by the author with high-profile Chinese scholars, Beijing, Fall 2010.

2. Linda Jakobson and Dean Knox, *New Foreign Policy Actors in China*, SIPRI Policy Paper 26 (Stockholm: Stockholm International Peace Institute, September 2010) (http://books.sipri.org/files/PP/SIPRIPP26.pdf).

3. David Kerr and Liu Fei, eds., *The International Politics of EU-China relations* (London: Oxford University Press for The British Academy, 2007), p. 3.

4. As John Fox and Francois Godement put it, "China is a skilful and pragmatic power that knows how to manage the EU," in *A Power Audit of EU-China Relations* (London: European Council on Foreign Relations, 2009), p. 8.

5. See Roderick MacFarquhar and John K. Fairbank, eds., *The Cambridge History of China,* Vol. 14: *The People's Republic, Part I: The Emergence of Revolutionary China 1949–1965* (Cambridge University Press, 1987), p. 532 onward; and Werner Meissner, "Cultural Relations between China and the Member States of the European Union," *China Quarterly*, no. 169 (March 2002): 186.

6. On this point, see Zhang Yanbing, "China's Views on Europe's Role in International Security," in *China, Europe and International Security*, edited by Frans-Paul van der Putten and Chu Shulong (London: Routledge, 2011), p. 26 onward.

7. For a detailed discussion of China's "core interests" and the ensuing debate, see Michael D. Swaine, "China's Assertive Behavior—Part One: On 'Core Interests,'" *China Leadership Monitor* (2011): 34 (http://media.hoover.org/sites/default/files/documents/CLM34MS.pdf).

8. State Councilor Dai Bingguo, Closing Remarks for U.S.-China Strategic and Economic Dialogue, Washington, D.C., July 28, 2009 (www.state.gov/secretary/rm/2009a/july/126599.htm).

9. Zhu Liqun, "China's Foreign Policy Debates," *Chaillot Paper* (Paris: European Union Institute for Security Studies, 2010): 121.

10. Barry Buzan and Richard Little, *International Systems in World History: Remaking the Study of International Relations* (Oxford University Press, 2000), p. 359.

11. Kay Möller, "Diplomatic Relations and Mutual Strategic Perceptions: China and the European Union," *China Quarterly*, no. 169 (March 2002): 11.

12. NATO secretary general Anders Fogh Rasmussen openly warned that European nations "cannot afford to get out of the security business," February 8, 2011 (www.acus.org/natosource/nato-chief-warns-europe-over-defence-budgets).

13. SIPRI data indicate that China's military expenditure accounts for 6.6 percent of the world total (www.sipri.org/research/armaments/milex/resultoutput/trends).

14. On securitization/desecuritization, see Barry Buzan, Ole Wæver, and Jaap de Wilde, *Security: A New Framework for Analysis* (Boulder, Colo.: Lynne Rienner, 1998), esp. p. 68.

15. Interview by the author with Chinese scholars and officials, Beijing and Brussels, Fall and Winter 2010–11.

16. Qin Yaqing, "International Society as a Process: Institutions, Identities, and China's Peaceful Rise," *Chinese Journal of International Politics*, no. 3 (2010): 148.

17. *China's National Defense in 2010*, White Paper released by the Information Office of the State Council of the People's Republic of China, Beijing, 2011 (www.gov.cn/english/official/2011-03/31/content_1835499_3.htm).

18. John Hillen, "Address to the 18th Annual Global Trade Controls Conference," London, November 3, 2005 (www.fas.org/asmp/campaigns/control/Hillen09nov05.htm).

19. Most analysts, including the International Monetary Fund leadership, believe the Chinese currency to be significantly undervalued, a policy of artificial monetary management pursued by China's leadership to prop up its exports, whose growth is estimated to account for anything between 10 and 60 percent of China's GDP growth over the past two decades. On China's export-led growth model, see John Horn, Vivien Singer, and Jonathan Woetzel, "A Truer Picture of China's Export Machine," *McKinsey Quarterly* (September 2010) (www.mckinseyquarterly.com/PDFDownload.aspx?ar=2676). IMF director Dominique Strauss-Kahn is on the record as saying that "the renminbi [is] substantially undervalued" (www.imf.org/external/np/tr/2010/tr100710.htm).

20. Shi Jianxun, "RMB Appreciation Pressure Harmful to Interests of China, EU," *People's Daily*, Beijing, October 9, 2010 (http://english.peopledaily.com.cn/90001/90780/91421/7161021.html).

21. On December 3, 2010, the far-reaching impact of the Market Economy Status issue became apparent as a World Trade Organization (WTO) Dispute Panel ruled in China's favor for the first time in a case against the European Union. The panel refused to uphold Brussels' practice to impose blanket anti-dumping duties on products that the EU deemed exported by China to Europe at below the cost of production. The fact that China is regarded as a nonmarket economy (a transitory condition Beijing accepted when it entered the WTO in 2001, and which is due to expire by 2016 unless individual countries decide to bring forward the deadline for the purpose of their

bilateral exchanges) allowed EU trade authorities to calculate whether Chinese products were sold at below domestic costs based on statistics from other nations, given the alleged impossibility of determining the market cost of production in China. While the specific case being discussed did not involve especially significant interests (it dealt with screws and bolts), the fact that the WTO panel stated that extra duties should not be applied to all Chinese exporters indiscriminately but on a company-by-company basis is a critical victory of principle for China, and a precedent that might have potentially vast repercussions for a number of other pending anti-dumping cases.

22. European Commission, "EU-China Trade in Facts and Figures," Brussels, July 20, 2010 (http://europa.eu/rapid/pressReleasesAction.do?reference=MEMO/10/352&format=HTML&aged=1&language=EN&guiLanguage=en).

23. Pew Research Center, "Pew Global Attitudes Project," section devoted to the opinion survey on China in 2010, asking the question, "Do you have a favorable or unfavorable view of China?" (http://pewglobal.org/database/?indicator=24&survey=12&response=Favorable&mode=chart).

24. *Transatlantic Trends 2010*, Q24_1 (http://www.gmfus.org/trends/doc/2010_English_Top.pdf).

25. European Parliament, Committee on International Trade, *Draft Report on Trade and Economic Relations with China*, October 17, 2008.

26. For more information on the PCA, see European Commission, DG Trade, *Trade Sustainability Impact Assessment of the Negotiations of a Partnership and Cooperation Agreement between the EU and China—Final Report*, Brussels, August 2008.

27. Toby King, "Human Rights in European Foreign Policy: Success or Failure for Post-Modern Diplomacy?" *European Journal of International Law* 10 (1999): 336.

28. Daniel Deudney and G. John Ikenberry, "The Myth of the Autocratic Revival," *Foreign Affairs* (January–February 2009).

29. Yasheng Huang, *Capitalism with Chinese Characteristics: Entrepreneurship and the State* (Cambridge University Press, 2008).

30. Richard Baum, "The Limits of Consultative Leninism," in *New Challenges and Perspectives of Modern Chinese Studies*, edited by Shinichi Kawai (Tokyo: Universal Academic Press, 2008).

31. Hu Jintao, *Report to the Seventeenth National Congress of the Communist Party of China*, Beijing, October 15, 2007 (http://english.peopledaily.com.cn/90001/90776/90785/6290120.html).

32. François Duchêne, "The European Community and the Uncertainties of Interdependence," in *A Nation Writ Large? Foreign-Policy Problems before the European Community*, edited by Max Kohnstamm and Wolfgang Hager (London: Macmillan, 1973), p. 20. Interestingly, the concept of "civilian power" has recently been reinjected into the international relations debate according to a more operational reading offered by U.S. secretary of state Hillary Clinton: "Washington will have to strengthen and amplify its civilian power abroad. . . . By drawing on the pool of talent that already exists in U.S. federal agencies and at overseas posts, the United States can build a global civilian service of the same caliber and flexibility as the U.S. military." Hillary

Rodham Clinton, "Leading through Civilian Power: Redefining American Diplomacy and Development," *Foreign Affairs* 89, no. 6 (November–December 2010): 16.

33. Accession negotiations with Croatia were opened by the European Commission in October 2005, and in December 2009, based on the Commission's recommendation, a working group was set up to draft the Treaty of Accession with Croatia. With the proviso of further reforms to reinforce the rule of law in the country and the independence of the judiciary, Croatians "should be able to vote for their representatives in the next elections of the European Parliament." "Statement by Štefan Füle, European Commissioner for Enlargement and Neighborhood Policy on Croatia," Plenary Session of the European Parliament, Strasbourg, February 16, 2011 (http://europa.eu/rapid/pressReleasesAction.do?reference=SPEECH/11/107&format=HTML&aged=0&language=EN&guiLanguage=en). See also European Commission, *Croatia 2010 Progress Report*, Brussels, November 9, 2010 (http://ec.europa.eu/enlargement/pdf/key_documents/2010/package/hr_rapport_2010_en.pdf).

34. European Union, *Report on the Implementation of the European Security*, Brussels, December 11, 2008 (www.consilium.europa.eu/ueDocs/cms_Data/docs/pressdata/EN/reports/104630.pdf).

35. This contradiction is cursorily mentioned in Kalypso Nicolaïdis, "The Power of the Superpowerless," in *Beyond Paradise and Power: Europe, America, and the Future of a Troubled Partnership*, edited by Tod Lindberg (London: Routledge, 2004), p. 115.

36. On civilian power, see Hanns Maull, "Europe and the New Balance of Global Order," *International Affairs* 81, no. 4 (2005).

37. On preventive revisionism, see Giovanni Andornino, "China and Global Governance," in *A Handbook of China's International Relations*, edited by Shaun Breslin (London: Routledge, 2010).

38. Ian Bremmer and Nouriel Roubini, "A G-Zero World," *Foreign Affairs* (March–April 2011): 1.

39. Hanns Maull, "World Politics in Turbulence," *Internationale Politik und Gesellschaft* (January 2011): 17.

40. At the Seoul Summit of November 2010 the G20 countries proposed to shift more than 6 percent of IMF quota shares to dynamic emerging market and developing countries. In December 2010 the IMF Board of Governors approved the proposed reform, paving the way for final ratification by member states by 2012. "Board of Governors Approves Major Quota and Governance Reforms," Washington, December 16, 2010 (www.imf.org/external/np/sec/pr/2010/pr10477.htm).

41. Effective multilateralism is a key concept in the EU Security Strategy. European Union, *A Secure Europe in a Better World. European Security Strategy*, Brussels, December 12, 2003.

PART FIVE

A New Security Architecture?

JAN TECHAU

15

A Saturated Alliance? Assessing the Prospects for Further NATO Enlargement

The enlargement of the North Atlantic Treaty Organization (NATO), executed in three rounds in 1999, 2004, and 2009, marks the biggest geopolitical shift in Europe since the end of the cold war.[1] And while the intended effects of that enlargement—increasing stability and supporting democracy in the transforming societies of the former Eastern Bloc—materialized brilliantly, the side effects of these enlargements were largely unexpected. What were these side effects?

How NATO Underestimated Its Own Enlargement

First, enlargement fundamentally changed the geopolitical function of the alliance. Having previously been an exclusively military coalition with a defensive posture aimed at a singular threat posed by the Warsaw Pact, it now turned into an active agent of change in political transformation processes. By creating the Membership Action Plan (MAP), a strictly supervised mechanism managing democratic reforms of the military in candidate countries, and more generally, by establishing political prerequisites for membership, NATO turned into one of the key stewards of the post–cold war development in Central and Eastern Europe and in the Balkans. And while the results of this stewardship for the countries in question are widely considered to be a success, it added a dimension to NATO's activities, and to the external perception of the alliance, that has been little understood so far.

This perception becomes most visible in NATO's relationship with Russia. Knowing very well that NATO does not pose a military threat to its national sovereignty and territorial integrity, Russia remains skeptical of NATO precisely because it has transformed itself into an agent of political change.[2] The political elite in Moscow, having no interest in importing overly democratic reform movements from its immediate neighborhood, opposes NATO expansion not primarily for military reasons, but for fear of being unable to halt Western ideas of open liberal societies and accountable government. To this day, however, the discourse about NATO-Russia relations remains largely focused on military affairs, which have long ceased to be of primary concern for most of the nations involved (Poland and the Baltic states being the notable exceptions). And while it is understandable that the Russian government wants to keep it this way (as it camouflages the real reasons for its uneasiness), it is highly unfortunate that this is also the prevailing discourse in the United States and other capitals within NATO. As long as NATO does not fully understand its new political role, the aftereffects of NATO enlargement will continue to surprise some of its members.

Furthermore, while NATO enlargement has muted the old geostrategic interests of its neighbors, it has simultaneously created new ones in their place. Most notably, Germany, which for the first time in its history is surrounded entirely by friendly nations, all of them NATO members (except Austria), has lost almost all strategic interest in further expansion, especially to the east (Ukraine, Georgia). Poland, however, is now in the same position that Germany was in before enlargement (that is, with an open eastern flank it eagerly wishes to protect) and is heavily promoting NATO membership for its neighbor Ukraine. These new geostrategic realities have created foreseeable frictions within NATO, requiring member states to develop new strategic modes of thinking. For some, this has been a rather difficult endeavor.

There is another notable mental shift observable within NATO that has been brought about by enlargement. Naturally, the end of the cold war was welcomed by all NATO member states as the resolution of a dangerous, and potentially existential, geopolitical quagmire. In some member states, however, this historic turn of events also created an unjustified sense of permanent relief from guard duty. Some nations cashed in on the peace dividend and did not expect to engage in security-related geostrategic considerations anytime soon. However, the incoming member states of the alliance were joining the club to acquire precisely that: a security guarantee in what they still perceived to be a potentially dangerous world. As a consequence, enlargement required the strategy-weary member states to engage in debates they had hoped would never return. When that did not happen, irritation followed. In many ways, NATO accepted new members who took the very purpose of NATO significantly more seriously than many older ones did. This new gap in threat perceptions and expectations has so far not been fully resolved.

To sum up, the new divisions within NATO were very much unanticipated by an alliance that had hoped it could grow without changing too much itself. But there was never a chance for that. It was clear from the outset that enlargement would have important ramifications. More important, however, they could not have been prevented had enlargement been postponed or canceled. Geopolitically, nonenlargement would have sent shockwaves through Europe. It would have meant, first, that NATO did not take seriously the pledge laid down in article 10 of its founding treaty—that is, that the alliance was open to "any other European State in a position to further the principles of this Treaty."[3] In addition, it would have signaled to the newly liberated countries of Central and Eastern Europe that the democratic West had no interest in filling the vacuum that had been created by the demise of the Warsaw Pact. The potential fallout from that kind of decision would have been much graver than that created by enlargement.

Overstretch through Enlargement?

Ideas about overstretch have long preoccupied military strategists. Imperial overstretch is said to have caused the downfall of empires, including the British Empire, Napoleonic France, and the Spanish and Swedish reigns over widespread territorial entities.[4] In accordance with these theories, with the relative decline of its hegemon, the United States, NATO would at least be rendered irrelevant if it outgrew itself, even if it did not entirely break apart.[5] As long as nations still desire to become full members of the alliance, these fears are unlikely to be realized. On the other hand, fears of overstretch are not entirely unjustified, but probably for reasons other than usually expected. It is true that, unlike in the European Union, a large increase in the number of member states, although making consensus-building more tedious, does not necessarily make NATO any more difficult to govern. This is due to the limited scope and the comparatively low degree of political integration that a military alliance requests from its members. However, a more fundamental question arises from NATO enlargement: is its territory still defensible?

Defensibility, arguably, is the most important consideration for an alliance whose raison d'état is a provision that proclaims that an attack on one of its members will be considered an attack on all of them. Defensibility in itself, essentially, rests on two pillars: first, military capabilities to stage a successful defense if need be; second, the political will of the alliance's members to use these capabilities in collective defense. The issue is further complicated by the fact that in modern times the meaning of "defense" is multifaceted and might mean a lot more than just physical defense against an enemy intruding on an alliance's territory or its air space. Some of the "new threats," such as cyber war or energy dependence, have already stretched the classic concept of defense.

But even in strictly traditional terms, defensibility has become a large issue for NATO. In times of ever-decreasing military capabilities (at least in Europe), full-fledged territorial defense might already be beyond NATO's capacity. But as the threat of a general invasion has practically disappeared, this seems to be an acceptable state of affairs. What is more dangerous is the question of political will, or rather the lack thereof. Doubts have arisen in some of the newer member states that there is still enough resolve to defend them against any kind of Russian military assault on their territory. Would allies be willing to risk escalation with Russia if such a scenario came to pass? How reliable will the American nuclear umbrella be for its European allies if a conflict with another nuclear power escalated? (This, alas, is an age-old question pondered by many strategists at almost every stage of NATO history.) NATO was hard-pressed to alleviate these fears by tasking its military planners to think about possible contingency plans.[6]

Even if we assume that all current member states will live up to their mutual promise to defend each other, the defensibility question remains valid for possible future rounds of expansion. Will all NATO member states really come to the rescue of any given member state—say from the Balkans—should that state get itself entangled in one of the many lingering regional conflicts? Will Europeans and Americans be willing stakeholders in Ukrainian-Russian disputes or in disputes concerning the notoriously opaque ethnic conflicts in the Caucasus? Bluntly put: will these countries, in the end, be important enough for all NATO member states to invest political and financial capital and significant military assets in coming to their aid?

With affirmative answers to these questions in doubt, the real overstretch of NATO is one of political will, not of territorial outreach. It is political will, based on shared interests and attachment to common values, that lies at the core of the alliance. If this will is strong enough, no territorial expansion would necessarily overstretch NATO. (One should not forget that long before NATO expanded eastward, the geographic spread of NATO from Alaska to East Anatolia and from Hammerfest to Gibraltar had been quite substantial—without raising serious talk of overstretch.) But anyone who wants to make the case for further NATO enlargement must first generate the sustainable political will to do so. This is tedious work. When U.S. president George W. Bush pushed for including Georgia and Ukraine in the MAP before the NATO summit in Bucharest in 2008, his initiative was destined to fail. There had been no convincing long-term effort to create the required political will.

Bush's initiative to enlarge NATO failed because the political will was stretched beyond its limits. To this day, this type of overstretch seems to be the largest risk to NATO's relevance.

The Future of the Great Bargain

The former U.S. ambassador to NATO, Harlan Cleveland, once famously described NATO as the product of a great transatlantic bargain.[7] This bargain, Cleveland explained, put Europe under U.S. military protection in return for serious commitments by the war-weary European allies to carry a part of the defense burden. More recently, this bargain has been described slightly differently by Robert Shapiro, a former economic adviser to President Bill Clinton. In his version of the deal, the United States gave protection to Europeans in return for a disproportionate American say in European political affairs (through NATO). But the Europeans did not only gain in security. As a result of the deal, they were also able to invest the money they saved on defending themselves to create substantial and far-reaching welfare states.[8] U.S. engagement (and investment) not only kept the Warsaw Pact at bay; it also enabled Europeans to maintain the fragile social peace in their conflict-ridden postwar societies. In both versions of the deal, NATO serves as the keystone that keeps the construction together. European security is administered through NATO, which is also the place where Europeans chip in their contribution, and through which the United States can express its stake in European politics.

Despite the end of the cold war, NATO's various rounds of enlargement, its military missions in Kosovo and Afghanistan, and the fundamental changes in its geopolitical function, the great transatlantic bargain remains intact today. It is still the foundation of Europe's security architecture. But this historically unprecedented deal is under threat from various sides. First, all signs seem to indicate that Europe will become far less of a strategic interest for the United States in the future. Already considerable resources are being withdrawn from the "old continent" to be invested in the Asian arena instead. For many, Europe is simply a pacified, stable continent that warrants much less American attention than it used to. Second, the Europeans seem to be increasingly unable to fulfill their side of the deal. With military assets in Europe already at an all-time low,[9] and with further cuts in defense spending already announced in major European countries,[10] Europe could well irreversibly uncouple itself from its commitments within NATO. As a consequence, talk is rife—and not only in the United States—about Europe becoming increasingly obsolete as a meaningful player in global affairs. Third, with the United States also being forced to reduce its global footprint, it might soon be unable to pick up the tab for European geopolitical interests around the world. This is not the place to debate the future of the great transatlantic bargain. But if this bargain is key to the alliance, then what does it have to do with enlargement?

The most obvious explanation is that the continued existence of the great bargain is the prerequisite for any future enlargement. Should America and Europe part ways on defense issues, nations will most likely cease to be interested in seeking membership. NATO's attractiveness as an alliance depends on America being part of the deal. Only with American participation is the security guarantee credible. The substantial (and still growing) capabilities gap between European allies and the United States has already created suspicions about NATO's military credibility, which in turn has led even some NATO allies to intensify their efforts to strengthen bilateral ties with the United States. This illustrates to what extent the great bargain, which makes the United States the decisive security player in Europe, is a *conditio sine qua non* not only for enlargement but also for NATO's existence.

Less obvious, but of similar importance, is Russia's role in connecting the bargain with enlargement. During the cold war, the Soviet Union, led by Russia, was the key outside enabler in bringing the great bargain about. By threatening both the United States and Europe it provided the external incentive that made the bargain necessary and possible. And while still today a good number of new (Eastern European) NATO members try to keep the bargain intact in order to receive American protection from Russia, this is hardly why the United States needs to sustain the bargain. After all, the military assets that Eastern Europeans can provide to the United States in return for being protected are rather negligible. Instead, the United States needs the bargain intact because it needs Russia's cooperation on almost all crucial foreign policy issues it wants to resolve. These include the proliferation of weapons of mass destruction (WMD), international terrorism, Afghanistan, energy security, missile defense, and Iran. For this reason, the United States cannot afford to have its Russia relations hijacked by a number of hard-nosed Eastern European nations. The United States needs the bargain (that is, its own security guarantee for its European allies) to keep the European front calm, and to not convolute the already rather messy Russia relations with geopolitical disturbance in Europe. This might seem counterintuitive at first: why should the United States issue a security guarantee against Russia when it really wants to cooperate peacefully with Moscow? Because a Europe calmed and stabilized by that guarantee is the key to productive U.S.-Russian relations. Keeping the bargain intact to improve America's relations with Russia might indeed seem counterintuitive, but it is a relatively cheap way of keeping one of its crucial bilateral relationships free from messy complications. And this is also why the United States will most probably, at least for the time being, not press for further NATO enlargement into the former Soviet space. For America, Russia's cooperation will for the foreseeable future remain more important than bringing Ukraine and Georgia into the NATO fold. America will continue its high-wire act: keeping Eastern Europeans silent by granting them protection while not extending that protection to too many other crucial countries within Russia's sphere of influence. The great bargain has indeed become a whole lot more complicated!

A Future for Enlargement?

After the sixth round of enlargement in 2009, which brought Albania and Croatia into the NATO fold, the drive toward further rounds of enlargement has clearly run out of steam.[11] This is clearly not due to a lack of potential candidate countries. But the timing seems off, and political support for further enlargement is not very strong for the moment. U.S. support for the candidacies of Georgia and Ukraine has been muted under the administration of President Barack Obama for geopolitical reasons (see above), and also because of an internal rift within the alliance on this issue. Macedonia is the strongest current candidate, but it lingers on the sidelines as the notorious name dispute with Greece is nowhere near a conclusion.[12] Serbia, Montenegro, and Bosnia-Herzegovina are possible candidates, but all of them have substantial internal problems and lack sufficient popular support for joining NATO. Moldova and Belarus—if one deems them possible candidates at all—are unlikely to even be considered for a MAP invitation. Also, initiatives to take in Israel, Australia, Japan, or other Western or Western-minded countries located in non-Western regions have regularly failed to spark real support. NATO's new Strategic Concept, adopted at the alliance's summit in Lisbon in late 2010, has further muted these plans. In this document, NATO stresses its role as a regional organization, thereby effectively rejecting any notions of a "global NATO."

As for Russia, despite some efforts by prominent Western figures to promote its inclusion in NATO,[13] membership seems highly unlikely. Some Eastern European NATO members deem it unthinkable to grant Russia a veto over its security matters; more crucially, Russia itself has very little interest in joining the alliance. Russia will not readily bind its national security to NATO procedures, which demand unanimity, transparency, and full inspections. Furthermore, the idea of granting the United States or other NATO member states a veto over its security affairs goes against Russia's hypersensitivity about sovereignty and independence. Most important, however, Russia perceives NATO as a merely regional organization of dwindling importance.[14] Russians believe that the Anglo-Saxon world is, slowly but surely, losing power, and that

NATO, as the primary agent of this world, will suffer accordingly. Since Moscow perceives itself to be the beneficiary of this process, it has no inclination to press for membership.

NATO, at this point in time, seems to be a saturated alliance. The sense of historical obligation that Western NATO members felt toward countries such as Poland, Hungary, and the Baltic states, and which lent their accession processes the required momentum, has disappeared. The countries of the Western Balkans had (and still have) a much more difficult time than their predecessors creating a sense of implicitness for their candidacies. With the sense of obligation gone, more sober considerations seem to prevail in member states: What added value can new candidates bring to the table? How do they—and can they—contribute to the maintenance of peace and stability in the Euro-Atlantic sphere? And, as pointed out above, are they defensible? Very few countries seem to pass the test, even though it is usually not discussed in public.

But NATO also worries not just about the contributions others could make, but also about its own strength. Will a security guarantee issued to new member states be sustainable? Or will membership provide them with a false sense of security, while in reality NATO will not be able or willing to fulfill its commitments if push comes to shove? The overstretching of political will that is behind these questions seems rather obvious. Fully absorbed by its military mission in Afghanistan, NATO is already struggling to manage a full plate.

Finally, with Russia portraying a new assertiveness in its immediate neighborhood, and with many Russia-related energy questions unresolved, Western countries feel substantially less inclined to push for eastward expansion. Such a move is considered to be of very unpredictable strategic value and thus has very little attraction, especially for the rather risk-averse old member states of Western Europe.

The answer to the question of whether there will be future rounds of enlargement will to a large extent depend on how NATO develops in the post-Afghanistan era (with the exception of Macedonia, whose accession hinges on a different consideration). Will Afghanistan-style operations become the daily bread of the alliance? Or, as some observers suggest, will NATO give up on costly and demanding out-of-area missions of such magnitude in order to refocus on its classic article 5 obligations?[15] In the latter case, new resources might be dedicated to resolving lingering conflicts in the Balkans and on NATO's eastern frontier, thereby paving the way for further expansion.

But even if, at some point in the future, enlargement should become fashionable again among NATO member states, the number of possible new entries will most probably be very limited.[16] The time of enlargement as a *grand projet* seems to be over, one way or another. NATO played a decisive role in managing the peaceful transition after the fall of the Berlin Wall. That transitory period, and with it enlargement, is over now. In this post-transition and post-Afghanistan period, NATO will have to sort out its own new role, consolidate its inner workings, and manage the substantial decline of defense spending among its members. In light of all this, enlargement will probably not be high on the list of priorities for some time to come.

Notes

1. For detailed historical analysis of the enlargement process, see, for example, Robal D. Asmus, *Opening NATO's Door: How the Alliance Remade Itself for a New Era* (Columbia University Press, 2002); James M. Goldgeier, *Not Whether but When: The U.S. Decision to Enlarge NATO* (Brookings, 1999); Stanley R. Sloan, *NATO, the European Union, and the Atlantic Community: The Transatlantic Bargain Challenged* (Lanham, Md.: Rowman and Littlefield, 2005), pp. 145–80; Zoltan D. Barany, "NATO's Peaceful Advance," *Journal of Democracy* 15 (January 2004): 63–76; James M. Goldgeier, "NATO Expansion: The Anatomy of a Decision," *Washington Quarterly* 21 (Winter 1998): 58–102; Johannes Varwick, *Die NATO: Vom Verteidigungsbündnis zur Weltpolizei?* (Munich: C. H. Beck, 2008), pp. 97–118.

2. These Russian concerns over the political ramifications of enlargement are in contrast to the assumed military fallout predicted by George F. Kennan. Kennan had called NATO enlargement "the most fateful error of American foreign policy in the entire post–Cold War era." See George F. Kennan, "A Fateful Error," *New York Times*, February 5, 1997.

3. See North Atlantic Treaty, Washington, D.C., April 4, 1949, Art. 10 (www.nato.int/cps/en/natolive/official_texts_17120.htm).

4. See, most notably, Paul Kennedy, *The Rise and Fall of the Great Powers* (New York: Random House, 1988).

5. For a typical example of theories about NATO overstretch, see Stanley Kober, "Cracks in the Foundation: NATO's New Troubles," *Policy Analysis*, no. 608 (Washington: Cato Institute, January 15, 1998).

6. See "Trust, but Make Military Plans," *The Economist*, July 29, 2010.

7. Harlan Cleveland, *NATO: A Transatlantic Bargain* (New York: Harper and Row, 1970).

8. Robert Shapiro, *Futurecast: How Superpowers, Populations, and Globalization Will Change the Way You Live and Work* (New York: St. Martin's Press, 2008), p. 219.

9. For a detailed analysis of Europe's dwindling military capabilities, see James J. Sheehan, *Where Have All the Soldiers Gone? The Transformation of Modern Europe* (Boston: Houghton Mifflin Harcourt, 2008).

10. The financial crisis that started in 2008 has led the three largest countries in Europe—Germany, France, and the United Kingdom—to announce drastic cuts in military spending over the next few years.

11. Rafael Biermann, "NATO Enlargement—Approaching a Standstill," *Security Insights*, no. 4 (December 2009) (Garmisch-Partenkirchen: George C. Marshall Center for Security Studies), p. 2.

12. For an illustration of the complexity of the name issue over "Macedonia," see the remarks by the Greek ambassador to the United States before the NATO summit in Bucharest in 2008. Alexandros P. Mallias, "NATO Enlargement—the View from Athens," *Huffington Post*, March 27, 2008 (www.huffingtonpost.com/amb-alexandros-p-mallias/nato-enlargement-the-view_b_93812.html [September 2010]).

13. See Volker Rühe and others, "Die Tür öffnen," *Der Spiegel*, March 8, 2010, p. 100; Radek Sikorski, "Russia in NATO? Why Not? " *Gazeta Wyborcza*, March 31, 2009 (www.wyborcza.pl/1,86871,6445605,Sikorski__Russia_in_Nato__Why_Not.html [September 2010]).

14. Andrew Monaghan, "'Russland, vorwärts!'" *Internationale Politik* 65 (September/October 2010): 52.

15. Karl-Heinz Kamp, "Nach Afghanistan," *Frankfurter Allgemeine Zeitung*, May 20, 2010.

16. See also the recommendation by Rafael Biermann, who believes that establishing clear geographic boundaries for NATO would be a strategically wise idea. Biermann, "NATO Enlargement," p. 6.

MARK ENTIN

16

Imperatives of Constructing a New Security System in the Euro-Atlantic Region: The Russian Perspective

The European Union and its member states are too focused on themselves. They have many critical internal problems, but they are not fully aware of what is going on around them. They do not fully realize how alarming and explosive the situation in the world is becoming.

The European Union and its member states rashly take for granted the reports their think tanks produce to the effect that it's business as usual. They believe that the security structures they have created are reliable because they are self-sufficient, and that all the other countries, including the Russian Federation, are quite ready and willing to content themselves with the status quo or are even seeking to preserve it.

This is an erroneous interpretation of our recent common history. The economic crisis that began in 2008, the first truly global economic and financial crisis, has taught us plenty of things. We should have learned a lot from the range of armed conflicts at different stages of escalation that we see unfolding. No less important are the lessons we should learn from the potential threats and new security challenges on the rise everywhere.

Power and influence as well as economic, military, and political might in the world are becoming ever more diffused. The factors undermining international stability are becoming increasingly multidirectional in character. In this environment, it is impossible to cope with the negative trends by applying specific ad hoc measures, which NATO, the EU, and their member states are still banking on.

The situation dictates the need to pool the efforts and resources of all the states, the alliances and unions that are ready and willing to do so in order to ensure genuinely indivisible security. The situation requires that all the prejudices and biases of the past, which continue to poison international relations, including those between Russia and NATO, as well as Russia and the EU and its member states, should be relinquished. It moves to the fore of public policy the main priority—that is, inclusive joint management of international processes, international cooperation, and above all, coordination in countering common and global threats.

The Cold War's Accursed Legacy

After the Berlin Wall fell in 1989, a refreshing wave of velvet revolutions swept the continent. A large group of new countries emerged in the territory of the former Soviet Union, which were seeking renewal and whose foreign and domestic policies were being shaped. All the participants in those events, all the political forces, and the populations at large sincerely believed that change was in the offing, that life would get better, that the family of European peoples would be reunified, and that the dividing lines of the past would disappear. In this new world, hostility and confrontation would give way to allied relations, because mutually incompatible ideologies would no longer place countries and political elites on opposite sides of the barricade. Ideological conflict would also become a thing of the past.

Two decades have since passed. But not even a minimal program in that direction has yet been implemented. The tenets and stereotypes of the cold war have proved to be extremely tenacious, thwarting all bold and innovative initiatives. Cold war ghosts are still very much a part of the political discourse and of political decisionmaking mechanisms. This is evident from the press accounts of the five-day war in the South Caucasus in August and September of 2008. The old political forces, keen on keeping the cold war stereotypes intact, have survived, and similarly minded new political forces have emerged. They continue to skillfully cultivate the image of an external enemy in the minds of the political class of Europe, to nurture and foster it. They need the image to secure new military orders, rally the nationalist-minded electorate behind them, fight their political opponents, cling to power, and sustain the illusion in the United States, NATO, and the EU that they are important, influential, and reliable. The set of cold war instruments remains in demand, both ideologically and in practical policies.

The EU and NATO declare with heartfelt emotion that the division of the continent has come to an end. They triumphantly report that the historic mission has been accomplished, that they succeeded in reunifying the continent. This is an undisguised distortion of the facts—an error of either omission or self-delusion.

In fact, what they did was to move the line of division and the dividing lines eastward, absorbing the former countries of the socialist camp and some of the countries that emerged in the post-Soviet space. These accomplishments should not be downplayed: Central and Eastern European countries needed political certainty and support of their choices. But the point I am making is different altogether.

The expansion of NATO and the EU did not accomplish the historic mission of reunifying the whole continent. Indeed, it could not have accomplished it. It was the USSR that had been seen as the West's adversary and a threat to it. Thus, without Russia's participation as the main successor state to the Soviet Union, no reunification of the continent is possible.

The configuration of the cold war division in Europe, despite NATO and EU enlargement or, to be more precise, because of it, has remained intact. Consequently, so has the bitter, unfair, and unbearable legacy of the cold war. This legacy slows down disastrously the economic growth of the countries in the region, hampers the establishment of a common economic space, and leads to ever more lost opportunities. Owing to this legacy, political stability on the continent is weaker than would be desirable by an order of magnitude, and weaker than it could have been under different circumstances.

Institutional Deficiency, or the Absence of a Security System in the Euro-Atlantic Region

The security structure on the continent credibly reflects the situation. NATO was created to countervail the USSR, to contain and deter it, to defend its member countries from a possible attack by the USSR. This military-political alliance has never had any other functional mission as important as this one. But lately, instead of defense, which has actually ceased to be necessary, NATO has embarked on out-of-area military operations.

Indeed, Stalin, to no less a degree than Jean Monnet and Robert Schuman, was one of the midwives of the EU. Talking about this is considered inappropriate, and more often than not this fact tends to be ignored. But the EU was created during the cold war, and the ideology underlying the EU activities and its practical policies bears the unerasable imprint of the cold war.

The Organization for Security and Co-Operation in Europe (OSCE) also came into being as a product of the cold war. Yet the purpose of the Helsinki process had been quite different. It was launched to defuse tensions in relations between the two blocs. One of its most significant upshots, the Conventional Forces in Europe (CFE) Treaty (the original one, not its adapted version) was built on an inter-bloc foundation and permeated by inter-bloc ideology.

The OSCE has never found its role in the new environment. It did not become an umbrella structure with regard for NATO and the EU, as Russia had insisted. It did not acquire a new mission. Even worse, Moscow believes, NATO and the EU have turned the OSCE into a screen, a political cover-up for pursuing their lopsided and narrow-minded egotistical policies in the Balkans and in the post-Soviet space. The crisis in the OSCE was vividly illustrated by the impasse it encountered when Russia's proposals were debated for reforming the organization, on the need to adopt its charter and regulate its functioning. The depth of the crisis was borne out by the unraveling of the CFE Treaty regime.

The Collective Security Treaty Organization (CSTO) is another important geostrategic actor in the sphere of security on the continent. Russia is the fulcrum and the major driving force of the CSTO. However, because of the adamantly obstructionist stand of NATO and the EU with regard to the CSTO, there is no interaction between them. All the proposals to this effect have been rejected under the pretext that the CSTO is still in an embryonic state. This argument is only partly true, though it can hardly be doubted that the CSTO is only building up its authority and influence.

In the long term, the Shanghai Cooperation Organization (SCO) will increasingly contribute to maintaining security in Eurasia. Even now it is active and has taken various initiatives. Its missions include maintaining security. The role the SCO intends to play is determined by the fact that it is the world's biggest regional organization. Yet so far it has no contacts with the Euro-Atlantic structures, which also seems strange. Common sense and objective needs make it clear that there is no logic in such a state of things. What can be discerned there, however, is the logic of political rivalry.

Thus, in the Euro-Atlantic region there seem to function quite a few international structures, organizations, and associations, but none of them deals with overall regional security. They do not ensure or guarantee it. Security space remains fragmented, divided, and patchy. In practice, there is no collective security, as has been demonstrated in the case of Yugoslavia and, subsequently, Serbia. Nor is there indivisible or equal security for all, which had been histrionically proclaimed by the OSCE documents and joint statements and declarations of NATO member states and Russia.

Moreover, the security space is structured in a way that automatically generates contradictions, misunderstandings, and suspicion. In turn, these give rise to mutual distrust and destabilize the situation in the Euro-Atlantic region. Such partnership and cooperation structures as the NATO-Russia

Council (NRC) and the EU-Russia political and sectoral dialogues at summit, ministerial, and high-ranking civil servant levels, including the Permanent Partnership Councils in different configurations, purportedly are called upon to serve as bridges between Russia and NATO and between Russia and the EU. But let us not delude ourselves. In fact, they only serve to legalize a divided Europe and legitimize the absence of a common security space, while the opposite is necessary.

All these structures proceed from the assumption that, on the one hand, there is NATO and the EU; on the other, there is Russia, and an insurmountable barrier exists between them, which it would be desirable to overcome. Yet these structures only perpetuate the existence of this barrier and confrontation. They are designed in a way that makes it impossible for them to overcome it. They have neither the powers nor the set of instruments—virtually nothing—to do it.

They are not authorized to make binding decisions. No one vested such powers in them. Brussels would not hear of it. No other mechanisms of making binding decisions have been established, however makeshift, primitive, or palliative.

Nor do these structures have built-in obligatory mechanisms and procedures of dispute settlement. They are not provided for. They do not exist. Even those nonobligatory ones that do exist are easily transformed into their opposite. This was graphically evidenced by the crisis in relations between Russia and NATO and between Russia and the EU in connection with Georgia's military attack against South Ossetia and Russian peacekeepers, Russia's response measures, and NATO's and the EU's inadequate reaction. Political documents proclaimed that the NRC was to prevent such things and render assistance in situations like that. However, it was blocked.

The mechanisms designed to manage interactions between Russia and the EU and its member states envisaged by the Partnership and Cooperation Agreement also failed. The French president, Nicolas Sarkozy, undertook mediation, given his country's presidency of the EU at the time. Russia and the EU quickly found an ad hoc solution for that specific case. It worked. But it is impossible by definition to build long-term cooperation on the basis of ad hoc solutions.

At the same time, the EU and NATO countries have mastered to perfection the methods of politicizing bilateral disputes with Moscow and giving them Europe-wide resonance. By the same token, they took on board the techniques of conflict escalation. Examples are numerous. The simplest one is the deployment of NATO fighters to the Baltic countries at their insistent request to police the air space along their border with Russia. There was no need to do so. It caused a storm of anger and indignation in Russia. A somewhat more complex example is the negotiations between Brussels and Moscow on a new fundamental EU-Russia agreement, which both sides need greatly. The negotiations were delayed for almost two years because of a routine trade dispute between an EU member state and Russia.

The security agenda of the above structures viewed as strategies for promoting indivisible security and a profound deepening of partnership relations is confined to strictly peripheral matters, whereas the core issues of dramatic importance concerning internal military planning and development are excluded from the agenda. The EU's and NATO's prime concern consists in preventing Russia from obtaining a veto on matters of security. However, without multilateral diplomacy and mechanisms to prevent incorrect, incautious, and one-sided decisions, no common security is possible.

Therefore, a common security is nonexistent. A couple of joint missions of the kind performed by combat helicopters and their crews to support the EU operations in tropical Africa or coordinated action against the Somali pirates do not count, nor does the work on a crisis resolution agreement started by Moscow and Brussels.

Shifting the Blame

Yet in the current security vacuum characterized by the hoax of equal and indivisible security and a lack of common security structures, many statesmen, politicians, military commanders, and experts in NATO and EU member states are clearly playing with the facts. It is being alleged that Russia seeks to maintain the status quo, based on the Kremlin's extremely negative attitude toward plans to draw Ukraine and Georgia into NATO. As one can see, there is nothing to maintain.

It was in his famous Munich speech following unsuccessful attempts to bring home his concerns to the EU and NATO leaders that Vladimir Putin, then president, publicly expressed Russia's dissatisfaction with the existing situation. Putin's speech caused an almost unanimous uproar in the West and was immediately stuck with all the traditional labels of cold war rhetoric. The only reason for this criticism was that instead of whitewashing the reality as befits the unwritten rules of political correctness, the Russian politician had dared call a spade a spade.

With regard to the initiative of the incumbent Russian president, Dmitry Medvedev, on signing a European security treaty (EST), it does not seek to maintain the status quo, which is unacceptable to Russia. Rather, it aims to set in motion, albeit with a twenty-year delay, the building of common security foundations in the Euro-Atlantic region. A second, equally untrue allegation may be summed up as follows: Medvedev's initiative must be caused by Russia's dissatisfaction with its place in the system of Euro-Atlantic security where, having failed to become part of it, Russia has no role to play. Indeed, Russia is dissatisfied and finds the current situation unacceptable. Russia will never tolerate attempts to portray the legacy of the cold war as an ideal Euro-Atlantic international system. But it would be absolutely impossible to occupy a dignified place in or become integrated into something that does not exist. Hence Moscow's clear and unequivocal call for a Euro-Atlantic security system in which it will play a natural and substantial role. The difference is evident.

The above issues, however, are but one aspect of the problem. There is another, which is that Moscow also finds the existing Euro-Atlantic security configuration ineffective, and therefore unacceptable. Unable to prevent disregard of peace and stability ideals, the current system condones lawlessness while failing to address any of the key tasks needed to diminish the threats and challenges facing the world.

Over the past twenty years the United States, NATO, and the EU have occupied the leading positions in the world, a factor that now defines the security configuration in the Euro-Atlantic area. They have turned into de facto custodians of international peace and stability while Russia remained self-absorbed and China was building up muscle. As to the nonaligned movement, it has lost all influence. The Euro-Atlantic leadership has produced catastrophic results.

Nuclear arms are spreading inexorably across the planet, while the triumvirate has done nothing to nip this process in the bud. India and Pakistan have gate-crashed the nuclear club, making the world a hostage to their rivalry. The half-hearted sanctions temporarily imposed on them have been pointless and ineffective from the outset. Now Israel and North Korea also have nuclear weapons of their own, with others seeking possession, both openly and in secrecy. The world is on the brink of bursting into flame, like a barrel of gunpowder. If that happens, all rational perceptions of world politics and international relations will have been futile and no measure of missile defense will give protection. After all, a nuclear device could be exploded anywhere, not to mention the nightmare of potential blackmail should a nuclear warhead fall into the hands of a terrorist network.

At the same time, the Middle East conflict is sending waves of tension around the globe, fueling a veritable clash of civilizations, impeding progress in various negotiation processes, and undermining the normal functioning of many international organizations by diverting attention away from other issues of equal importance. The triumvirate, however, has contributed next to nothing to resolving it. Just as it has many times in the past, the conflict in the Middle East is likely to boil over at any given moment.

All around the world a growing number of wars—internal and international armed conflicts—are both blazing and smoldering, and record numbers of human lives are being lost. Some of those wars have been provoked or unleashed by the triumvirate itself, thus making it directly responsible. Mankind has made no significant progress toward eliminating the endogenous causes of such conflicts; nor has the number of failing states diminished, despite the many billions of dollars in development aid money sent in assistance of local and regional problem resolution.

The United States and NATO have stood at the head of the antiterrorist coalition in which the EU and its member states are playing a vital role. But they are losing their battle against terrorism—first and foremost in Afghanistan, but also elsewhere, as terrorism takes strong root in all troubled nations and regions. The war against organized crime, illicit drug trafficking, and other international corruption seems to be following a similar defeatist scenario, which renders the internal and the external security of all Euro-Atlantic nations ephemeral. Russia, in particular, is feeling painfully affected.

Regrettably, even without venturing into the spheres of financial, economic, or energy security, the above list of grievances could be longer. However, the conclusion is evident. The existing security configuration, with its extremely poor record, does not meet the current needs and should be transformed as soon as possible. A reformatted and an upgraded system will need to take account of everyone's interests, including those of NATO and the EU member states as well as of Russia.

Positive Change Program

The sphere of security is known to be almost inert, because all change has to be preceded by both objective and subjective prerequisites.

The objective prerequisites are already there, consisting in the concurrence of interests on the scope of issues between Russia and NATO on the one hand, and between Russia and the EU on the other. A synergy will likely result from their pooling of resources, capabilities, and efforts. Another consideration is that the rivalry will be destructive and lead nowhere, and those indulging in it are only inflicting damage to themselves by undermining their own positions. Only through joint effort will they be able to prevent further degradation of the security sphere, reverse the situation, and overcome global threats and challenges, providing a universal security for all.

As regards subjective prerequisites, they have been nonexistent so far. However, President Medvedev's EST initiative has made some progress. Initially it was received with outright hostility. But the harder the Russian politicians, diplomats, and expert community worked to promote the idea, through discourse and closer attention to the issue, the more it became evident that there was something to it. The initiative did not materialize out of thin air. It takes account of actual needs.

Hence there is a need to maintain the effort to explain Medvedev's initiative both politically and professionally. It is necessary to multiply the number of negotiating forums by engaging more knowledgeable persons in the debate. Concrete proposals and documents need to be drafted. Then the realization of the need to reconstruct the Euro-Atlantic security structures can be expected to take root. Meanwhile, subjective prerequisites for real practical steps and strategic decisions will also mature.

In order to achieve this outcome, one ingredient is necessary: the support of the media, nonprofit organizations (NPOs), and civil society in the nations concerned. They must be engaged as allies capable of neutralizing the negative messages that are constantly injected into the public consciousness. Indeed, it is an open secret that the Russian media demonize NATO while also predicting the disintegration of the EU. The media in the EU and NATO member states, for their part, engage in slandering the Kremlin's domestic and foreign policies while NPOs are fixated on attaching strings to constructive cooperation. All of them should take a panoramic, bird's-eye view of the security situation, rather than a narrow parochial one, to allow for a realistic assessment. Having taken such a view and having become appalled by the spectacle, the media, NPOs, and civil society will be able to serve as social pillars in the process of modernizing international relations and the security sphere in the Euro-Atlantic area. They will transform themselves into an intellectual pool of ideas and considerations to be implemented in further practical work.

That, among other things, is what Medvedev's initiative aims to achieve. Moscow has never before intended and has no intention now to impose ready-made solutions on anyone. The initiative says: there is a problem to address, let us address it together. It sends an invitation to an open, sincere, and meaningful dialogue. It suggests building security safeguards and structures together, for only together can common approaches be found and a political culture of partnership, mutual understanding, and trust be formed. Only with an open and flexible approach will viable, strategic, and mutually acceptable solutions be found.

To a considerable extent, the Russian initiative relies on self-development fueled by its stated objectives being tuned to the needs of the region as a whole. The approach seems to be bearing fruit, with intensive bilateral consultations already under way and the Corfu Process launched within the OSCE framework. Concrete proposals have been made at the political level, and many interesting new ideas concerning the disarmament agenda, confidence-building measures, and institution-building mechanisms have been aired at expert community forums.

The EST project officially delivered by Russia to NATO, the EU, the OSCE, and their respective member states will neither obliterate nor replace the aforesaid efforts. Rather, it could be incorporated into them as a single-theme project seen as key by Moscow. It is meant to incorporate the mutual and indivisible Euro-Atlantic security commitments into a formal treaty process and to establish international conflict prevention and de-escalation procedures to underpin joint security structures. In conjunction with many other confidence-building and cooperation measures needed in the common struggle against common and global threats, the EST initiative would lay down a new foundation for Euro-Atlantic security.

Medvedev's initiative deserves serious consideration, along with other worthy ideas and proposals that have been offered for public scrutiny. Some are designed to specify the norms of international law and the key notions of cooperative, collective, and inclusive indivisible security, while others foresee measures to establish joint structures for evaluating and monitoring potential threats and suggesting recommendations for their prevention. Still others analyze ways and means of building a new umbrella framework to allow coordinated effort of international organizations operating in the security sphere. There are also new ideas and proposals in a number of related areas.

The Russian initiative looks particularly promising because it dedicates all effort, discussions, and negotiations to achieving its principal goal—that of providing more and better security for all of the Euro-Atlantic nations and their peoples.

KURT VOLKER

17

The EU Concept of Security from a U.S. Perspective

From 1945 to 1989—and despite periodic tensions, crises, and opportunities—the division of Europe was for all practical purposes frozen in place by the Iron Curtain. Even in the earliest years of the cold war, however, the United States strongly encouraged European integration—to build a bulwark against Soviet communism, to foster economic growth to overcome the legacy of World War II, and to create a new culture in which cooperation, rather than rivalry, would become the norm. Post-Nazi West Germany would thus be anchored peacefully in a modern Europe.

Though it was less often stated, an implicit assumption of this support for European integration was that if indeed the communist system collapsed from within, Central and Eastern European nations would be restored to a place within a broader European family of nations. This was clearly part of the thinking behind Germany's cold war "Ostpolitik," and it was the essence of the call by former presidents George H. W. Bush and Bill Clinton for a Europe whole, free, and at peace.

The original European Coal and Steel Community (ECSC) grew during the cold war from its six founding ECSC members to twelve members of the European Community (EC) by 1989. Its growth enjoyed strong U.S. support, but remained within the Western nations of Europe, with what were then called Eastern European states being frozen out and the European neutrals steadfastly remaining apart from the Western bloc. Thus in 1989, all twelve members of the EC—save Ireland—were also members of NATO.

No Ambiguity on Defense

At the same time, while the United States strongly supported European integration, it looked at the EC almost exclusively as an economic association, even though it had a political purpose, and the Western European Union nominally created a security arm. For hard security, the United States looked to NATO as *the* security framework for Europe, as well as the key venue for transatlantic political consultations.

The collective defense clause of the Western European Union (WEU) Treaty did of course mean that there was a strong commitment to mutual self-defense among most European members of the EC. But because all of the WEU nations were also members of NATO, as a practical matter this WEU commitment was subsumed by the mutual defense commitment of NATO's Article 5, which included all the EC (and WEU) members except Ireland, as well as the United States, Canada, Turkey, Norway, and Iceland.

Thus the EC member states' defense commitments to each other through the WEU did not extend any more broadly than U.S. commitments to European states—everything fell within the confines of the Article 5 commitments of the NATO Treaty. This meant that there was no moral hazard for the United States: that is, there was no situation where an EC/WEU member state's defense commitments on behalf of a fellow EC/WEU member who was not a NATO member risked involving the United States in a conflict beyond the scope of the NATO Treaty.

Though seemingly pedantic now, this clarity was significant at the time: ambiguity over security commitments weighed heavily on the minds of U.S. strategists who believed that a lack of clarity over the U.S. commitment to defend South Korea encouraged the North to launch an attack. In a world where the risk of war in Europe was quite real, where America had hundreds of thousands of troops on the line in European territory, and where the doctrine of extended deterrence meant that even the U.S. mainland was at risk from possible conflict in Europe, ensuring that there was no ambiguity in defense commitments was absolutely critical.

The Fall of the Wall

The fall of the Berlin Wall changed all of this, though it took time for the changes to work their way through the system.

First was the question of German unification, and establishing that a united Germany, with all its territory and population, could be a full member of both NATO and the European Community. Again, while in retrospect this seems obvious, at the time, the question was seriously debated both within the West, and between the Western powers and the Soviet Union. It was resolved only through a variety of assurances developed in the two-plus-four negotiations (between the two German states and the four powers, the United States, the United Kingdom, France, and the Soviet Union).

Second was the aspiration of newly free nations in Central Europe to join both NATO and the EU. In the wake of the major expansions of both organizations in the late 1990s and early 2000s, it is easy to forget that this was also highly controversial at the time. The United States and the key Western allies wanted to ensure a stable and peaceful end to the cold war. President George H. W. Bush specifically admonished that the West should not act in a "triumphalist" manner toward the Soviet Union; nor should the West take any steps that would result in the drawing of a new dividing line in Europe a few hundred miles east of the old one. Because of this "anti-enlargement" policy, NATO's Partnership for Peace, launched in early 1995, was originally criticized as being a sellout—a substitute for NATO enlargement, rather than the pathway it eventually became.

At the same time that NATO was holding off any extension of security commitments at the end of the cold war, the European Community was in the process of becoming the European Union, and it wanted to accomplish a significant "deepening" of Europe before "widening." The EU also knew that it would be tremendously challenging for former communist command economies to meet the economic and legal requirements of membership, and it did not want to give false hope of speedy accession.

Thus as far as Central Europe was concerned, from both the United States and the EU, the initial reaction to the fall of the Berlin Wall was caution concerning any expansion of membership in either organization. As a result, the question of diverging defense commitments between the EU and NATO that could have arisen was not a factor. Although scholars and pundits raised the issue of NATO enlargement much earlier, it was only in the course of the 1996 U.S. presidential campaign that candidates Bill Clinton and Bob Dole went on the record as advocates of future NATO enlargement, a position that led eventually to changing the policy of both the United States and NATO as a whole.

The third effect of the fall of the Berlin Wall—and subsequent collapse of the Soviet Union—was that the old cold war concept of neutrality had lost its meaning. An increasingly integrated European Union became more attractive economically to states such as Sweden, Finland, and Austria. And at the same time the political and security policy rationale for those states remaining outside the European Union was vanishing.

It was this third phenomenon, changes in the concept of neutrality, that ultimately forced the United States and Western Europe to think beyond the cold war mentality of potentially diverging defense commitments. Even though they never joined the WEU (whose defense cooperation aspects were subsumed by the EU), there could have been hesitation over extending a moral commitment to collective defense of EU members who were not members of NATO.

But by 1995, when the core group of European neutrals joined the EU, the United States and the European Union states had all internalized the fact that the risk of a war in Europe was now minuscule—based both on the collapse of the former Soviet military capabilities and on the growing cooperation between the West and post-Soviet Russia. In U.S. eyes, any potential risk based on ambiguities in defense commitments was now far outweighed by the positive benefits of expanding the geography of an increasingly democratic, prosperous, and integrated Europe.

Role Reversal—U.S. Warms to EU Enlargement While Europe Cools

While the EU moved to include the European neutrals among its members, NATO began the process of including Central and Eastern European democracies among its members. For the states in Europe's East, however, it was seen as part of a package. There was no "either-or" in joining NATO or the EU, but a firm desire to join both, and joining one facilitated movement toward the other. As a practical matter, NATO membership came first for Central Europe, and EU membership second.

In the United States, this was seen as a virtue. Not only had the United States overcome its hesitancy over diverging commitments—it instead saw the inclusion of new members in both NATO and the EU as good for Europe as a whole. Though there were the "historical exceptions" of NATO states that never joined the EU, and European neutrals who felt comfortable joining the EU but not NATO, the broader effect was to create a wider space where freedom, democracy, market economy, rule of law, *and* long-term security and collective defense could flourish. As the growth of this space progressed, the United States assumed that it would have a positive influence on adjoining areas, so they too would begin to come closer to a Europe whole, free, and at peace. Certainly, the progression between the first (1999), second (2004), and third (2009) rounds of NATO enlargement seemed to demonstrate this point.

This belief that expanding membership in NATO and the EU helps cement a larger space of freedom, democracy, prosperity, and security—while at the same exerting a positive influence on neighboring areas—remains an important element in the thinking of many U.S. experts today. It helps to explain the continued U.S. support for further NATO enlargement in the Balkans and Europe's East, and for expanding EU membership in the Balkans. It also contributes to U.S. support for Turkish EU membership, though that is determined principally by larger strategic considerations. And because of both the overlap of NATO and EU enlargement—as well as the fundamental shift in the strategic environment away from conventional military threats in Europe—there is almost no concern over creating ambiguous security obligations for the United States in Europe.

A further consideration for the United States is that while most new NATO members may have relatively small military capacities, they have proven themselves strong advocates of NATO solidarity, and are willing to contribute to NATO-led operations across the board. Indeed, the forces of some new members have proven themselves to be well skilled and willing to take on tough missions. Though perhaps less significant to Western European members of NATO, this new member enthusiasm is welcome to a United States that often feels Western Europe is under-resourcing its defense establishments and applying conditions to troop deployments.

But while U.S. enthusiasm for EU enlargement has grown, the EU's own enthusiasm has diminished sharply.

This shift in EU thinking can be attributed to several factors. Among them:

—the growing pains of absorbing the EU's existing new members, including the influx of workers from new members into old member states (which is exacerbated in its effect by significant migration from North and sub-Saharan Africa)

—economic downturn in Europe, again making these labor market pressures seem more acute

—perceptions that some new EU members have not performed well enough on reform, anti-corruption, and political maturity since becoming EU members—and thus that any potential new members, who are starting from further behind, would have even more catching up to do, imposing even greater risks to existing EU states

—growing opposition to Turkish membership, which dampens enthusiasm for enlargement in general

—the eurozone crisis, which has exposed significant differences even among old members of the EU on core fiscal and financial performance issues

—in the Balkans, a perceptions of stagnation—from the recognition of Kosovo to the argument over Macedonia's name to the Bosnian nationalist stalemate

—in the East, a much more assertive Russia that has made clear it is seeking to reassert a sphere of influence around itself. Even though Russia's irritation is aimed more at NATO enlargement than EU enlargement, it casts a pall over EU thinking about the East.

Lack of EU Enlargement Now a Liability?

The United States, far from worrying about the EU creating new security commitments, is more concerned that the EU's fears about further enlargement will contribute to slower development in many neighboring states. By failing to provide a credible "light-at-the-end-of-the-tunnel" and purposeful accession negotiation, there is little incentive for leaders to take the risks required to tackle the thorny issues necessary to build the kind of mature, democratic, prosperous, and secure space that the United States and the EU ultimately seek. This applies equally to nationalists in Bosnia, hardliners in Macedonia (over the name), and reformers fighting corruption and organized crime.

Clearly, the EU has a rhetorical commitment to further enlargement in the Balkans, as well as strong policies in place to help advance reforms in both the Balkans and in the Eastern Partnership nations. Yet the EU's commitment to further enlargement lacks credibility in most of these states, and willingness to make hard decisions on reform suffers as a result.

In turn, continuing political and economic stagnation perpetuates security risks, which could extend or create new demands on the United States. Although the Dayton Accords were signed in 1995, Bosnia remains deeply divided and at risk of increased tension along ethnic lines. Kosovo continues to require a NATO-led security presence (KFOR), with U.S. participation. The risk of tension between ethnic Albanians and Macedonians increases the longer the name issue is unresolved, and Macedonia remains outside NATO and EU structures.

Moreover, by keeping a "partnership" distance from Georgia and Ukraine, the EU inadvertently reinforces Russia's perception that it has a right to a "sphere of influence" extending over the Eastern Partnership countries. This in turn can contribute to assertive behavior by Russia, which also can affect U.S. security interests.

All that being said, the risk of traditional security threats in Europe is dwarfed by the risk of nontraditional threats. Energy vulnerabilities, cyberthreats, terrorism, and insecurity and societal ills stemming from weak states are all more likely to affect Europe than state-to-state conflict, or even ethnic or civil violence within states. The most effective means of countering these new threats is through stronger societies and states and closer cooperation among them, rather than traditional military means.

In addition, the United States is increasingly engaged in addressing more pressing security challenges outside of Europe—from Afghanistan to Iraq and elsewhere—and would prefer to reduce its security presence and contributions within Europe itself. The solidification of strong political, economic, and security foundations in a wider Europe is fundamentally in the interest of U.S. security and would afford the United States the ability to divert resources elsewhere.

From the perspective of the challenges of 2011, the more the project of establishing a Europe whole and free can advance, the more the historical security challenges of Europe can be put into the past, the more Europe can withstand new, nontraditional challenges, and the more Europe and the United States can together address security challenges affecting them both, well beyond the territory of Europe itself.

PART SIX

Democracy Promotion and the Rule of Law

AMICHAI MAGEN

18 The Rise and Stall of Democratic Enlargement

The boundaries of the European Union today are by and large also the boundaries of consolidated liberal democracy on the continent and in its surrounding frontiers. With the happy but small exceptions of Iceland, Israel, Norway, and Switzerland, an EU of twenty-eight member states resides in proximity to a vast and varied medley of weak states (Albania, Bosnia-Herzegovina, Iraq, Kosovo, Lebanon, Moldova); pseudo-democracies (Georgia, Macedonia, Turkey, Ukraine); competitive authoritarian states (Armenia, Egypt, Kazakhstan, Morocco, Russia); as well as many of the world's most closed and repressive regimes (Algeria, Azerbaijan, Belarus, Jordan, Iran, Kyrgyzstan, Libya, Tajikistan, Turkmenistan, Syria, and Uzbekistan).[1]

That the EU now extends so far northward and eastward, and that its members, old and new, are today without exception consolidated liberal democracies attests to the extraordinary process of democratic enlargement that took place on Europe's frontiers over the past two decades. That expansion—a major feature of the so-called third wave of global democratization—has now largely stalled. The stagnation, and in some cases decline, of democracy in regions neighboring the EU over the past several years ought to both concern Americans and Europeans and prompt the transatlantic community into fresh thinking on how best to consolidate recent gains, stem democratic erosion, and help renew positive democratic development on Europe's new frontiers.

The first part of this chapter substantiates the claim that there has been a "rise and stall" pattern in the fortunes of democracy since the onset of the third wave in 1974, placing the European experience within the broader global one on both counts—the rise and the stall. The chapter then zooms in to briefly examine American tradition and thinking about democracy promotion on Europe's frontiers, and analyze in greater detail the unique engagement strategy developed by the Union itself in an effort to secure and promote democratic regimes on its shifting borders—initially among the fledgling democracies of Central and Eastern Europe (the CEECs), and later in Turkey, the Balkans, Ukraine, North Africa, and parts of the Middle East.

Understanding Europe's "transformative engagement" philosophy and existing toolbox is essential for appreciating its past achievements and contemporary limitations. The EU's existing capacities for building a ring of well-governed countries on its eastern and southern peripheries are inadequate. Stemming and reversing democratic decline on Europe's frontiers, the chapter concludes, requires new transatlantic thinking, initiative, and determination.

Global Democracy and Europe's Expanding Frontiers

On April 25, 1974, the Portuguese Revolução dos Cravos (Carnation Revolution) overthrew the longest standing dictatorship in Southern Europe. In that year, the number of democracies in the world stood at a mere forty, concentrated overwhelmingly in Western Europe, North America, and some of the other former British colonies. Among countries with a population larger than 1 million people, only thirty were electoral democracies—fewer than a quarter of all states existing at the time. In parallel, dictatorships of various types (one-man, one-party, or military junta) controlled most of Africa, Asia, Latin America, and the Middle East, while the countries of Eastern Europe and the Soviet Union were entirely subject to communist rule.[2]

Portugal's domestic revolution heralded the onset of a global democratic transformation. The "third wave" of democratization quickly spread to the rest of the Iberian Peninsula and Greece, then in the 1980s to Latin America, several countries in Asia, and—with the demise of Soviet communism at the turn of the 1990s—to Central and Eastern Europe and parts of Africa.[3] A fourth wavelet of transitions in Serbia (2000), Georgia (2003), and Ukraine (2004) extended democratic gains on Europe's eastern and southern edges.[4] By the turn of the millennium, eighty electoral democracies had been created, or restored, and the percentage of democracies worldwide had increased to sixty-three.[5] For the first time in human history, democracy had become not only a universal aspiration, but the predominant system of government practiced in the world. This transformation constituted arguably the most profound reorientation of the international system since the dawn of the modern state system, and has carried with it far-reaching consequences for human well-being, in terms of individual freedom, security, and wealth.[6]

The triumph of democracy in Europe was particularly meaningful. Two generations ago political ideologies inimical to liberal democracy all but overran the continent and Britain. As Samuel Huntington observed, the dominant political development of the 1930s and early 1940s was the shift away from democracy and "either the return to traditional forms of authoritarian rule or the introduction of new mass-based, more brutal and pervasive forms of totalitarianism."[7] At lowest ebb, in the early years of the Second World War, there existed a mere eleven democracies on earth.[8] A generation later, the fortunes of democracy had improved somewhat, yet Europe itself remained deeply divided in the cold war struggle between open and authoritarian regimes.

Moreover, the triumph of democracy in Europe, while not complete, was more extensive than that attained in other regions of the world. As overtly authoritarian regimes have disappeared from many parts of Latin America, Asia, and Africa, they have tended to be replaced, especially since the end of the cold war, not by high-quality liberal democracy, but by weak electoral regimes displaying deep flaws in government accountability, the rule of law, protection of political rights and civil liberties, and responsiveness to citizen needs.[9] Not so in Europe, where even the laggards among the new democracies that eventually joined the EU as full members—Bulgaria, Romania, and Slovakia—achieved relatively high levels of democratic consolidation and quality.

Gains in political freedom worldwide reached a zenith in the decade between 1995 and 2005, yet even at the turn of the millennium ominous signs of stagnation and decline began to appear. Most dramatically, a series of democratic breakdowns, either by coup or through rigged elections, took place in a number of large strategic states—Pakistan (1999), Russia (2000), Nigeria (2003), Venezuela (2005), Thailand (2006)—prompting eminent analysts to warn of the possibility of an impending "reverse wave."[10] After a decade of nearly uninterrupted gains in freedom outpacing losses by a ratio of at least two to one, the trend was broken in 2006, with Freedom House noting in its annual report that year "a series of worrisome trends that together present potentially serious threats to the stability of new democracies."[11] In addition, powerful authoritarian states that had previously displayed various degrees of liberalization—Belarus, Egypt, Saudi Arabia, Syria, and Uzbekistan—began constricting internal space for public dissent and shutting down channels of international assistance as a means of reducing democratizing pressures.[12]

Since 2006, global levels of freedom have witnessed continued, indeed accelerated, deterioration. For four consecutive years, a decline in levels of political freedom, as measured by Freedom House, has exceeded gains, leading to the longest continuous period of democratic erosion since the advent of the third wave.[13] It remains to be seen whether the February 2011 popular removal from power of dictators Zine El Abidine Ben Ali in Tunisia and Hosni Mubarak in Egypt will help reverse the trend by instigating genuine democratic breakthroughs in the Middle East, or whether renewed hopes for an Arab spring will be dashed by a new wave of authoritarian adaptation, or worse, descent into chaos.

The situation in regions neighboring the EU is mixed. On the upside, as Europeans celebrated the twentieth anniversary of the fall of the Berlin Wall, the democratic institutions and political cultures of the post-communist Central and Eastern European and Baltic countries proved resilient enough to weather considerable economic stresses. Broad improvements were also recorded in the Balkans, with Croatia moving rapidly toward liberal democracy, and Kosovo, Macedonia, Moldova, Montenegro, and Serbia all bucking the global trend to make positive gains.[14]

In contrast, the countries of the non-Baltic former Soviet Union continued their decade-long decline, reaching levels of authoritarianism comparable only to those of North Africa and the Middle East. Indeed, as Arch Paddington observes, with the exception of the three Baltic republics (which joined the EU in 2004) and Ukraine, the countries of the former Soviet Union now lag "far behind sub-Saharan Africa on the average scores for political rights and civil liberties, as well as on the majority of individual indicators, including freedom of expression, freedom of association, and the rule of law."[15]

Despite promises made by President Dmitry Medvedev to curtail corruption, free up public space for civil society, enhance freedom of speech, and strengthen judicial independence, Russia continued deteriorating in 2008 and 2009. Kazakhstan and Kyrgyzstan also experienced declines, with the latter moving from the "partially free" to the "not free" category of countries. Belarus remained the last truly closed regime in Europe itself. Georgia, whose 2003 Rose Revolution raised hopes of a powerful democratization trend, declined in 2007–08, and has stagnated since. Ukraine, though still within the "free" category of the Freedom House scale, has been shaken by economic downturn and remains burdened by enormous corruption and a high degree of political instability. Elsewhere on Europe's frontiers, levels of freedom in North Africa and the Middle East remained extremely low, with Jordan, Morocco, and Turkey actually dropping in 2009. A staggering 88 percent of the region's population still live in countries ranked "not free" on the Freedom House scale.[16]

By historical standards, the state of democracy in the world generally, and in Europe in particular, has clearly improved greatly since the advent of the third wave in 1974, and especially since the end of the cold war. Fears of a major reverse wave have not materialized, and are highly unlikely to do so in Europe itself. The countries of Western, Central, and Eastern Europe are now all consolidated liberal democracies, and encouraging gains continue to be made in the Balkans.

At the same time, it is clear that, as in other regions of the word, democratic expansion beyond the enlarged EU itself has stalled and in some important cases declined over the past several years. With relatively minor exceptions, the EU now faces a set of frontiers largely hostile to democracy.

Democratic Enlargement: A Brief American Perspective

In the summer of 1993, six months after coming to power, President Bill Clinton's national security team met in Washington to coin a phrase that would replace George Kennan's cold war doctrine of "containment" with a new all-encompassing sobriquet for the post–cold war foreign policy of the United States. The eventual winner of the "Kennan sweepstakes," as the exercise came to be known, was the concept of "democratic enlargement."[17]

In a speech in September of that year, Clinton's national security adviser, Anthony Lake, articulated Washington's new grand strategy: "The successor to a doctrine of containment must be a strategy of enlargement—enlargement of the world's free community of market democracies."[18] Now that Soviet communism was no longer, Lake explained, the United States would be more secure, more prosperous, and more influential, while the wider world would be more humane and peaceful, to the extent that democracy and market economies became entrenched in other nations.

The new "strategy of enlargement" would have four core components: (1) it would "strengthen the community of major market democracies . . . which constitutes the core from which enlargement is proceeding"; (2) it would "help foster and consolidate new democracies and market economies, where possible, especially in states of special significance and opportunity"; (3) it would "counter the aggression" and support the liberalization of states "hostile to democracy and markets"; and (4) it would "pursue our humanitarian agenda not only by providing aid" but by helping democracy and market economics take root in the poorest regions of the world.[19] Several days after Lake's SAIS speech, President Clinton made "democratic enlargement" the centerpiece of his major policy address to the UN General Assembly.[20]

The opportunity to begin implementing the new strategy of enlargement came soon thereafter, and it did so on Europe's new eastern frontiers. At the January 1994 NATO summit in Brussels, Clinton urged NATO allies to "enlarge" the transatlantic defense community eastward, having in mind the three Visegrad countries—Poland, Hungary, and the Czech Republic—in particular.[21] NATO partners concurred, declaring that they "welcome NATO expansion that would reach to democratic states to our East, as part of an evolutionary process, taking into account political and security developments in the whole of Europe."[22]

The Clinton administration, like the earlier administration of George H. W. Bush, understood that NATO and EU enlargement would be important for anchoring the fledgling new democracies of Central and Eastern Europe in the Western values system, as well as for preserving NATO's relevance (and so U.S. influence) in the emerging post–cold war European space. It was primarily through NATO enlargement that Clinton and Lake saw a means for the United States to help complete European integration, leaving behind them a legacy of a Europe "whole and free."[23]

Seeking to ensure NATO membership expansion took place in a gradual and stable manner, the Americans also instigated the Partnership for Peace (PfP) initiative. Drawing on work already under way in the North Atlantic Cooperation Council (NACC), the PfP offered all states participating in the Conference on Security and Cooperation in Europe (CSCE) the prospect of cooperation with NATO in six areas, including democratic control of defense forces, transparency in defense budgeting, and building capacity for partners to participate in NATO-led peacekeeping operations sanctioned by the UN or CSCE. "Partnership," Lake declared, "will serve one of the most important goals in our enlargement strategy . . . building a stable environment in which the new democracies and free markets of Eastern and Central Europe and the former USSR can flourish."[24] A year later, the concept of "democratic enlargement" remained at the core of the Clinton administration's National Security Strategy.[25]

The early to mid-1990s did constitute a rare historical juncture when a victorious West could seek to reshape world politics in the malleable aftermath of the cold war. Yet President Clinton's seizing upon the opportunity to promote democracy abroad through the expansion of the liberal international order established following the Second World War, far from amounting to a novel departure from the United States' foreign policy traditions, in fact reflected an affirmation of one of its oldest.

Since gaining their independence, and even before, many Americans believed not only that their system of government and civic culture was responsible for America's own freedom and prosperity, but that it made America a democratic example and a moral force to be emulated overseas. At least since Woodrow Wilson's April 1917 call for the world to be "made safe for democracy," some American leaders, both Democrats and Republicans, have extrapolated from this belief an operational conclusion: that it was in the very nature, even a moral imperative, of the United States to share its values and institutions universally.[26]

Different administrations have attached different weight to different aspects of democracy, and they have offered various justifications for American involvement, from "realism" that stressed the benefits of a liberal political and economic order for American interests, to "idealism" that enunciated the morality of democracy and the universality of its promise. The priority accorded to democracy promotion in U.S. foreign policy has also varied, both between administrations and even within the tenure of one president. Still, no American head of state has ever denied the importance of the objective, and the goal of promoting democracy abroad has never been completely jettisoned by an American president.[27]

Europe and its immediate frontiers have historically been the prime location in America's global efforts to defend democracies, extend them where possible, and thwart the spread of totalitarian regimes. From Woodrow Wilson's call to replace balance-of-power politics in Europe with a commonwealth of democracies governed by international rules; Franklin Roosevelt's concern to save democracy on the continent from fascism; Harry Truman's and George Marshall's determination to democratize Germany during the Allied occupation and rebuild a shattered Western Europe; Dwight Eisenhower's and John Dulles's promise to "roll back" communism and liberate the "captive nations" of Eastern Europe; to Ronald Reagan's and George Shultz's insistence that communism not be contained but transformed through "democratic revolution"—Europe has been at the very core of America's efforts to promote democracy.[28] And when the boundaries of democratic Europe expanded, when the goal of seeing a Europe whole and free came to fruition, it is Europe's new frontiers, in Russia, Central Asia, the Balkans, North Africa, and the Middle East, that have become prime focal points of American concern and policy.

Democratic Enlargement: The EU's Rules and Engagement Strategy

In the summer of 1993, European leaders too had democratic enlargement very much on their minds. After hesitating for several years following the tearing down of the Berlin Wall, at a June meeting of the EU heads of state in Copenhagen they decided to offer "the associated countries of central and eastern Europe that so desire" the prospect of full membership. The offer was strictly conditional, subject to those countries demonstrating their ability "to assume the obligations of membership by satisfying the economic and political conditions required." Membership would demand comprehensive socio-economic modernization, first and foremost: "that the candidate country has achieved stability of institutions guaranteeing democracy, the rule of law, human rights and respect for and protection of minorities."[29]

The articulation of the Copenhagen criteria meant not only the launch of a massive, decade-long EU drive to secure democracy on Western Europe's post-communist frontiers. It also heralded the transformation of the EU itself into an active promoter of democracy.

At a fundamental level, the process of European integration itself has, from its inception, been intimately linked to the goal of defending liberal democracy in Europe against the dual perils of fascism and communism. As early as 1952, French foreign minister Robert Schuman stressed that the nascent European Coal and Steel Community (ECSC) would be open to all "free" European states, and to them alone.[30] Since that time, integration has been continuously legitimated by an ideology that perceived the Community as a community of liberal economic and political values.[31]

Yet the EC/EU did not proclaim a commitment to promoting democracy *outside* its own borders until the turn of the 1990s, and then only after several of its member states and other international actors (notably the UN and World Bank) endorsed the objective. Before the end of the cold war, Western European leaders drew largely pessimistic lessons about the efficacy of democracy promotion, and the substantial role played by the EC in underwriting democratic consolidation in Greece, Portugal, and Spain in the late 1970s and 1980s was only gradually appreciated by European policymakers. At the same time, the consuming task of postwar reconstruction within Western Europe and the restrictions imposed on its governments by bipolarity meant that democracy promotion emerged as a significant European foreign policy objective only after the collapse of Soviet communism. In comparison with the United States, therefore, the EU is a relative newcomer to promoting democracy abroad.[32]

A related historical consequence is the fact that the key formative experiences that have shaped American and European thinking about promoting democracy abroad have varied greatly. The postwar transformations of Germany and Japan mark America's clearest and most profound success in building democracy. In contrast, Europeans rightly view the enlargement of the EU to Central and Eastern Europe as having proven to be the Union's most successful foreign policy strategy to date.

The laying out of the Copenhagen criteria for membership heralded the transformation of the EU from an inward-looking democratic community to an outward-oriented democratic magnet. Fast on the heels of the June 1993

Copenhagen statement came the launch of a Commission-designed and -led pre-accession strategy; a strategy whose underlying logic, core institutional features, and methodologies form, to this day, the template for the EU's transformative engagement strategy with Turkey, the Balkans, and, in diluted form, the wider European neighborhood.[33]

The EU's approach to promoting liberal market and political reform on its eastern and southern frontiers—from Central and Eastern Europe in the 1990s to the European Neighborhood Policy (ENP) today—has been variously described as "external Europeanization," "EU external governance," "transformative Europe," or "transformative engagement."[34] In essence, it entails the EU prescribing laws, norms, regulatory models, and administrative standards with which targeted neighboring states are expected to comply (rule setting), coupled with the conditional offer of powerful incentives—in some cases the golden carrot of full membership—and other mechanisms intended to induce compliance with the mandated rules (engagement).

In terms of rule-setting, the corpus of EU law itself, the *acquis communautaire*, constitutes the bedrock of democratic substance promoted outward by the Union. The *acquis*-export approach carries several distinct advantages. With 85,000 pages and growing, the *acquis* (covering everything from human rights to customs and excise standards, financial regulation, and corporate governance) forms a legal and regulatory framework of extraordinary scope and density, extending in its fullest application to practically every area of economic, social, and political life in the modern democratic states of Western Europe. This attribute, which stems from the sheer breadth and density of regulation at the EU level itself, is unparalleled in international society. It means that under the aegis of a single concept—a concept enjoying broad legitimacy, since it is the law of no fewer than twenty-seven Western democratic states—the EU is in principle able to project any part, or a complete comprehensive model, of socioeconomic existence.[35]

Reliance on the *acquis* as the standard with which third countries seeking closer relations with the EU are required to comply also helps couch deeply political reforms in depoliticized, technocratic terms. As Jiri Pehe attested immediately after the May 2004 "Big Bang" round of enlargement to include countries of Central and Eastern Europe:

> While stock-market and privatization transparency, banking reform, anticorruption measures, and simplified bankruptcy laws might not at first glance seem to have much to do with democratic consolidation, in truth they all helped greatly to give democracy solid underpinnings in Eastern Europe.[36]

Rather than wielding the rhetoric of "liberty" and "freedom," or declaring that the goal of the external power is "transformational diplomacy," a reference to the Union's *acquis* and other regional instruments (notably the Council of Europe and OSCE) and global standards (notably UN treaties and recommendations), it is a means of promoting EU-mandated rules while blunting resistance from veto players who oppose external intervention. The Commission in particular is highly conscious of this feature of the *acquis*, with its officials stressing the tactical advantages of promoting what amount to highly intrusive demands on national sovereignty through formally legalistic, depoliticized language.[37]

Alongside rule-setting, EU transformative engagement with weakly or undemocratic neighbors involves the application of compliance-inducing mechanisms. While not always fully coordinated or applied with equal stringency, engagement has become more methodologically sophisticated, and has demonstrated an appreciation for rationalist, norm-based, and managerialist theories of compliance.[38]

Chief among the EU's compliance-inducing tools, as exemplified by the Copenhagen criteria for membership, is the use of political conditionality. In this, the pioneering successes of the EU have not gone unnoticed by the architects of recent development programs, notably the Millennium Challenge Corporation (MCC) created by the Bush administration in 2002.

EU conditionality is distinguished by two key features: the ability to deliver powerful tangible rewards and the emphasis on compliance *before* the granting of such rewards. All European regional organizations have practiced some form of conditionality since the end of the cold war, but as Frank Schimmelfennig observes, in Europe tangible conditionality has been limited to the two organizations capable of providing substantial material security and economic and political incentives: the EU and NATO.[39]

The Organization for Security and Cooperation in Europe (OSCE), in contrast, seeks to place peer pressure on member states by monitoring elections, investigating alleged human and minority rights abuses, and distributing praise or condemnation through fact-finding missions, official reports, and regular intergovernmental meetings. Similarly, Europe's oldest regional political organization, the Council of Europe (CoE), seeks to socialize member states into liberal-democratic practices. In 1993 it formalized a set of membership criteria requiring a multiparty system with free and fair elections, protection of minority and religious rights and the freedom of expression, as well as ratification of the European Convention on Human Rights (ECHR). Yet both the OSCE and the CoE have forgone stringent pre-accession conditionality for an approach favoring post-accession socialization. Their pre-accession procedures, therefore, have been slack, leading some commentators to lament the two as instances of wasted leverage on the part of the West.

The type of conditionality practiced by the EU on its frontiers is largely one of "reinforcement by reward"—granting tangible benefits ex post where the targeted government complies with the conditions, and withholding the benefit where it does not.[40] This form of conditionality is distinguished from both punitive conditionality, characterized by sanctions or the use of force, and from from ex ante conditionality, where benefits are provided before compliance or as a simple matter of support. A government that fails to respond to incentives to introduce democratic reforms is mainly left to bear the costs of exclusion until such time as it, or a successive government, decides to comply. Only exceptionally has the EU resorted to punitive measures in its near abroad. Furthermore, over time the EU has stretched conditionality, introducing additional "gatekeeping" junctures in relations with neighboring third countries, as a means of maximizing leverage.

A second constitutive feature of EU policy toward its immediate neighbors has been the individual bilateral nature of links established with targeted countries. Whereas globally EU external relations tend to be structured as region-to-region dialogues—as exemplified by EU relations with the African, Caribbean, and Pacific (ACP) group of countries in the Lomé/Cotonou framework, in EU-ASEAN, and in EU-Mercosur relations—the pre-accession strategy and its progeny in the Balkans and ENP are decidedly differentiated and bilateral in orientation. The negotiation of Association Agreements, Accession Partnerships, Commission opinions (*avis*), annual progress reports, national programs for screening domestic legislation and aligning it with the *acquis*, inclusion in EU agencies and programs, as well as the release of EU controlled political and financial benefits, are all country-specific.

By negotiating separately with each targeted state the EU establishes a bargaining dynamic where power asymmetries in its favor are enhanced. EU bargaining with individual applicants separately reduced the ability of neighbors to form collective negotiation alliances among themselves, and supports the Commission's goal of promoting an atmosphere of competition among candidates and associates for closer ties with the EU.[41]

Third is the use of financial and technical aid to facilitate compliance with conditionality and help build institutional and administrative capacity in targeted states. The worldwide distribution of EU development aid indicates a strong littoral focus, with geographically proximate regions attracting large shares of total aid. Whereas in the period 1986–90 ACP countries received 67 percent of total European Communities (EC) foreign aid, by the time the enlargement process to the CEECs had been set in motion, in 1996–98, the share of aid to these primarily sub-Saharan Africa and Caribbean countries had dropped to 29 percent. During the same period, the CEECs attracted 23 percent of aid, the Commonwealth of Independent States (CIS) member countries with whom the EU signed Partnership and Cooperation Agreements (PCAs) received 11 percent, and the Southern Mediterranean countries received 20 percent (up from only 12 percent in the period 1986–90).[42] Moreover, the granting of EU funds has, over the past two decades, become more tightly linked to performance on the internalization of the *acquis* and the meeting of EU-prescribed benchmarks. Alongside the allocation of financial aid, EU technical assistance, notably TAIEX (Technical Assistance Information Exchange Office) and "twinning"—the long-term secondment of officials from EU member states to corresponding bodies in targeted countries to assist transfer of administrative and technical know-how—represents a related mechanism of compliance induction.

The progressive, conditional inclusion of candidate and other associated countries in EU programs and agencies is a fourth distinguishing feature of the EU's compliance-inducing strategy toward its immediate frontiers. Initiated in 1997 for the CEECs, the practice of selectively opening EU programs and agencies to participation by nonmember states has been extended to Turkey, the Balkan countries, and now the ENP countries. This entails gradually bringing targeted states into existing EU programs covering a wide array of technical and professional agencies and affording access to EU funds (research and development, energy, transportation, the environment, public health) to business networks (small and medium-size enterprises), as well as programs for mass student exchange such as ERASMUS. Transnational political party networks and parliament-to-parliament committees also help anchor candidates and noncandidate neighboring countries in a thick web of EU-run and -managed epistemic communities at mass technical, professional, and political levels.

Finally, systematized Commission-led monitoring and reporting—naming, praising, and shaming—that targets neighboring states for compliance with EU-mandated rules, has been a key feature of induction. The practice of monitoring and reporting, which began with the CEEC candidate states in 1997–98, has also been extended to Turkey, the Balkans, and the ENP countries. The method combines continuous "private" review of progress within the association committees and subcommittees established in bilateral relations between the EU and a targeted state, as well as periodic "public" reporting, designed to place social and civic pressure on the government of targeted countries to comply with mandated reforms. As Marc Maresceau observed before the 2004 enlargement round, systematic reporting at a time of intense accession negotiations put enormous pressure on some of the candidates for full membership: "The publication of progress reports, or even the simple fact that such reports are anticipated, creates an atmosphere of permanent follow-up," contributing considerably to pressure to comply with EU-mandated reforms.[43]

The Boundaries of Democratic Enlargement

By 2007 twelve new member states, largely post-communist, were added to the Union: Bulgaria, the Czech Republic, Cyprus, Estonia, Hungary, Latvia, Lithuania, Malta, Poland, Romania, Slovakia, and Slovenia. The perspective of membership was extended to an additional six "Western Balkan" countries—Albania, Bosnia-Herzegovina, Croatia, Macedonia, Montenegro, and Serbia—and more tenuously, to Turkey. Croatia will become the twenty-eighth member state of the EU in 2012, and Iceland, which formally opened accession negotiations on July 27, 2010, is likely to progress quickly toward accession.

In an effort to replicate the perceived success of enlargement without paying the high price of full membership, the EU has since 2004 extended the conditional prospect of partial integration ("a privileged relationship") to an additional sixteen states and territories, under the aegis of the European Neighborhood Policy: to Algeria, Armenia, Azerbaijan, Belarus, Egypt, Georgia, Israel, Jordan, Lebanon, Libya, Moldova, Morocco, the Palestinian Authority, Syria, Tunisia, and Ukraine. Progress in attaining ENP benefits is conditional on demonstrating a commitment to "common values," defined as democracy and human rights, the rule of law, good governance, market economy principles, and sustainable development. All in all, therefore, thirty-six states and territories, roughly 18 percent of the world's total, have been engaged by the EU over the past two decades in proximate regions—an extraordinary grand experiment in exporting democratic governance.

The impact of European integration on the enlargement of the group of democratic countries in surrounding countries and regions has been intensely debated over the past decade. While the exact causes and mechanisms of influence remain hotly contested, the evidence points to substantial positive influence—particularly by the EU—where three cumulative conditions exist: (1) the "golden carrot" of full EU membership was conditionally and credibly extended; (2) targeted states had already made a fundamental democratic choice and were, at the very least, fledgling electoral democracies at the time of engagement; and (3) targeted states see membership in "the West" generally, and the EU especially, as their main strategic orientation—where Europe (in other words, not Russia or the Islamic world) represents the community of association to which the targeted state wishes to be a part.

Where these conditions existed, the prospect of full EU membership served to both discourage backsliding and "lock in" broad and deep processes of economic, societal, and political liberalization. Yet even in Central and Eastern Europe, EU conditionality worked through the transfer of the *acquis* once reformist states had already made a transition to electoral democracy; instances of "shallow compliance"—where EU rules are formally adopted but not fully implemented—were rife, and the laggards on democratic reform held out for some time against EU pressure.[44]

Elsewhere, visible European influence has been generally weak to insubstantial. President Alexander Lukashenko's Belarus, although it shares borders with three EU member states, is theoretically eligible for full EU membership, and has been subjected to alternating EU sanctions (in 2007–08) and sunshine policies of engagement (since 2008), remains one of the world's most closed and repressive regimes.

In other autocracies targeted by the EU that do not have even a remote prospect of membership—Algeria, Azerbaijan, Egypt, Jordan, Kazakhstan, Kyrgyzstan, Libya, Morocco, Syria, Turkmenistan—normative gaps in regime type are so large that EU "incentives," already diluted, are rightly perceived by ruling elites to be a threat to their rule. Since EU positive conditionality is dependent on voluntary acceptance and implementation by state decisionmakers, its influence is largely determined by the preferences of the targeted government and other "veto players" (bureaucracies, militaries, business elites, and in some cases powerful tribes) whose acquiescence is a necessary condition for changing the status quo. Civil society and public discontent alone have, to date at least, proven incapable of generating sufficient coherence and pressure to drive their governments toward substantial compliance with EU rules.[45]

Prospects for democratic convergence with the EU have grown slightly but are still weak in the neighboring pseudo-democracies of Turkey, Georgia, and Ukraine. Between 2000 and 2005 the credible prospect of EU membership undoubtedly provided Turkey with a powerful external impulse for democratization. Yet the pernicious combination of growing European doubts about whether the 73 million strong, largely Muslim country should ever be permitted to join the EU club (regardless of its progress toward democratic consolidation) and the Islamist-oriented government's worrying overtures to Iran, Syria, and Hamas largely halted the virtuous cycle of reform. Growing hostility towards Israel, once a staunch ally of Ankara's, is also read in Brussels and Washington as evidence that Turkey is turning away from the West. At the same time, a resurgent Russia, the weakening of the "EU magnet" as the result of the euro crisis, and the lack of a concrete accession horizon for Georgia and

Ukraine undermine prospects of democratic consolidation in the two eastern neighbors.

Concluding Remarks

Over the past three decades an extraordinary process of democratic enlargement has taken place globally, with levels of democracy attained on Europe's expanding frontiers distinguished favorably in terms of both endurance and quality. Anchoring the fledgling democracies of Central and Eastern Europe, the Baltics and the Balkans in the EU system have helped lock in democratic reforms, as well as achieve broad and deep liberalizing changes in acceding states' administrative, regulatory, and market structures. The European Union's impact on democracy on Europe's frontiers has been unique. No other entity—the UN, the World Bank, the North American Free Trade Agreement (NAFTA), the Organization of American States (OAS), ASEAN, or the African Union (AU)—has developed anything comparable to the EU's strategy of transformative engagement. In this sense, the Union's experience, with both its successes and its failures, while not a model to be emulated *stricto senso*, contains valuable lessons for worldwide multilateral efforts to promote democracy.

For example, the Arab Human Development Reports published by the United Nations Development Program (UNDP) in 2002, 2003, 2004, 2005, and 2009 constitute an innovative and potentially important mechanism for encouraging socioeconomic development, women's rights, and political freedom in Arab countries. Yet this valuable monitoring and reporting mechanism has not been annualized, and no institutionalized structures have so far been created to maximize its leverage. By drawing on the "rule-setting and engagement" strategy developed by the EU (creating links between progress on benchmarks and the granting of benefits), the Arab Human Development Reports could become a far more potent instrument for positive change in the least democratic group of states in the world.

The wave of democratic expansion has stalled, and Europe's existing toolkit is now outmoded, inadequate for engaging the difficult neighboring regions that today surround the enlarged Union. Enlargement fatigue, the 2008–10 euro crisis, and the general sense that the West is currently in relative decline (and is therefore a less attractive magnet) all raise concern about the enduring ability of the EU to play a transformative role in its neighborhood. Perhaps in the short to medium term the most that can be expected from Europe is the maintenance and continued consolidation of the gains it has achieved over the past two decades, the continued democratic socialization of the new member states, coupled with the gradual inclusion of the remaining Balkan candidates as full members.

More ambitiously, the EU could exercise greater differentiation among its neighboring states, rewarding with greater inclusion democratic states that have already displayed a commitment to liberal values and who possess a Western orientation. The revamping of a credible membership perfective for Turkey would be a decisive though by no means risk-free decision in this direction. Georgia and Ukraine, both of whom fulfill the "Europeanness criteria" for membership, would be provided with a concrete membership horizon, even if long term. Israel, the only liberal democracy in the Middle East, will be offered a privileged relationship akin to that enjoyed by Norway and Switzerland.

Less immediate or visible, but potentially no less profound, are broader lessons from the rise and stall of democratic enlargement—lessons that may renew the transatlantic community's commitment to encourage democratization on Europe's volatile frontiers and reorient their democracy assistance strategies in the future. In contrast to the era of bipolarity, both Americans and Europeans now share the fundamental liberal insight that regime type truly matters—that, as the 2006 National Security Strategy of the United States put it: "In the world today, the fundamental character of regimes matters as much as the distribution of power among them." Indeed, as the European Security Strategy of December 2003 (a strategy unanimously endorsed by EU heads of state) stated: "The quality of international society depends on the quality of the governments that are its foundation. The best protection for our society is a world of well-governed democratic states. Spreading good governance, supporting social and political reform, dealing with corruption and abuse of power, establishing the rule of law and protecting human rights are the best means of strengthening the international order."

At the same time, the U.S. and European preoccupation with democracy promotion over the past decade, in particular, has resulted in an accumulation of knowledge and experience in the field that was simply not there in the past. As Thomas Carothers has observed, international democracy assistance is to some extent maturing, with the leading international actors, America and Europe, moving away from early tendencies to follow a one-size-fits-all strategy toward more nuanced and diversified strategies of engagement.[46] In America, Europe's developmental approach to democracy promotion—one that adopts a broad notion of democracy and focuses on deep, long-term processes of socioeconomic, administrative, and regulatory transformation through institutionalized engagement—is gaining greater recognition and respect.

Notes

1. As of June 2011, Croatia will become the twenty-eighth EU member state sometime in 2012. Iceland, which formally opened accession negotiations with the EU on July 27, 2010, is expected to progress quickly toward accession, becoming the twenty-ninth member state.

2. S. Huntington, *The Third Wave: Democratization in the Late Twentieth Century* (University of Oklahoma Press, 1991), p. 26. See also L. Diamond, "The State of Democratization at the Beginning of the 21st Century," *Whitehead Journal of Diplomacy and International Relations* 6 (2005): 13–18.

3. Ibid.

4. Michael McFaul, "The Fourth Wave of Democracy and Dictatorship: Noncooperative Transitions in the Post-Communist World," *World Politics* 54, no. 2 (2002): 212–44.

5. See Freedom House, *Freedom in the World 2010: Global Data* (www.freedomhouse.org/uploads/fiw10/FIW_2010_Tables_and_Graphs.pdf [July 2010]).

6. On the consequences for the international system and the benefits of democracy, see B. Russett and J. Oneal, *Triangulating Peace: Democracy, Interdependence, and International Organizations* (New York: Norton, 2001); M. Halperin, J. Siegle, and M. Weinstein, *The Democracy Advantage: How Democracies Promote Prosperity and Peace* (London: Routledge, 2005).

7. Huntington, *The Third Wave*, p. 17.

8. Ibid., p. 16.

9. On hybrid regimes, see L. Diamond, "Elections without Democracy: Thinking about Hybrid Regimes," *Journal of Democracy* 13, no. 2 (2002).

10. See, for example, L. Diamond, "Is Pakistan the (Reverse) Wave of the Future?" *Journal of Democracy* 11, no. 3 (2000): 91–106.

11. Arch Paddington, "The 2006 Freedom House Survey of Freedom: The Pushback against Democracy," *Journal of Democracy* 18, no. 2 (2007): 119.

12. For a detailed discussion of the democratic recession, see L. Diamond, *The Spirit of Democracy* (New York: Times Books, 2008), pp. 56–87.

13. Arch Paddington, "The Freedom House Survey for 2009: The Erosion Accelerates," *Journal of Democracy* 21, no. 2 (2010): 136–50.

14. Ibid., pp. 142–43.

15. Ibid., p. 146.

16. Ibid., p. 141.

17. See D. Brinkley, "Democratic Enlargement: The Clinton Doctrine," *Foreign Policy* 106 (1997): 110–27.

18. Remarks of Anthony Lake, assistant to the president for national security affairs, "From Containment to Enlargement," Johns Hopkins University School of Advanced International Studies, Washington, D.C., September 21, 1993, *U.S. Department of State Dispatch* 4, no. 39 (September 1993): 658–64.

19. Ibid.

20. Brinkley, "Democratic Enlargement," p. 111.

21. See J. Borawski, "Partnership for Peace and Beyond," *International Affairs* 71, no. 2 (1995): 233–46.

22. Declaration of the heads of state and government participating in the meeting of the North Atlantic Council ("The Brussels Summit Declaration"), January 11, 1994, clause 12 (www.nato.int/docu/basictxt/b940111a.htm).

23. The goal of a "Europe whole and free" was declared by President George H. W. Bush in May 1989. See "A Europe Whole and Free," remarks to the citizens of Mainz, Federal Republic of Germany, May 31, 1989 (http://usa.usembassy.de/etexts/ga6-890531.htm).

24. Cited in Brinkley, "Democratic Enlargement," pp. 122–23n17.

25. The White House, *National Security Strategy of Engagement and Enlargement* (February 1995) (www.au.af.mil/au/awc/awcgate/nss/nss-95.pdf [July 2010]).

26. See Tony Smith, *America's Mission: The United States and the Worldwide Struggle for Democracy in the Twentieth Century* (Princeton University Press, 1994); Michael Cox, G. John Ikenberry, and Takashi Inoguchi, *American Democracy Promotion: Impulses, Strategies, and Impacts* (Oxford University Press, 2000).

27. Amichai Magen and Michael McFaul, "Introduction: American and European Strategies to Promote Democracy—Shared Values, Common Challenges, Divergent Tools," in *Promoting Democracy and the Rule of Law: American and European Strategies*, edited by Amichai Magen, Thomas Risse, and Michael McFaul (New York: Palgrave Macmillan, 2009), pp. 1–33. This is essentially true for President Barack Obama as well, although Obama has been criticized for backtracking on important initiatives developed under George W. Bush, especially regarding the Arab Middle East and Iran. See Shadi Hamid, "Can Obama Erase 'Bush Nostalgia' in the Middle East?" *Christian Science Monitor*, April 12, 2010; Barbara Slavin, "Obama's Middle East Democracy Problem," *Foreign Policy*, March 5, 2010.

28. See Smith, *America's Mission*, n26.

29. Presidency Conclusions of the European Council in Copenhagen, June 21–22, 1993.

30. Andrea Ott and Kirstyn Inglis, eds., *Handbook on European Enlargement: A Commentary on the Enlargement Process* (New York: Springer, 2002), p. 93.

31. See Jeffrey Henderson, "Introduction," in *Regional Integration and Democracy*, edited by Jeffrey Anderson (Lanham, Md.: Rowman and Littlefield, 1999), pp. 1–20.

32. Magen and McFaul, "Introduction," n27.

33. For a detailed discussion, see Amichai Magen, "The Shadow of Enlargement: Can the European Neighbourhood Policy Achieve Compliance?" *Columbia Journal of European Law* 12, no. 2 (2006): 383–427.

34. See Frank Schimmelfennig and Wolfgang Wagner, "External Governance in the European Union," *Journal of European Public Policy* 11, no. 4 (2004): 657–60; Sandra Lavenex and Frank Schimmelfennig, "EU Rules beyond EU Borders: Theorizing External Governance in European Politics," *Journal of European Public Policy* 16, no. 6

(2009): 791–812; Heather Grabbe, *The EU's Transformative Power—Europeanization through Conditionality in Central and Eastern Europe* (New York: Palgrave Macmillan, 2006); Richard Youngs, "Engagement: Sharpening European Influence," in *Global Europe: New Terms of Engagement*, edited by Richard Youngs (London: Foreign Policy Centre and British Council, 2005), pp. 1–14.

35. See Amichai Magen, "Transformative Engagement through Law: The Aquis Communautaire as an Instrument of EU External Influence," *European Journal of Law Reform* 9, no. 3 (2007): 361–92.

36. Jiri Pehe, "Europe Moves Eastwards: Consolidating Free Government in the New EU," *Journal of Democracy* 15, no. 1 (2004): 36–47, at p. 38.

37. Interview with senior Commission officials, Brussels, June 2005.

38. See Magen, "The Shadow of Enlargement," n34.

39. Frank Schimmelfennig, "Strategic Calculation and International Socialization," *International Organization* 59 (Fall 2005): 827–60, at p. 833.

40. Frank Schimmelfennig, Stefan Engert, and Heiko Knobel, "Costs, Commitment and Compliance: The Impact of EU Democratic Conditionality on Latvia, Slovakia and Turkey," *Journal of Common Market Studies* 41, no. 3 (2003): 495–518, at p. 496.

41. Interview with senior Commission officials, Brussels, June 2005.

42. Figures cited in Franck Petiteville, "Exporting Values? EU External Cooperation as a 'Soft Diplomacy,'" in *Understanding the European Union's External Relations*, edited by Michele Knodt and Sebastian Princen (London: Routledge, 2003), pp. 127–41, at p. 129.

43. Marc Maresceau, *The EU Pre-Accession Strategy: A Political and Legal Analysis*, in *The EU's Enlargement and Mediterranean Strategies: A Comparative Analysis*, edited by Marc Maresceau and Erwan Lannon (London: Palgrave Macmillan, 2001), pp. 3–28, at p. 22.

44. Richard Youngs, "Democracy Promotion as External Governance?" *Journal of European Public Policy* 16, no. 6 (2009): 895–915, at p. 896.

45. Amichai Magen, "The Shadow of Enlargement," pp. 417–18.

46. Thomas Carothers, "Democracy Assistance: Political vs. Developmental?" *Journal of Democracy* 20, no. 1 (2009): 5–19.

JOAQUÍN ROY

19 European–Latin American Relations in the Twenty-First Century

The future of relations between the European Union and Latin America—after an expected important enlargement in the decade 2010–20—will depend on the confluence of at least four factors necessary to accomplish a considerable change (positive or negative) from the current inertia. Two of these factors depend on the role of Latin American governments and the regional integration system they are developing. The other two factors depend on events in Europe and its vicinity.

The Setting: Between a Casino and a Customs Union

While the Latin American factors are based on the will and success of Latin American entities to develop an institutional framework for regional integration, the European factors depend on the nature of the next enlargements, and the attitude of the main EU actors in shaping the EU's relationship with Latin America. What will be the shape of Latin American integration in the next decade? How important will Latin America be for a refurbished Europe? These are the two crucial questions under consideration here.[1]

In the Argentine city of San Juan, capital of the northern province of the same name, four Latin American countries took a decisive step toward the consolidation of a customs union: the members of Mercosur (Brazil, Argentina,

I am grateful to Federiga Bindi for the kind invitation to participate in the seminar "Frontiers of Europe," held in Rome in July 2010. Thanks also are due to José Antonio Sanahuja for providing extensive bibliographical data. Astrid Boening provided final editing and reading.

Uruguay, and Paraguay, plus Venezuela, which is still awaiting membership ratification) committed to abolish the double external tariff.[2] This tariff, which violates the principles of a customs union, has also been one of the most formidable obstacles for an Association Agreement with the European Union toward the establishment of a free trade area between the two regions. If implemented, the customs union would meet the conditions of that pact, made at the EU–Latin America (LA)–Caribbean summit held in Madrid in May 2010, to proceed toward an Association Agreement.

The importance of Mercosur is multidimensional, including the fact that this bloc of countries, founded in 1991, represents the largest global producer of food. In addition to the four permanent members, it has four associate members (Chile, Colombia, Peru, and Ecuador); Venezuela and Bolivia have agreed to become members as well. Such an expanded Mercosur would allow the EU to deal with a unified South American entity and fulfill one of the historical aims of Brussels, to witness the formation of an integrated system in the image of the European model—that is, with a supranational profile. This type of system, beyond making basic economic cooperation possible, represents a priority in all the Western hemisphere schemes, from the North American Free Trade Agreement (NAFTA) to the current working stage of intra–Latin American subblocs. The implementation of the four freedoms of a common market (the free movement of goods, capital, services, and people) has never included the mobility of labor in Latin America, with institutions there nonexistent or powerless.

This requirement was matched at the same time by a decision with its own significance on the surface: in the Uruguayan capital of Montevideo, on one of its most beautiful corners facing the ocean, a building celebrated its centenary last year, and at the same time changed its functions and tenants. Visitors to this city are often drawn to this most impressive example of art-deco architecture, an architectural style of which Montevideo is a centenary jewel. The former Hotel Parque (completed in 1909) stands in front of a calm beach. It now houses the headquarters of Mercosur, where its small secretariat and offices of the member state governments are located, with some extra offices rented to other international organizations. Meetings and briefings are held in the former dining rooms and ballroom of the hotel. At the entrance, facing the four flags of the organization plus Venezuela's, one still can see on the marble floor the inscription "Hotel Parque."[3]

What was most odd was the sight of a side building, flashing the word "Casino" in fluorescent lights, and its shared parking lot with Mercosur. This scene has been the talk of the town. Mercosur can be thought of as a roulette table, according to local humor. A photo focusing on the two buildings was a must for tourists. Not anymore. After almost two decades of negotiations, the casino is being relocated to a much smaller building belonging to a Spanish society, the Casa de Andalucía, located in the vicinity within the Rodó park.[4] As good news for the backers of a stronger Mercosur, the casino building will now house the offices and meeting rooms of the Parliament of Mercosur. This composite of representatives of the national parliaments of the member states, which for years resembled a parliamentary assembly, will be directly elected beginning in 2011.[5]

Lobbyists for a "deepening" of Mercosur and a higher supranational profile with strong institutions are celebrating. Staff members of the European Commission in Brussels share the joy. There is no doubt that the remodeling of the building and future maintenance, along with funding of some of its activities, will be supported by the EU's budget for relations with Latin America. However, this is not new, since the EU has been subsidizing the foundation and development of several Latin American institutions already, even paying for their infrastructure.

What remains to be seen is if the new use of the casino building will lead to substantial advancement in the progress of Mercosur. The result is of utmost importance for the EU, because this southern bloc organization has been since its inception the favorite daughter of European institutions. Reasons for this enthusiasm include its sheer size—its huge economic reality as well as its potential—and its historical and social proximity to Europe. European immigration is an integral part of the national soul of the region, especially for its two main partners (Brazil and Argentina), but also for Uruguay itself.

However, the long road of the EU's policy toward Latin America is marked by ups and downs, solid data on facts, contradictions, and hope, mixed with uncertainty about the future. In a way, the gambling spirit of Mercosur's former neighbor is still present in the form of facts and trends beyond the reach of the leadership and staff of the EU. On the one hand, this complex relationship has made notable advances developing integration schemes in Latin America. And the backing of the EU for the region is not in question.[6]

On the other hand, Latin America has changed. It is not a solid bloc; there are differences in the internal political and economic fabric of the countries, and in their approaches to foreign policy. Other foreign actors, such as China, are now acting aggressively in the region. Attitudes toward regional integration are as many as the number of countries. Neo-populist regimes coexist with full democracies. Temptations to return to authoritarian solutions are evident. Europe is seen in an ambivalent way.

Europe has also changed. It is not the same as at the end of the cold war, or when the Maastricht Treaty was signed in 1992. The adoption of the euro and internal mobility have increased the pace of integration. But the failure of the constitutional project has raised doubts about the nature of the process. The spectacular enlargement of 2004 has modified the EU forever. All of these things, in addition to the internal shifts in Latin America, have forced observers to reanalyze the relationship between the two blocs, based on the tenets of the vanishing dictatorships of the 1960s and 1970s and part of the 1980s, and the status of regional integration as a panacea that it has enjoyed since then. Nonetheless, what still counts are the facts, mechanisms, and resources that dominate this relationship today.

How the EU Deals with Latin America

The official story of today's relationship between the European Union (EU) and Latin America boasts that for the past decade the two regions have regulated their diverse links through a formula known as "strategic partnership."[7] Crafted in the context of the first biregional summit in Rio de Janeiro in 1999, the concept, spirit, and details of this agreement have influenced all other agreements and conduct between the two blocs.[8] Major decisions are made in those biannual summits, whose meetings alternate between Latin America and Europe and are attended by all member states' representatives on both sides of the Atlantic at the highest level.[9] The 2010 summit took place in Madrid,[10] and previous gatherings took place in Rio de Janeiro (1999), Madrid (2002),[11] Guadalajara (2004),[12] Vienna (2006),[13] and Lima (2008).[14]

In addition to this decision-making framework, during the years when the EU-LA-Caribbean summit does not take place there is a meeting between the EU and the Rio Group, composed of ministerial representatives of Latin American and Caribbean countries. The most recent EU–Rio Group Ministerial Meeting took place in Prague in 2009.[15]

Like the United States and Europe, the two regions are "natural allies," bonded by solid cultural, historical, and economic ties. Their political differences are more prominent, given their different interpretations of democracy and political approaches, although the regions maintain an intensive "political dialogue" at all levels. They also conduct many nuanced exchanges regionally and subregionally. Brussels respects Latin America's subregions as defined by Latin Americans themselves. Thus the EU (as a whole) deals with the entities known as Central America, the Andean Community, and Mercosur. It has special bilateral agreements with Mexico and Chile and has also entered into agreements with individual members of the existing blocs (Peru, Colombia, and Brazil, with others on the horizon).

On a juridical level, the EU revealed its policy preferences toward the greater region referred to as Latin America in a 2009 document, "EU-Latin America: Global Players in Partnership."[16] This statement updates a previous communication, "Stronger Partnership between the European Union and Latin America" (2005).[17] In addition to traditional themes and issues, the EU and Latin America are engaged in specific and crucial areas in the new century, including macroeconomic and financial matters; the environment, climate change, and energy; science, research, and technology; migration; and employment and social affairs.

The perspective of the EU is clearly expressed in more concrete terms in a regional strategy paper,[18] in which the Commission defines EU policy and financial details toward Latin America, most specifically in the sensitive areas of economic and social development cooperation programs: Brussels has budgeted in excess of €3 billion in assistance to Latin America for the current seven-year budget period,[19] on top of development assistance programs provided by each EU member state and NGOs. Spain is Europe's major donor to the region.[20] In addition, the European Investment Bank (EIB) is ready to use €2.8 billion.[21]

Beyond those programs, whereas the European Commission has a commanding role as a major agent of the interests of the European Union, relations between the European Parliament and its counterparts in Latin America have also increased over the past decade. Joint efforts are channeled through EUROLAT, a biregional body composed of representatives of the European Parliament and the Parlatino (the conglomerate of the representatives of the Latin American parliamentary assemblies) whose meetings alternate between Europe and Latin America. Their decisions have a great impact on reshaping programs crafted by the Commission and ultimately approved by the Council (with the co-decision-making powers of the EU Parliament representing a dimension to reckon with in the future).[22]

Global Economic Relations

International financial flows indicate that European Union member states represent the leading investors in Latin America. In turn, Europe is for the Latin American countries, as a whole region, the second most important trade partner. Moreover, the EU is the primary trading partner with the important subregion of Mercosur. Chile as an individual country does not belong to any of the Latin American subgroups and has bilateral free trade agreements with other countries.

Figure 19-1. *Trade between the EU-27 and Latin America*

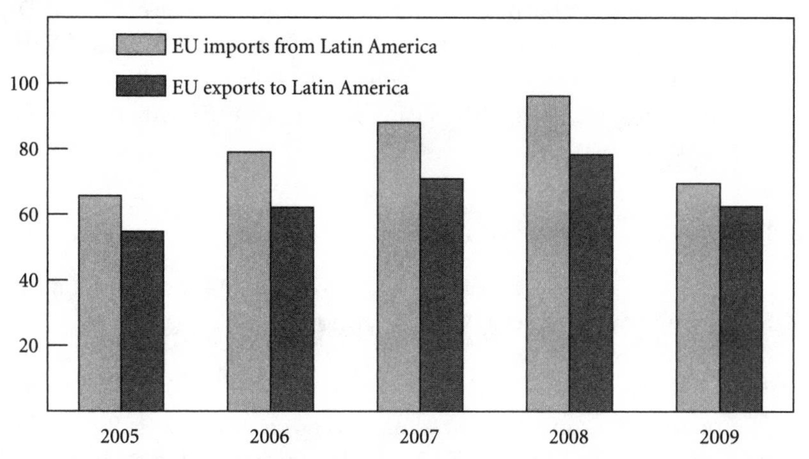

Source: European Commission.

The economic and commercial links between the two regions increased dramatically in the first decade of the twenty-first century. Trade doubled between 1999 and 2008. EU imports from Latin America increased from €42.5 to €97 billion; European exports to Latin America rose from €52.2 to €79 billion. In 2009 the EU's trade with Latin America reached €71 billion for imports and €63.4 billion for exports (which represent 6 percent of total EU trade, a figure that has remained steady over the years). Trade in services was estimated at €19 billion for imports and €28 billion for exports, representing 4.35 percent and 5.44 percent of world flows respectively.

Although the volume of trade with Latin America has more than doubled since the turn of the century, the balance is negative for the EU in the area of goods but positive in services. EU imports from Latin America are mainly raw materials (70 percent). European exports are most important in machinery and transport equipment (85 percent).[23] Although trade figures have been negatively impacted and trade volume decreased in 2009 in line with general trade patterns, the overall positive trend has not been seriously disrupted by the financial crisis that began in 2008.[24]

Figure 19-1 shows that both imports from and exports to Latin America increased from 2005 to 2008. It is worth noting that in 2009, however, both suffered a decrease. This can be explained by the impact of the economic crisis, which has not been as severe in Latin America as in Europe. In any case, the fact remains that the EU-27 bloc imports more from Latin America than it exports to Latin America.

The EU has become the primary source of foreign direct investment (FDI) in Latin America. FDI to Latin America was €46 billion in 2000. Total European investment in Latin America grew from €189.4 billion in 2000 to €227.8 in 2007. In 2009 EU direct investment in Latin America rose to €275.4 billion.

Relations with the Subregions of Latin America

The EU has well-established relations with several Latin American countries. Here I explore how those relations affect regions.

Central America

The European Union and the Central American countries (Costa Rica, El Salvador, Guatemala, Honduras, Nicaragua, and Panama) have maintained a solid relationship for at least a quarter of a century, composed of political dialogue, important development cooperation, and a favorable trade regime for both regions.[25] Their political relationship stems from the San José Dialogue of 1984, which was set up to support democracy in the region after the internal armed conflicts affecting most of the Central American countries during this period. Europe, with its experience in resolving centuries-old animosities, saw a golden opportunity to contribute to the pacification of the area—paradoxically in the backyard of the United States in a dangerous era when the threat of a Marxist takeover of certain countries (Nicaragua, El Salvador) was more than a hypothesis. At first, the U.S. government was reluctant to see the European involvement, but by the early 1990s the record was extremely positive. In June 2007 the EU and Central America began negotiating an Association Agreement, using as a base the previous EU–Central America Political Dialogue and Cooperation Agreement of 2003.

Since then, several stages of negotiation have taken place, although progress has been slow, due to disagreements over regional integration.[26] Beyond this, separate negotiations have taken place pertaining to the full participation of Panama in the process of integration, known as SIECA (in English, the Central American Secretary for Economic Integration). Finally, as a result of the Madrid summit of 2010, Central America and the EU have found a way to complete their Association Agreement.

In terms of financing for development cooperation, the regional strategy paper for the period 2007–13 shows the EU as the major donor to the area.

Figures from 2008 show that the EU was the second largest trading partner with Central America after the United States.[27]

The Andean Community

The Andean Community was founded in 1969 through the Andean Pact.[28] Today it has four members (Bolivia, Colombia, Ecuador, and Peru), each with a different attitude toward the collective entity. The EU's approach of political dialogue was initiated in 1996 with the Declaration of Rome and was consolidated in 2003 with a Political Dialogue and Cooperation Agreement, which regulates the current relationship. As in the case of the other subblocs, the EU and the Andean Community also maintain institutional links within the framework of the forums between the EU and the Rio Group.

Negotiations for a complete Association Agreement failed in 2008, but were followed by a new approach, including an option to deal with individual countries—a reverse of past policy, in part due to the difficulties imposed by Bolivia, and in part to comply with the requirements of the World Trade Organization. Negotiations subsequently began with Peru, Colombia, and Ecuador in February 2009, and were successful in March 2010 for Peru and Colombia, with Ecuador opting for a delay. This tour de force angered Bolivia, which complained about Venezuela's decision to leave the Andean Community and join Mercosur. The forming of the Bolivarian Alliance of the Peoples of the Americas (ALBA, in Spanish) under the aegis of Venezuela was a major obstacle to progress by the Andean group, which seemed at moments on the verge of dissolution. Meanwhile, Chile, formerly a member (and today only an associate), decided to wait for better times. The fact that Peru and Colombia have also engaged in free trade arrangements with the United States only added more fuel to the fire.

Mercosur

As mentioned above, Mercosur has been the favorite subregional bloc in Latin America for the EU.[29] Formed in 1991 by the Treaty of Asunción, it is today officially composed of four countries (Argentina, Brazil, Paraguay, and Uruguay). Venezuela has agreed to join the group, but full membership is still pending because a new member must be approved unanimously. Paraguay, however, has not yet endorsed the presidency of Hugo Chávez and Venezuela's accession, questioning its democratic credentials. In spite of the difficulties of the past in fulfilling its aim of building a common market, the EU has supported Mercosur via several initiatives, among them an Interinstitutional Agreement to deliver technical and institutional support.

As early as 1995 the EU and Mercosur signed an Interregional Framework Cooperation Agreement, which took effect in 1999. In 2001 both blocs opened negotiations for a much anticipated Association Agreement based on the usual three pillars for this relationship between the EU and Latin American groups: political dialogue, cooperation, and a free trade area. However, negotiations were suspended in 2004 because fundamental differences existed in the sensitive realm of trade. The other issues continued to advance, and at the EU-LA summit in Lima in 2008 new areas were added to the relationship: science and technology, infrastructure, and the trendy issue of renewable energy. At the Madrid summit in May 2010, considerable progress in the negotiations toward an Association Agreement was announced, which would lead to a free trade area. The Mercosur decision of August of 2010 to complete the requirements for a customs union reopened the path toward that end.[30]

In 2009 EU-Mercosur trade equaled all of the remaining trade between the EU and the rest of Latin America. A year earlier, the EU was Mercosur's primary trading partner, with 20.7 percent of total trade of the southern bloc. In 2008 the EU was the already the largest investor in Mercosur. In 2009 globally the subregion ranked eighth among EU trading partners, with 2.7 percent of total EU trade.

Development assistance from the EU to Mercosur is provided via its 2007–13 regional program, adopted in 2007 within the context of the regional strategy for Mercosur. This program sets aside €50 million for projects in the main areas of cooperation: institutional strengthening, preparing for implementation of the Association Agreement, and participating of civil society. The record shows that the EU is the major donor of assistance to Mercosur.

Special Relationships

Respectful of individual links enjoyed by some Latin American countries with the EU, the latter has signed special agreements with certain states that do not belong to any of the Latin American subgroups, or are partners of other regional networks beyond the Latin American territory. This is the case for Mexico and Chile, which enjoy special free trade agreements with the EU. Since their inception, EU trade with these two countries has increased by more than 100 percent.

The South American republic of Chile was a member of the Andean Community in the past, but abandoned this membership during the years of military dictatorship under General Augusto Pinochet. With the return to democracy, Chile proceeded to develop one of the world's most open economies, including free trade agreements with many countries and regions, including the United States and the EU. In December 1990 the EU signed a first Framework Cooperation Agreement to restore political relations as a bloc with Chile. This agreement was replaced in June 1996 by another Framework Cooperation Agreement, with the primary objective to establish a political and economic association. The EU and Chile negotiated and signed an Association Agreement in 2002, effective as of 2005, covering fundamental areas in the traditional trio formed by political, commercial, and development assistance issues.[31] In addition, the EU and Chile signed an Agreement on Scientific and Technological Cooperation in 2002. In 2005 the two parties adopted a horizontal agreement on air transport. All of these agreements have had a positive impact on trade and development cooperation.[32]

Mexico for its part has enjoyed membership in the North American Free Trade Agreement (NAFTA) for two decades, with the United States and Canada. In 1997 it signed a partnership agreement with the EU, the Economic Partnership, Political Coordination, and Cooperation Agreement.[33] This agreement is an expression of the commitment that governs all sectors of the relationship between the two parties, including sensitive topics such as democracy and human rights, which Mexico was reluctant to address previously. On a purely commercial level, the agreement means that the establishment of a free trade area also fostered an increase in investment. Furthermore, social cohesion, a crucial area in any Latin American country, represents an integral part of these processes.[34]

Although considered to be outside the strictly Latin American context, reference should be made to the special relations between the EU and the Caribbean. Mostly dotted by former British colonies, in addition to independent and semi-colonial islands of Dutch and French origin, the majority of the autonomous states are members of the Caribbean Community (Caricom). Inspired partially by the institutional example of the EU, Caricom's path toward true integration has been slow. Cariforum is the framework established with the support of the EU as way of coordinating the Caribbean portion of benefits for the Africa, Caribbean, and Pacific (ACP) group of seventy-six nations, which receive benefits originally under the Lomé Convention, and now under the Cotonou Agreement.[35]

In this setting, the Dominican Republic and Haiti have been added. The first was endorsed by Spain, the second by France. Cuba, which is the only Latin American country with no established cooperation or trade agreement, became a member of the ACP, pending its application to sign the Cotonou Agreement—which never took place owing to the confrontations between Brussels and Havana.[36] The relationship with Cuba has been one area of disagreement between some of the earlier EU member states and the new member states since the 2004 enlargement. While Spain, due to its historical special relationship with Cuba, has a record of maintaining solid links with its former colony irrespective of who is in power, some new members of the EU that were formerly under communist domination have taken a hard-line attitude, making a full normalization of relations difficult.

Clouds, Uncertainties, and Hope

One of the EU's main objectives in its involvement in Latin America has been to spread European values, as they were understood after the Second World War. The European model of integration as a base for economic and social progress and political reconciliation is an integral part of the EU ideals that have been shared with Latin American countries. But on balance EU institutions have expressed some frustration about the accomplishments of regional integration.

One wonders why the Latin American systems of integration lag so much behind the point of reference (or the outright model) of the European Union. Why has that region of the world that is closest to Europe in history and cultural origin not succeeded in adopting the European path in spite of the considerable financial efforts dedicated by Brussels to Latin America? Why is there a recurring contrast between official declarations over the past quarter-century vowing to pursue the goal of integration modeled on that of the EU and an empirical reality riddled with shortcomings and failure? What do Latin American leaders mean when they declare that the region needs "its own model of integration," sidelining the influence of the EU precedent? What is this elusive Latin American alternative?

The Nation and the State

The main obstacle to the development of an ambitious regional integration entity mirroring the model of the EU is the unfinished task of consolidating a polity that meets the needs of national identity. National cohesion still takes precedence over continental integration. For this reason a limited number of intellectuals and technocrats have found it very difficult to convince Latin American elites and society of the benefits proposed by what appears to be a "loss" of national "personality."

In these circumstances, the inability of certain governments to cope with the pressures of instability, corruption, poverty, inequality, and endemic criminality presents endogenous threats to achieving regional integration in Latin America. The prospect of the appearance of "failed states" is daunting. The usual conclusion is that the "state" has failed the citizens in providing basic services and protection. The monopoly of economic control and force has been translated in Latin America as a guarantee that income disparities and social exclusion will continue, as well as outright racial, gender, and economic discrimination. Personal security has been translated into repression. Human rights are reduced to the maintenance of law and order (although crime is endemic). Judicial and legislative institutions are found to be weak and impotent. In the few places where police and the armed forces are present, they serve to maintain the traditional structures where the possibilities for change are few. It is then said that what has failed is the "state."

In reality, what has failed is the "nation." The nation-state as a European invention, mostly crafted by wars, is an elusive dream in Latin America. The concept of nationality based on will, option, and a desire for a better future (as in the French and U.S. traditions) is an attractive project on paper, but it has never been accomplished. Paradoxically, an unfinished nation could be the ideal base for an effective regional entity, in which displaced and marginalized people could identify themselves.

Emigration has recently built an identity (*latinoamericano*) that does not exist in the normal operation of each of these countries. The use of this term is further reinforced when the phenomenon of immigration is set in the domestic context of the United States. "Hispanic" and "Latino" are words that originated from the experience of a new life in the United States. Ironically, the force of migration could manage to produce what treaties and declarations have failed to accomplish. However, for that project to be successful, the current and future regional integration schemes would have to achieve the four freedoms of a common market, as in the EU: free trade and a customs union, with full freedom of movement of capital and services. But the key for full integration is the free mobility of labor, something that the existing integration and economic cooperation networks do not seem to be able to fully contemplate.

Latin America has lacked a Jean Monnet, someone who could sell a brilliant idea to be transformed into a "bold step," as in the initial phase of the EU. Well-intentioned, some of the most influential *pensadores* seldom managed to infiltrate the centers of power, which are still obsessed with maintaining domestic control and imitating the model of the combination of *prócer*—"founder" and "father of the land"— sometimes fused with the concept of the nation, with semi-religious connotations, as in the notorious cases of Bolívar and, most specifically, Cuba's José Martí. Some recent attempts to give rise to such a "technical" person have been detected in the work of technocrats behind the scene, though their impact has been limited.[37]

As a result, the overwhelming centrality of the presidential figure in the Latin American nation-states is a formidable obstacle to moving toward shared sovereignty. The recent appearance of neopopulist regimes (a trademark of the history of Latin America) is not helping to tame this endemic regional characteristic. Moreover, the scarcity of economic capital resources and the deficient use of natural resources make the pooling of products a cumbersome task, subject to a lack of confidence and competition to protect scarce resources. As a result of national competition, the building of joint institutions, which are viewed as new competing bureaucracies and therefore distrusted, is a never-ending process. Finally, the pressure posed by invitations to sign flat and direct individual trade agreements with the United States makes the advantages of a supranational Latin American integration even more uncertain. However, there are other positive factors that make the pursuit of a Latin American path of integration viable, with a moderate prognosis for the future.

A Tortuous Path toward Integration

The endemic confrontations between France and Germany and among most of the European empires and modern countries that led to the formation of the "EU as remedy" cannot be likened to wars involving Latin American countries. Brazil, the largest nation-state, owes its independence not to an anti-colonial struggle, but to the abandonment of the Portuguese monarch, who ironically took refuge there after the Napoleonic invasion of the Iberian Peninsula.[38] The independence struggles in most of the rest of the Latin American area were initially resistance against the Napoleonic invasion of Spain.

In theory, then, the comparatively peaceful background of Latin America should result in a deeper integration, stronger than in Europe. Instead, war cannot not be used as a springboard for the foundation of integration schemes as it was in Europe. Latin America lacks that "foundational justification." And other factors—geography, political resentment, concrete border disputes—have presented difficulties for the strengthening of regional projects.

Recently Latin American sectors skeptical of the deepening economic cooperation arrangements welcomed the endorsement of what they perceive as an ambivalent European example. This trend stresses the negative approach to what is erroneously interpreted as "loss of sovereignty" or "cession of national prerogatives." An expression in English, the de facto official EU language (with the futile resistance of France), supplies a perfect illustration of its innate nature and its practical functioning: the reference to sovereignty as "pooled" means that it is shared, not ceded or lost as is often claimed in Latin American discourse when considering the benefits and disadvantages of regional integration. Since "pool" as a verb does not exist in Spanish, the concept of "shared sovereignty" is incorrectly understood. Like equivalent expressions that try to fill a linguistic vacuum, this misunderstanding reveals more a conceptual shortcoming than a linguistic deficiency. The result is that the European model fails to project an effective message throughout the Americas.

What is missing in Latin America is "political commitment" to integration. Without it, there can be no regional integration. In all the effective stages of the EU, the commitment of the political leadership has been notable, mirroring the mandate of Jean Monnet that "nothing is possible without the work of men." For the project to survive, it also requires the existence of effective institutions, ruled by a juridical structure that is accepted by all. Monnet added that "nothing is lasting without institutions," which he considered to be the pillars of civilization. Political commitment backed by institutions makes the implementation of common policies and actions possible. This element is missing in Latin America.

An additional factor, close to the "presidential syndrome," that makes the advancement of systems for Latin American integration difficult is the lack of juridical respect for norms and codes. This is a paradoxical phenomenon in a subcontinent obsessed with codification of laws in the tradition of Roman and Napoleonic law bestowed by Spain. But the enshrining of presidential decisions sidelines accepted law, as well as the basic principles of international norms. From the speed used to announce new alliances and frameworks to the rush to terminate commitments subject to international treaties—such as the withdrawal of Venezuela from the Andean Community—the current panorama is truly disappointing, and even alarming.

The Community of South American Nations, later rebaptized the South American Union (Unasur), has not advanced to the level of expectations and grandiose declarations.[39] Nonetheless, optimistic analyses still believe the process can produce an entity that follows in the path of the EU.[40] The key to this assessment is the leading role played by Brazil.

Those in charge of the Latin American process of integration have been more inclined to make spectacular announcements about the founding of new entities. One recent addition (besides the birth of Unasur) is the Bolivarian Alternative of the Americas (ALBA), founded by Venezuela to compete with what remains of the U.S.-dominated Free Trade Area of the Americas (FTAA). At the same time, there is formidable resistance to the consolidation of independent institutions. Amidst claims that these entities without budgets and authority were actually the culprits in past failures, the process was left in the hands of a Latin American leadership consumed by a fever for "summitry." The result has frequently been a string of media declarations and publicity-grabbing headlines.

Results depend on the political will of the diverse leadership of the Andean countries. Some countries, questioning the validity of the deepening of indigenous blocs, seem more inclined to opt for a free trade pact with Washington. Faced with the choice of only one wish offered by a genie, these countries would likely choose the perceived stability of a deal with Washington over the uncertainty of a regional pact.

The conditional backing of Europe may reach a similar fate. Threats of Bolivia to leave the Andean group, following the path of Venezuela, have been alarming. The radicalization and nationalization process exercised by Chávez has raised more questions about the reinvigoration of Mercosur than it has provided answers. Across the pond, facing the disintegration of the Andean Community and the instability of Mercosur, Brussels seems to have exhausted its energies for pushing true integration. It is not surprising then that the EU has crafted a strategic partnership with Brazil, and offered separate deals to Peru and Colombia. In turn, European governments have been reevaluating their global relationship with a Latin America that in reality does not exist as a bloc, making bilateral approaches a must.[41] It is safe to say that the subtle and then clear shift to a bilateral approach has not been caused directly by a change of philosophy in Brussels, but by the force of the arguments posed by the internal crisis of the Andean Community. It remains to be seen if this new approach will be applied to Mercosur. For the moment, the EU continues with its bloc-to-bloc strategy, although the special move toward Brazil is noteworthy.

Other obstacles make the EU-LA front difficult. On the one hand, the EU resists reforming its Common Agricultural Policy (CAP). That move would open its market to Latin American products, which are still subject to quotas and quality regulations. Europe has now also irritated Latin American governments and societies by restricting immigration in response to economic pressures and the rise of unemployment in Europe. The argument that Europe needs to replenish its aging population with a new work force provided by immigration has been neutralized by the financial crisis, which has affected some sectors (construction, agriculture, the service sector) that have traditionally employed immigrants. Facing huge payments of unemployment subsidies, some countries have even opted to sponsor the repatriation of idle immigrants.

On the other hand, most Latin American countries refuse to liberalize their economies (the countries of Mercosur and Central America, for example) to the level of European expectations. They also have not responded to the request of the EU for the formation of effective customs unions. However, the most daunting obstacle for progress and regional integration is the endemic level of poverty and inequality, which is the worst in the world. Social exclusion and discrimination fuel the rise of criminality, which affects all sectors of society and in turn leads to the establishment of authoritarian regimes. The alternative is for populist regimes to take charge, but they are usually not inclined to undertake market-oriented regional integration experiments. Hence, the appearance of the ALBA is subject to the whims of Venezuela's Hugo Chávez.

Conclusion

Latin America has been caught between, on the one hand, moving toward regional integration following a traditional framework and, on the other, the attraction of EU influence. Another challenge is the "new regionalism," a trend in which the performance of Latin America has been mixed.[42] Experience shows enough positive signs. The current third wave of regional integration in Latin America is dominated by a variety of options for market insertion that can be used simultaneously and not exclusively and with mutual benefits.[43] The prevailing dissatisfaction with the existing subblocs may lead to different scenarios. The first is to continue on the path of "business as usual"; the second is the perennial temptation of opting for a tabula rasa.

However, there is also a third way. It is based on learning from all the experiences and applying them to new entities, such as Unasur.[44] Instead of ignoring its accumulated experience, Latin America should give regional integration a chance to provide stability and create an indigenous trademark, combined with the acceptance of what is now becoming the trend in Europe: the so-called variable geometry, the idea that not every country needs to agree to every policy, but that some can cooperate more closely than others. At all times, there is a need to respect and implement agreements while being willing to change and adapt to new circumstances. However, while populist temptations have been spreading and the demands for a hard line on security are growing, protests against inequality and pressure for unfettered mobility could make such an agenda impossible to carry out.

All in all, the EU model is still valid to a certain extent in this context. Over the past decade, the survival of the original European project was based on learning from mistakes and adapting frameworks to new circumstances. Perhaps the latest of these self-corrections has been the reform of the institutions through successive treaties, and the return to a more methodical process after the ambitious "constitution project" failed. Europe has not decided to start from scratch or to do nothing. Latin America may adopt a similar approach to redress its own path of integration.

However, observers representing the most active and influential Latin American and Spanish think tanks have endorsed a synthetic analysis by a handful of Spanish experts under the sponsorship of government agencies.[45] Their conclusion is that the balance of EU-LA relations is a mix of successes and failures, of advances in the political dialogue counteracted by shortcomings in the global strategy. The reason for this is that general plans are still anchored in arguments prevalent in the 1990s. "Open regionalism" is seen as outdated. But blame is placed on both sides of the equation: the Latin American side lacks clearly shared ideas, while the two main policy priorities continue to be regional integration and social cohesion. Insistence on integration has diminished and needs to be reshaped or replaced by a bilateral strategy.

The fact is that the new times are dominated by "post-liberal" winds. As a consequence, programs have to adapt to this new climate.[46] One way to correct what is considered a faulty process is to adopt concrete objectives that have enough support to be implemented. Priority areas here are: better regional connections, support for permanent employment, policies to address climate change, and a solid educational strategy.[47] Consensus exists on the argument that social cohesion must be at the top of the biregional agenda, but the diverse array of programs for achieving it does not contribute to its accomplishment. The official documents elaborated by EU institutions are frequently ignored by its member states. Therefore there is the need to reinforce the role of the summits in the political area. This should lead to the targeting of national sovereignty as paramount in state policy. Given the reality that some Latin American governments will not adapt to a subregional framework, the bilateral approach is the right solution. Although full democracy is a goal to be fostered, the existence of populist regimes with little respect for political civil rights and lack of integration with neighbors makes it necessary for the EU to deal with them separately.[48]

In sum, there is a consensus based on the reality of an EU that has changed dramatically, primarily because of the 2004 and 2007 enlargements. Latin America has also changed, moving beyond the priority agenda dominated by transition to democracy and its consolidation. Regional integration and the use of the EU model were seen to be panaceas that would contribute to the advancement of Latin American societies. The traditional focus on relations between the Latin American and Caribbean regions and the EU needs to be reshaped. The summits must be redefined to deal with priority areas, to deliberate global issues, and to open up new avenues for cooperation. The agenda of the summits must recognize that both regions are important global actors that need to foster triangular frameworks. Bilateral and subregional approaches must be complementary, not competing. Latin American development must be seen as beneficial for both parties. Subnational actors must be incorporated into the agenda. Finally, some European states, with Spain in the lead, must take a more aggressive and trend-setting role.[49]

Regarding the overall impact of the 2004 EU enlargement on the European–Latin American framework of relations, it is safe to say that there are no signs of a decrease in the volume of development aid to Latin America. Internal EU declarations and evaluations after the turn of the twenty-first century boasted that the full implementation of the economic conditions of the 2004 enlargement would even increase the commercial links between the regions.

In some areas, especially for political and ideological reasons, the role of some of the new members has been more notable for opposing specific policies endorsed by old-timers than for making a positive contribution. This is the case of relations with Cuba, an issue where some of the Central and Eastern European countries (Poland and especially the Czech Republic) have opposed the project of Spain to reformulate the Common Position adopted toward Cuba in 1996.

A future, step-by-step enlargement of the EU (Croatia, Serbia, the rest of the Balkans, even Ukraine) is not expected to have a noticeable effect on relations with Latin America. Budgetary lines for development assistance are guaranteed at least until 2013, and are expected to remain at a similar level beyond that. Trade will probably show an increase, especially if the Association Agreements with Central America and Mercosur are successful. The lowering of barriers for products of the new members will lead to wider markets in Latin America. The accession of Turkey would mean that the EU had changed dramatically. Then external relations might be seen in a different framework. However, Latin American states that are classified as "emergent economies" (such as Brazil) and the members of the BRIC (Brazil, Russia, India, China) will propel the subcontinent to a new level of importance and attraction. European investors could then increase their involvement in Latin America to balance the new and aggressive insertion of China. By properly responding to this challenge, the EU–Latin American relationship will definitely benefit.

Notes

1. This chapter is supported by a considerable bibliography that is heavily of Spanish origin. Spain has more vested interests in the development of the EU–Latin American/ Caribbean relationship than any other EU member.

2. See Mercosur (www.mercosur.org.uy/).

3. See "History of the Parque Hotel" (www.rau.edu.uy/mercosur/ph.htm).

4. See "Comuna licitará el Parque-Hotel" (www.elpais.com.uy/100406/pnacio-480887/nacional/).

5. Clarification of certain details of this rather odd dimension of Mercosur was provided to me by Fernando González-Guyer.

6. Among the vast literature on the relationship between the EU and Latin America is a series of publications developed by the European Union Center/Jean Monnet Chair of the University of Miami: Joaquín Roy and Roberto Domínguez, eds., *The European Union and Regional Integration: A Comparative Perspective and Lessons for the Americas* (Miami: European Union Center/Jean Monnet Chair, 2005); Joaquín Roy and Roberto Domínguez, eds., *After Vienna: Dimensions of the Relationship between the European Union and the Latin American-Caribbean Region* (Miami: European Union Center/Jean Monnet Chair, 2007); Joaquín Roy and Roberto Domínguez, eds., *Regional Integration Fifty Years after the Treaty of Rome (March 25, 1957): The EU Model in the Americas, Asia and Africa* (Miami: European Union Center/Jean Monnet Chair, 2008); *España, la Unión Europea y la integración latinoamericana* (Miami: European Union Center/Jean Monnet Chair, 2010). All are available online; see "Publications-Books," www.miami.edu/eucenter.

7. Portions of this chapter are an update of several previous pieces, including Joaquín Roy, "Relations between the European Union and Latin America and the Caribbean," in *The Foreign Policy of the European Union: Assessing Europe's Role in the World*, edited by Federiga Bindi (Brookings, 2010); Joaquín Roy, "The European Union and Latin America: Relations and Model," *EUSA Review* (Winter 2009): 13–16 (www.eustudies. org/files/eusa_review/winter2009final.pdf); Joaquín Roy, "Why Do Latin American Integration Systems Differ from the EU Model?" in *Comparative Regional Integration*, edited by Finn Laursen (Dalhousie University, Halifax, Nova Scotia, 2010) (http://euce. dal.ca/Files/Joaquin_Roy_paper.pdf); Joaquín Roy, "The European Union and Latin America: Relations and Model," *Novos Estudos Jurídicos* (Universidade do Vale de Itaiji, Brazil) 14, no. 1 (January–April 2009): 147–53.

8. For an overview, see Christian Freres and José Antonio Sanahuja, eds., *América Latina y la Unión Europea: estrategias para una asociación necesaria* (Barcelona: Icaria/ Instituto Complutense de Estudios Internacionales [ICEI], 2006).

9. For analytical essays on the summits see Alejandro Chanona, "An Assessment of the Summits," in *After Vienna*, edited by Roy and Domínguez, pp. 35–49; Thomas Cieslik, "The Future of the Strategic Association," in *After* Vienna, edited by Roy and Domínguez, pp. 51–62.

10. European Commission, EU-LAC Madrid summit, May 18, 2010 (www.eeas. europa.eu/lac/index_en.htm); Declaración de Madrid (www.eu2010.es/export/sites/ presidencia/comun/descargas/Cumbre_UEALC/may18_madriddeclarationES.pdf). For an evaluation, see Carlos Malamud, "La Cumbre ALCUE de Madrid y el estado de la relación birregional Europa–América Latina (Madrid: Real Instituto Elcano, 2010), ARI 98/2010, June 16, 2010 (www.realinstitutoelcano.org/wps/portal/rielcano/ contenido?WCM_GLOBAL_CONTEXT=/elcano/elcano_es/zonas_es/america+latina /ari98-2010); Facundo Nejamkis, "Consideraciones preliminares acerca de la reciente CV Cumbre ALC-UE," Fundación Alternativas, Memorando OPEX-CEPES, no. 145/2010. For an overall assessment, see Celestino del Arenal and José Antonio Sanahuja, "La cumbre ALCUE de Madrid: un nuevo impulso a las relaciones birregionales" (Madrid: Fundación Carolina, 2010).

11. European Commission, EU-LAC summit, Madrid 2002 (http://ec.europa.eu/external_relations/lac/madrid/dec_02_en.pdf). For a review of this summit, see José Antonio Sanahuja, "Cumbre Unión Europea–América Latina, Madrid 17–18 de mayo de 2002," in *La responsabilidad de la Unión Europea en la lucha contra la pobreza. Claves de la Presidencia española 2002. Una evaluación de Intermón Oxfam*, edited by P. Escudero, Informes no. 22 (Barcelona: Intermón Oxfam, 2002), pp. 47–72; José Antonio Sanahuja, "La II Cumbre Unión Europea–América Latina y el Caribe (Madrid, May 17–18, 2002); José Antonio Sanahuja, "Luces y sombras del vínculo eurolatinoamericano," in *Revista Española de Derecho Internacional y Relaciones Internacionales (REDI)* 14, no. 1 (Madrid): 181–90; José Antonio Sanahuja, "De Río a Madrid. Posibilidades y límites de las relaciones Unión Europea–América Latina," Jean Monnet/Robert Schuman Paper Series 2, no. 6 (University of Miami), April 2003).

12. European Commission, EU-LAC summit, Guadalajara, 2004 (http://ec.europa.eu/external_relations/lac/guadalajara/decl_polit_final_en.pdf).

13. European Commission, EU-LAC summit, Vienna, 2006 (http://ec.europa.eu/external_relations/lac/vienna/index_en.htm); for an evaluation, see Roberto Domínguez, "Between Vienna and Lima," in *After Vienna*, edited by Roy and Dominguez, pp. 23–32.

14. European Commission, EU-LAC summit, Lima, 2008 (http://ec.europa.eu/external_relations/lac/index_en.htm). For an update on relations after this summit, see Aimee Kanner, "European Union–Latin American–Caribbean Relations after Lima and Lisbon," EUMA 5, no. 6 (March 2008) (www6.miami.edu/eucenter/publications/KannerEU_LACrelationsEdiEUMA08.pdf).

15. See European Union, European External Action Service (EEAS), "The EU and the Rio Group" (www.eeas.europa.eu/la/riogroup_en.htm).

16. See "EU-Latin America: Global Players in Partnership" (http://www.eeas.europa.eu/la/docs/com09_495_en.pdf).

17. See European Commission, "A Stronger Partnership between the European Union and Latin America" (www.eeas.europa.eu/la/docs/com05_636_en.pdf).

18. See European Commission, "Latin America Regional Programming Document, 2007–2013" (www.eeas.europa.eu/la/rsp/07_13_en.pdf).

19. See European Commission, "External Assistance and Latin America" (http://ec.europa.eu/europeaid/where/latin-america/index_en.htm).

20. For an evaluation of Spain's assistance, see María Fernández Carcedo and Carmen Sánchez Miranda Gallego, "Madrid: Fundación Alternativas. La cooperación multilateral española: de la retórica a una práctica de calidad," in collaboration with AECID, no. 51/2010 (www.falternativas.org/opex/documentos-opex/documentos-de-trabajo/la-cooperacion-multilateral-espanola-de-la-retorica-a-una-practica-de-calidad).

21. See European Investment Bank (www.eib.org/projects/regions/ala/index.htm). For an evaluation, see Anna Ayuso and Christian Freres, "La cooperación con América Latina: hacia una estrategia europea comprometida con la calidad," Memorando Opex no. 138/2010, April 27, 2010.

22. The author would like to recognize the assistance of José Javier Fernández Fernández and Stelios Stavridis, who provided access to documentation and events related to this dimension of EU activities. For analysis, see José Antonio Sanahuja, *25 años de cooperación interparlamentaria entre la Unión Europea y América Latina (1974–1999)*, Dirección de Estudios del Parlamento Europeo, serie política (POLI 107-ES), Luxembourg, March 2009. For an updated study of this entity, see Stelios Stavridis and Natalia Ajenjo, "EU–Latin American Parliamentary Relations: Some Preliminary Comments on the EUROLAT" (University of Miami, European Union Center/Jean Monnet Chair, 2010).

23. For an evaluation of EU–Latin American trade, see CEPAL, *El comercio internacional en América Latina y el Caribe en 2009. Crisis y recuperación*, 2010. Global figures can be extracted from CEPAL, *Anuario estadístico de América Latina y el Caribe*, 2009 (www.cepal.org/cgi-bin/getProd.asp?xml=/publicaciones/xml/6/38406/P38406.xml&xsl=/deype/tpl/p9f.xsl&base=/tpl/top-bottom.xslt); www.eclac.cl/publicaciones/xml/6/38276/2009-914-Crisis_y_recuperacion_WEB.pdf).

24. Figures and data from EU sources (http://trade.ec.europa.eu/doclib/press/index.cfm?id=573&serie=344&langId=en).

25. See European Union, European External Action Service, "The EU's Relations with Central America" (www.eeas.europa.eu/ca/index_en.htm); and José Antonio Sanahuja, "Relations between the European Community and Central America in the 1990s: Continuity, Reactivation or Change?" in *Peasants beyond Protest in Central America*, edited by Kees Biekart and Martin Jelsma (Amsterdam: Transnational Institute, 2004), pp. 141–206.

26. For an assessment of Central American integration, see Claudia Beatriz Umaña, "Integración centroamericana: un proyecto en proceso de construcción" (Madrid: Real Instituto Elcano), ARI no. 68/2008, June 27, 2008 (www.realinstitutoelcano.org/wps/portal/rielcano/contenido?WCM_GLOBAL_CONTEXT=/elcano/elcano_es/zonas_es/america+latina/ari68-2008).

27. European Commission, "Latin America Regional Programming Document, 2007–2013."

28. See European Union, European External Action Service, "The EU's Relations with the Andean Community" (www.eeas.europa.eu/andean/index_en.htm).

29. See European Union, European External Action Service, "Mercosur—(Common Market of the South)" (www.eeas.europa.eu/mercosur/index_en.htm).

30. For a pre-summit evaluation, see Félix Peña, "Es factible que en la Cumbre de Madrid se relancen las negociaciones UE-Mercosur?" (Madrid: Real Instituto Elcano), ARI no. 65/2010, April 9, 2010 (www.realinstitutoelcano.org/wps/portal/rielcano/contenido?WCM_GLOBAL_CONTEXT=/elcano/elcano_es/zonas_es/america+latina/ari65-2010).

31. Europa Press Release, "EU-Chile Association Agreement to Be Signed Today in Brussels," November 18, 2002 (http://europa.eu/rapid/pressReleasesAction.do?reference=IP/02/1696&format=HTML&aged=0&language=en&guiLanguage=en).

32. See European Commission, "Chile: Country Strategy Paper, 2007–2013," April 11, 2007 (http://eeas.europa.eu/chile/csp/07_13_en.pdf)

33. See European Commission, European External Action Service, "Mexico (United Mexican States)" (http://eeas.europa.eu/mexico/index_en.htm); European Commission, "Towards an EU-Mexico Strategic Partnership," Brussels, COM (2008) 447 final, July 15, 2008 (http://eeas.europa.eu/mexico/docs/com08_447_en.pdf).

34. For another view of this experience, see José Antonio Sanahuja, "México y la Unión Europea, ¿Hacia un nuevo modelo de relación?" in *La regionalización del mundo: la Unión Europea y América Latina,* edited by Rosa María Piñón Antillón (Universidad Nacional Autónoma de México [UNAM], México DF, 1998), pp. 325–82.

35. European Commission, "Relations with the Caribbean" (http://ec.europa.eu/development/geographical/regionscountries/eucaribbean_en.cfm?CFID=1306536&CFTOKEN=53102587&jsessionid=2430648ae4ad105f444d). For a selection of analytical pieces on the status of Caribbean integration, see Wendy Grenade, "CARICOM: Coming of Age?" in *Regional Integration Fifty Years after the Treaty of Rome,* edited by Roy and Domínguez, pp.145–64; Mauricio Mesquita Moreira and Eduardo Mendoza, "Regional Integration: What Is in It for CARICOM?" INTAL 2007 (www.iadb.org/intal/aplicaciones/uploads/publicaciones/i_INTALITD_WP_29_2007_MesquitaMoreira_Mendoza.pdf).

36. For analysis, see Joaquín Roy, "Cuba and the European Union: Chronicle of a Dead Agreement Foretold," in *Redefining Cuban Foreign Policy: The Impact of the "Special Period,"* edited by Michael Erisman and John Kirk, pp. 98–120 (University of Florida Press, 2006); Joaquín Roy, "From Stubbornness and Mutual Irrelevancy to Stillness and Vigil on Castro's Crisis: The Current State of European Union–Spain–Cuba Relations," Occasional Paper, Jean Monnet Chair/European Union Center, August/September 2006 (www.falternativas.org/base/download/bc80_28-08-06_vigil-EN-paper. pdf); also, Joaquín Roy, The *Cuban Revolution (1959–2009): Its Relationship with Spain, the European Union and the United States* (New York: Palgrave Macmillan, 2009).

37. For a classic assessment of the difficulties and obstacles, see Carlos Malamud, "Frenos a la integración regional en América Latina" (Madrid: Real Instituto Elcano), ARI no. 134/2005, November 4, 2005 (www.realinstitutoelcano.org/wps/portal/rielcano/contenido?WCM_GLOBAL_CONTEXT=/elcano/elcano_es/zonas_es/america+latina/ari+134-2005).

38. The list includes: the war of Peru, Chile, and Bolivia (1879–84), which resulted in the loss of sea access for Bolivia); the actions of Brazil, Argentina, and Uruguay against Paraguay (War of the Triple Alliance, also known as the Paraguayan War, from 1864 to 1870); and the bloody conflict between this country and Bolivia over the rich natural resources of the Chaco (1932–35). Wars in Central America have been mostly civil skirmishes. The so-called "soccer war" between El Salvador and Honduras in 1969 had more to do with uncontrolled migration than with disagreement over the result of a sports match. War involving Mexico has been in essence the result of aggression by the United States.

39. For an in-depth analysis see José Antonio Sanahuja, "From 'Open Regionalism' to the Union of South American Nations: Crisis and Change in Latin American Regional Integration," in *Election Year 2006: Latin America at the Crossroads (Again)?* edited by L. Špičanová, P. Springerová, and J. Němec, pp. 187–210 (Prague: Association for International Affairs [AMO], 2008. Although it covers a wide range of integration trends in Latin America, the following edited volume places Unasur in the proper context: Manuel Cienfuegos and José Antonio Sanahuja, eds., *La construcción de una región. UNASUR y la integración en América del Sur* (Barcelona: CIDOB, 2010).

40. Felix Peña, "MERCOSUR or UNASUR?" paper presented at a symposium "Regionalism and the European Union," Miami-Florida European Union Center/Jean Monnet Chair, April 6, 2009.

41. Carlos Malamud, "España y América Latina: el pulso entre lo global y lo bilateral" (Madrid: Real Instituto Elcano), DT no. 58-2004, November 23, 2004 (www.realinstitutoelcano.org/wps/portal/rielcano/contenido?WCM_GLOBAL_CONTEXT=/elcano/elcano_es/zonas_es/america+latina/dt58-2004); Celestino del Arenal, "Relations between the EU and Latin America: Abandoning Regionalism in Favour of a New Bilateral Strategy," Working Paper (Madrid: Real Instituto Elcano, 2009).

42. For practical analysis, see Scott L. Baier, Jeffrey H. Bergstrand, and Peter Egger, "The New Regionalism: Causes and Consequences," *Integration & Trade Journal*, no. 26 (January–June 2007) (www.iadb.org/intal/aplicaciones/uploads/publicaciones/i_INTAL_I&T_26_2007_Baier_Bergstrand_Egger.pdf); Lorraine Eden, "Multinationals, Foreign Direct Investment and the New Regionalism in the Americas," *Integration & Trade Journal*, no. 26 (January–June 2006; Philippe de Lombaerde, "The Problem of Comparison in Comparative Regionalism," paper presented at the symposium "Regionalism and the European Union," Miami-Florida European Union Center/ Jean Monnet Chair, April 6, 2009; Germán de la Reza, "The Divide between New and Old Regionalisms: An Analytical Framework," *Asian Journal of Latin American Studies* 22, no. 2 (2010): 181–201; José Antonio Sanahuja, "Regionalismo e integración en América Latina: balance y perspectivas," *Pensamiento Iberoamericano* (nueva época), monográfico "La nueva agenda de desarrollo en América Latina," no. 0, Madrid (February 2007): 75–106; José Antonio Sanahuja, "Del 'regionalismo abierto' al 'regionalismo post-liberal'. Crisis y cambio en la integración regional en América Latina y el Caribe," in *Anuario de la Integración de América Latina y el Gran Caribe nº 7, 2008–2009*, edited by L. Martínez, L. Peña, and M. Vázquez (Buenos Aires: Coordinadora Regional de Investigaciones Económicas y Sociales [CRIES]), 2007), pp. 11–54.

43. Félix Peña, "The Experience of Half a Century: Regional Integration in the New Global Context," *International Trade Relations Newsletter*, April 2009 (www.felixpena.com.ar/index.php?contenido=negotiations&neagno=report/2009-04-regional-integration-in-new-global-context).

44. For a critical, in-depth review of the prospects of Mercosur and Unasur, see Noemí Beatriz Mellado, ed., *MERCOSUR* y *UNASUR*, *¿hacia dónde van?* (Córdoba: Lerner, 2009).

45. Instituto Cervantes, *Foro Eurolatinoamericano de Centros de Análisis* (Madrid: Fundación Carolina, 2010).

46. Celestino del Arenal, "Balance de la Asociación Estratégica entre la Unión Europea (UE) y los países de América Latina y el Caribe (LC)," Instituto Cervantes, *Foro Eurolatinoamericano de Centros de Análisis* (Madrid: Fundación Carolina, 2010), pp. 25–55.

47. José Antonio Alonso, "Hacia una nueva estrategia UE–América Latina: notas para un debate," Instituto Cervantes, *Foro Eurolatinoamericano de Centros de Análisis* (Madrid: Fundación Carolina, 2010), pp. 89–104.

48. Araceli Mangas, "Unión Europea y América Latina y Caribe: recomendaciones ante la VI Cumbre," Instituto Cervantes, *Foro Eurolatinoamericano de Centros de Análisis* (Madrid: Fundación Carolina, 2010), pp. 137–54.

49. Instituto Cervantes, *Foro Eurolatinoamericano de Centros de Análisis*, "Conclusiones."

FEDERIGA BINDI AND IRINA ANGELESCU

20 *Conclusion: The European Union Should Again Be "Open for Business"*

This book has shown that EU enlargement—and the EU's relations with its neighborhood—has never been an issue of exclusive European concern. As Federiga Bindi and Kurt Volker explain in their respective chapters, the very creation of the European institutions and the EU's successive waves of enlargement have been transatlantic issues because the United States has always viewed enlargement as a stabilization tool in Europe and therefore a matter of national interest. This will also be the case if the EU is to expand to the countries of the Western Balkans. Beyond that, the situation may change, depending on the EU's position. If the EU adopts a unified voice and acts a as a counterbalancing force to the U.S. (and Russian) influence in the neighborhood, the United States would likely reconsider its priorities. However, if Europe continues to be divided by the interests of its individual member states and to behave like a weak international actor, the United States is likely to continue to support it—as a matter of stability and, hence, national interest.

In the late 1990s and early 2000s, for example, the United States pushed for NATO enlargement to the east in a way that was at least partially counterproductive for the EU enlargement process. As Bindi and Jan Techau suggest in their chapters, the post–cold war NATO enlargement challenged the EU because the Central and Eastern European countries (CEECs) seemed to favor accession to NATO over the more burdensome EU accession process. In addition, the CEECs seem to attach more political importance to NATO than do the older member states.

The USSR—and after the end of the cold war, Russia—has had a different view of the EC/EU and its enlargements. During the cold war, it refused to recognize the EC's existence as a legal international entity. It did so in 1988, but only out of necessity (it was in need of financial assistance). However, despite the fact that the USSR initially viewed the EC as a U.S. Trojan horse in Europe, the EU's 2004–07 eastern enlargement was of only marginal concern to Russia. Russia was preoccupied with NATO's expansion toward its former Soviet satellites: as Mark Entin writes, NATO expansion has been seen in Russia as a shift of the cold war division to the east. Therefore, although NATO's expansion challenged the process of EU enlargement to the east, it also facilitated it because it was the focus of Russian attention and fear (read "opposition"), which otherwise would have been directed at the EU.

Should Russia join both NATO and the EU, as Mark Entin argues? The contributors to this book do not agree on the answer to this question, but share his concern that the tenets and stereotypes of the cold war have been slow to die. They are still alive in the leaders' minds, but they do not occupy the minds of the younger generations, those who are challenging regimes in the Middle East in a way that would have been unthinkable before 1989. In a way, the last legacies of the cold war are being challenged in the Middle East as we write, though it is hard to predict what will replace them when today's protesters assume leadership.

The Next Frontier: A Scenario for Future EU Enlargements

What is the foreseeable direction of EU enlargement? The clear picture provided by Ferdinando Nelli Feroci indicates that, in the short term, Croatia will become the only new member state. It is possible that Macedonia, Serbia, and Montenegro will follow by 2020. The other countries in the Balkans (Albania, Bosnia and Herzegovina, and Kosovo) face greater domestic and international challenges (for example, five EU member states have not yet recognized Kosovo's independence) and are unlikely to join before the next decade. Iceland, which had the best accession prospect, voted against accession in a referendum on April 9, 2011. In response to the Icelandic population's refusal to pay back the United Kingdom and the Netherlands for their assistance during the economic crisis that began in 2008, those countries made it clear that they would oppose Iceland's membership.

The prospects for Turkey's membership are more complex. There is general agreement among the contributors that Turkey's EU membership would be in the "national" EU interest. As an EU member state Turkey would give added value to the Union as a whole in both energy and geopolitical terms, as Massimo Gaiani clearly describes. Unfortunately, the EU appears to have chosen a short-sighted view in its approach to the Turkish case, putting subjective cultural and value-related issues ahead of a pragmatic analysis of its own interests. As a result, the EU may have lost a historic opportunity. Paradoxically, after decades of eagerly seeking and preparing for EU membership and fulfilling many of the conditions to join, Turkey may decide not to continue its pursuit of EU membership.

Over the past few years, Turkey has progressively affirmed itself as a broker in the Middle East and on the international scene. For example, Turkey is now part of the G20, which is slowly emerging as a major international forum. The unrest in the Arab world has confirmed the unique role Turkey can play in stabilizing the larger neighborhood. Furthermore, the country is now expanding its economic and diplomatic influence not only in the Middle East, but also in the Balkans. Should the Western Balkan states be rejected by the EU, they may well turn to Turkey as an alternative. Should Turkey decide to unilaterally halt or even break off the negotiations, the cost to the EU in political, economic, and, most of all, credibility terms would be enormous. There are signals that Turkey is already considering this scenario, as reflected in Prime Minister Recep Tayyip Erdogan's speech at the Council of Europe in April 2011, in which he asserted that the EU needs Turkey as a member perhaps more than Turkey needs the EU.[1]

Explaining the EU's Lack of Commitment to Enlargement

One reason for the EU's lack of commitment to enlargement is the absence of a sense of historical legacy and obligation that characterized past expansions to the south in 1986 and to the east in 2004–07. It is unclear why this feeling is not present with regard to the (Western) Balkans, which, for better or worse, are at the heart of European history. As Franco Frattini points out in the Introduction, the European "mission" cannot be considered accomplished until all of the Western Balkan countries have joined the EU. He also emphasizes the symbolic significance of Turkey's accession to the EU, comparing it to two crucial moments in Europe's recent history: the French-German reconciliation and the fall of the Berlin Wall.

European politicians have also been using the economic crisis as a justification for not enlarging further. But there is no correlation between the two. Past enlargements have taken place both in periods of stagnation (1973) and in periods of economic growth (1986). As Luca Einaudi explains, joining the EU does not automatically mean joining the eurozone, a process that is governed by its own rules and criteria in order to guarantee the stability of the area. For instance, of the twelve countries that acceded to the EU in 2004–07, only five joined the eurozone (Cyprus, Estonia, Malta, Slovenia, and Slovakia). Furthermore, a bigger EU also means a larger market. External trade by the

European Union rose by 20 percent after the EU enlarged to twenty-seven members and, from 2000 to 2006, intra-EU trade rose by 33 percent.[2] Although the consequences of the economic crisis that began in 2008 are not yet clear, it is certain—if, for instance, we compare this crisis with the one at the beginning of the 1990s—that the existence of the euro partially buffered the impact of the crisis, especially with regard to financial speculation. Therefore, as Einaudi underlines, the euro is unlikely to be abandoned. An expanding EU would contribute to projecting a perception of dynamism and thus make its economy more attractive for investors. This is what happened before the most recent wave of enlargement, when investors turned to the CEECs not only for lower prices, but also for the prospect of becoming part of the single market.

A third reason for the lack of enlargement enthusiasm in the EU is the lack of popular support and a sense of "enlargement fatigue." As Irina Angelescu, Gilles de Kerchove, Umberto Melotti, and Jean-Luc Marret explain in their respective chapters, there is a growing xenophobia among European citizens and politicians, who perceive immigrants as a threat to the social and economic order and their "way of life"; the threat is perceived to include terrorist attacks.

The official European discourse, which is supportive of enlargement, often does not seem to be complemented by the same message from the narrative and practices of its member states. As these conflicting messages reach countries outside the EU's borders, among them aspiring candidate countries and neighbors, they affect perceptions of the EU's commitment to enlargement and to close relations with its neighbors. and consequently influence their willingness to undertake costly reform. This may result in a catch-22 situation, in which neighbors are not willing to engage in costly reforms until they have a firm commitment (to enlargement) from the EU, while the EU is not willing to offer that commitment in the absence of thorough reforms.

Projections for the Future

What are the consequences of the EU's inability to think strategically about enlargement? We argue that this inability is likely to affect the EU's relations in two directions: first, with its neighborhood, and second, with the wider world. The first consequence, as mentioned already in the case of Turkey, is the possible disenchantment with the EU in the candidate and prospective member countries. The EU's inactivity and Turkey's increasingly proactive stance in foreign affairs could cause the countries of the Western Balkans to gravitate toward the latter. Should this happen, it would deprive the EU of its historical backyard and of a major geopolitical and energy asset (the pipelines planned in that area). Similarly, the countries in the East, driven by the EU's unwillingness to give them a concrete membership perspective, are likely to gravitate toward Russia.

As Gaiani and Alessandro Ortis point out, Russia occupies a preeminent role in ensuring Europe's energy supply. With unrest in the Arab world, the EU is even more dependent on Russian energy. Although Russia's role in ensuring Europe's energy needs has been a matter of contention between the United States and Europe and in Europe itself, the unrest in the Middle East will make Russia's contribution far more appealing. U.S. arguments against Europe's energy dependence on Russia will find Europeans less receptive than in the past. With its southern shore becoming increasingly problematic, Europe will need a stable eastern neighborhood, and it will be less opposed to Russia extending its influence to the former Soviet republics. The consequences for the "frozen conflicts" in the Caucasus would be substantial. Even the former Soviet satellites—now EU members—that joined the United States in vocal protest against Russia in the past may reconsider their position because of their domestic energy needs. The tragic events at Japan's Fukushima nuclear power plant are likely to contribute to this trend if nuclear power is no longer regarded as a secure energy alternative, as suggested by the June 2011 decision made by the German chancellor, Angela Merkel, to close all the nuclear plants in the country by 2020.

The EU will have a big opportunity to contribute to institution building in the post-Arab spring. As Amichai Magen points out, the EU has a record of excellence in institution building and support of democracy. It is hoped that the EU will be able to apply lessons from the past in this part of the world. Stable and well-functioning democratic institutions in this area are of direct interest to the EU, as the waves of immigrants and the energy shortages following the Arab crisis have clearly shown. Likewise, Maurizio Carbone notes that cooperation on development has been one positive example of the EU's transformative power. The EU now has the choice to build on this success. Should it fail to do so, the attractiveness of its soft power will decrease substantially.

The second consequence of the EU's inability to think strategically about enlargement and its neighborhood concerns the EU's role in the world. The United States has become disenchanted with the EU. The post–Lisbon Treaty Europe created enormous expectations. In 2010 the U.S. Department of State created for the first time a position with responsibility for managing relations with the European Union and Western Europe. However, the inability of the EU to speak with one voice because of the desire of its member states to achieve "privileged" status in Washington has, for the most part, voided the potential offered by the Lisbon Treaty in the field of foreign policy.

A similar pattern can be found in other parts of the world. Latin America, as Joaquín Roy points out, has long been attracted by the EU influence. Institutional frameworks such as Mercosur have facilitated dialogue between Mercosur and the EU. More recently, however, emerging economies have pushed for their own place in the sun within Mercosur, just as they have within the EU. Roy believes, though, that an eventual Turkish EU membership would have a positive impact on trade and political relations between Latin America and the EU.

China does not place the EU at the top of its political or foreign policy priorities, as Giovanni Andornino points out. The EU and China speak different foreign policy languages, the former driven by the postmodernist logic of enlargement, the latter guided by pragmatism. Eventual enlargements of the EU would only consolidate this divide. The lack of a proper EU strategy toward China based on a pragmatic analysis of the European "national" interest is striking. A willingness to meet halfway between the postmodern and pragmatic approaches could translate into greater cooperation and mutual benefits for the two actors.

Toward an EU "National" Interest?

As Entin suggests in his chapter, the EU's apparent incapacity to pragmatically determine what best constitutes its "national" interest appears to be linked to the fact that it was unable to understand the radical paradigm shift in international relations after the end of the cold war. The language of diplomacy in the twenty-first century has changed, moving from cold war diplomacy to geoeconomics, as Andornino explains in relation to the China case. The inability of the Europeans to understand the vastness of the change and how to cope with it is even more surprising since it is the second time in less than sixty years that they are facing a paradigm shift in international relations and in their role on the world stage.

A similar change occurred in the 1950s and 1960s, during the decolonization process. This failure to grasp the new reality may be linked, as discussed by Bindi, Angelescu, and Entin, to an inward-looking attitude that has characterized the EU since the 1990s. After 1996 the EU appeared obsessed by its need for institutional reform, which it was unable to properly achieve, while the 9/11 terrorist attacks provided new impetus for the European interior ministers to attempt to "seal the borders" of the EU and to "export" unwanted immigrants to third countries.

Both Frattini and Nelli Feroci point out that enlargement is a measure of success and a test of the EU's credibility in the world and at home. Christoffer Kølvraa and Ian Ifversen emphasized the power of attraction of the EU's "civilizational discourse" among its neighboring states. The EU's "soft power" is likely to become less effective if the EU continues to avoid defining its relations with the neighborhood and providing a vision for its foreign policy at large. Furthermore, the more self-centered and inward-looking the EU becomes, the more difficult it is to "sell itself," and its enlargement, to the media. The less the media write about the EU, the less informed the EU citizens are. This translates into less support for the European project as a whole and into lower turnouts for the elections of the European Parliament. (Turnout declined from 61.99 percent in 1979 to 43 percent in 2009.)[3] The result is a vicious circle in which elected politicians are unwilling to back further enlargement because of the lack of support and approval of their national constituencies.

However, the main responsibility for the current deadlock seems to lie with the European political leaders. As the former president of the European Commission, Jacques Delors, underlined in 2011, past leaders such as François Mitterrand, Helmut Kohl, Valéry Giscard d'Estaing, Konrad Adenauer, and Charles de Gaulle "have left their mark on the history of Europe because at a given moment they overcame their preconceptions towards the other for a European vision."[4] Without a European vision, it is impossible to define where the European interest lies and therefore to pragmatically determine what best to do about enlargement and relations with the neighborhood and the world.

There are three main beneficiaries of enlargement, as identified by John Peet: the candidate countries, which gain in economic, political, financial, and security terms; the existing member states, for which enlargement preserves stability and fosters prosperity in the neighborhood and in their own national economies; and the EU project itself because enlargements have historically led to more integration and a more active foreign policy. The contributors to this volume argue that there is a fourth and fundamental beneficiary of further EU enlargement: the United States. A further EU enlargement to include the Western Balkans and Turkey would serve the EU, the United States, and transatlantic relations in terms of political stability and economic growth. The United States, which is currently very concerned about public expenditures, would benefit from the EU taking on a greater share of responsibility in the neighborhood. The EU, on the other hand, should include, and prioritize, stability in all its considerations about enlargement and its relations with the neighborhood. This is not to say that the EU should enlarge tomorrow and at all costs (a mistake that has been made in the past), but that it should continue to engage in the process of enlargement in a dynamic and proactive way. It should also engage its larger neighborhood more consistently and be clear about putting the prospects for membership on the table. In other words, the EU should demonstrate no prejudice on the issue of enlargement and send a message to the neighborhood that the EU is (once again) "open for business."

Notes

1. *Euractiv*, "From Strasbourg, Erdogan Blasts France over Burqa Ban," April 14, 2011 (www.euractiv.com/en/enlargement/strasbourg-erdo-blasts-france-burqa-ban-news-504068).

2. Eurostat, *Internal and Intra-European Union Trade. Statistical Yearbook—Data 1958–2006* (the 2008 edition is available online).

3. "Public Opinion in the European Union," *Eurobarometer* 74, Autumn 2010 (Luxembourg: European Commission, 2011); European Parliament, "Turnout at the European Elections (1979–2009)" (www.europarl.europa.eu/parliament/archive/elections 2009/en/turnout_en.html).

4. *Euractiv*, "Delors: 'Superficial' Franco-German Engine Needs Kick-Start," April 14, 2011 (www.euractiv.com/en/future-eu/delors-superficial-franco-german-engine-needs-kick-start-news-503853).

Contributors

GIOVANNI B. ANDORNINO is lecturer in international relations of East Asia at the University of Torino and vice president of the Torino World Affairs Institute. He has taught and researched at the Catholic University of Milan, Zhejiang University (China), and the Transatlantic Academy (Washington, D.C.). His most recent publications include a chapter on China and global governance in *Handbook of Chinese International Relations* (Routledge, 2010) and *L'orizzonte del mondo* (Guerini, 2010). He is the editor of *OrizzonteCina*, a leading Italian monthly discussing contemporary China's politics and economy.

IRINA ANGELESCU is a researcher at the Center on the United States and Europe at the Brookings Institution, a researcher at the European Center of Excellence at the University of Rome Tor Vergata in Italy, and a PhD candidate at the Graduate Institute of International and Development Studies, Geneva. She has written extensively on European policies of migration, foreign policy, EU enlargement and neighborhood policies, and Romanian contemporary history and politics. Her most recent publication, a coedited volume with Sergiu Gherghina and Paul Flather, is *Facets of Migration in Contemporary Europe: Interdisciplinary Approaches to Specific Challenges* (Stuttgart: Ibidem Verlag, 2010).

FEDERIGA BINDI is Jean Monnet Professor and the founding director of the European Centre of Excellence at the University of Rome Tor Vergata and a senior fellow at the Paul H. Nitze School for Advanced International Studies, John Hopkins University, Washington, D.C. She is a leading expert on European affairs, including European governance and European foreign policy. She advises the Italian Foreign Ministry on global governance and transatlantic relations and is responsible for the EU modules and international training at the Italian National School of Public Administration. Bindi has published widely in Italian, English, Portuguese, and Spanish. Her most recent publications include *Italy and the European Union* (Brookings Institution Press, 2011) and *The Foreign Policy of the European Union* (Brookings Institution Press, 2010).

MAURIZIO CARBONE is a professor in international development in the School of Social and Political Sciences at the University of Glasgow, where he also holds the Chair in European Politics. He has published on the external relations of the European Union, foreign aid, the politics of international development, as well as European and Italian politics. He currently is working on books on the relations between the European Union and Africa (ed., Manchester University Press, 2012) and on the evolution of EU development policy (Oxford University Press, 2013).

LUCA EINAUDI, an economist and a historian, is a senior research fellow at the Joint Centre for History and Economics at the University of Cambridge, and is also at Harvard University. Einaudi has been an economic adviser to Prime Minister Romano Prodi, a cabinet member, and a senior economist in the Italian G-8/G-20 office. He is currently conducting research on the economic and financial crisis of 2008–09 and international cooperation in addressing policy and regulatory responses to it in a historical perspective.

MARK ENTIN is a lawyer and a professor at Moscow State University of International Relations and is an expert in Russian and the European Union legal systems and their functioning. He previously worked at the Russian Ministry of Foreign Affairs, where he was responsible for compatibility studies of evolving Russian legislation and the *acquis communautaire* as well as the relationship between the Russian Federation and the European Union. His experience includes in-depth work with Russian governmental and legislative bodies. Entin is also the author of many publications on EU Law.

FRANCO FRATTINI has served in a number of positions with the Italian government. Since 2008 he has been the minister for foreign affairs (he also served in this post from 2002 to 2004). Before this he served as vice president of the Barroso Commission, commissioner for justice, freedom, and security; deputy secretary general in the prime minister's office; and minister of civil service and regional affairs, as well as president of the Parliamentary Committee for

Intelligence and Security Services and State Secrets and minister for civil service and coordination of information and security services.

MASSIMO GAIANI is the diplomatic adviser to the Italian minister for European affairs and director general of the Inter-ministerial Committee for European Affairs at the Presidency of the Italian Council of Ministers. After entering the diplomatic service in 1982, he has held several offices in the Ministry for Foreign Affairs, including as legal adviser to the director general for human resources and head of the Office for EU External Relations. He also served in the Italian diplomatic missions in Montreal, Washington, and Brussels.

JAN IFVERSEN is associate professor at Aarhus University and has been head of the Department of History and Area Studies since 2004. His primary research interests include the question of European identity and contemporary European history, and he has conducted extensive research on the history of ideas and discourse from a European perspective.

GILLES DE KERCHOVE closely monitors the implementation of the EU counterterrorism strategy, coordinating the work of the EU Council in the field of counterterrorism, maintaining an overview of all the instruments at the EU's disposal, fostering better communication between the EU and third countries, and ensuring that the EU plays an active role in the fight against terrorism. He is also a European law professor at the Catholic University of Louvain, the Free University of Brussels, and the University Faculty Saint Louis (Brussels). He was deputy secretary of the convention that drafted the charter of the fundamental rights of the European Union from 1999 to 2000. He has published a number of books on European law.

CHRISTOFFER KØLVRAA is assistant professor in the Department of History and Area Studies at Aarhus University. He holds a PhD in history with a dissertation focusing on Europe as a global player. He has published a number of articles and chapters in edited volumes on European identity, the EU as a global power, and its neighborhood policies.

AMICHAI MAGEN is director of political development and senior fellow at the International Institute for Counter-Terrorism, The Interdisciplinary Center (Herzeliya, Israel), and visiting fellow, Hoover Institution, Stanford University. His recent publications include "Hybrid War and the Gulliverization of Israel," *Israel Journal of Foreign Affairs* 12 (2011), "The Rule of Law and Its Promotion Abroad: Three Problems of Scope," *Stanford Journal of International Law* 45 (2010); *International Actors, Democratization, and the Rule of Law* (ed. with

Leonardo Morlino, Rutledge, 2009); *Promoting Democracy and the Rule of Law: American and European Strategies* (ed. with Thomas Risse and Michael McFaul, Palgrave-McMillan, 2009). His research interests include the law and policy of global and regional governance institutions, political development in transitional and weak states, American and European democracy promotion, and the Middle East, especially Israeli and Turkish politics.

JEAN-LUC MARRET is a senior fellow at the Center for Transatlantic Relations of the Johns Hopkins Paul H. Nitze School of Advanced International Studies and a senior fellow at the Fondation pour la Recherche Stratégique, the leading think tank on international security issues in France. Prior to this, he was an associate professor of U.S. foreign policy, counterterrorism, and the Middle East at the École Spéciale Militaire de Saint-Cyr (the French West Point). He is currently working on counterterrorism, radicalism, WMD, and conflicts and conflict prevention issues and has published numerous books in French and in Arabic.

UMBERTO MELOTTI is full chair at the University of Rome La Sapienza, where he teaches political sociology. He previously taught sociology and cultural anthropology at the Accademia di Belle Arti in Brera, Milan, and at the University of Pavia. He has published extensively in the field of history of sociology, sociology of change, sociobiology, ethnic relations, immigration in Italy, and international migrations in Europe. He also founded the magazine *Terzo Mondo* (The Third World), which he still directs.

FERDINANDO NELLI FEROCI has been the permanent representative of Italy to the European Union since June 2008. After graduating in law from the University of Pisa and receiving a graduate degree in international relations from SIOI–Rome, he began his diplomatic career in 1972. He has held numerous diplomatic positions with the United Nations and the Italian government and has served in Italian diplomatic missions in Algiers, Paris, and Beijing. He is the author of several articles, fellow at the Center for International Affairs at Harvard University, and visiting professor at the University of Naples.

ALESSANDRO ORTIS was the chairman of the Italian Regulatory Authority for Electricity and Gas from 2003 to 2011. He was vice president of the Council of European Energy Regulators and president of the Association of the Mediterranean Regulators for Electricity and Gas. He also has been director general for energy and mineral resources at the Italian Ministry for Productive Activities and served in many roles in private industry, including management positions with the Zanussi Group, Pirelli Group, ENI Group, Ispredil—ANCE, Serono, and Tecnofarmaci.

JOHN PEET has been Europe editor for *The Economist* since September 2003 and was the journal's business affairs editor from 1998 to 2003. For this periodical, he has surveyed such issues such as management consulting, health care, Spain, the European Union, European Monetary Union, equity markets, Italy, and the future of Europe. He has written widely for a number of European publications.

JOAQUÍN ROY is Jean Monnet Professor of European Integration and codirector of the European Union Center of Excellence at the University of Miami. He has published over 200 academic articles and reviews and is the author, editor, or coeditor of many books, among them *The U.S. and the Helms-Burton Doctrine: International Reactions* (University of Florida Press, 2000), *Las relaciones exteriores de la Unión Europea* (México: UNAM, 2001), *Retos de la integración regional: Europa y América* (México: UNAM, 2003), and *La Unión Europea y el TLCAN* (México: UNAM, 2004).

JAN TECHAU, an expert on EU integration and foreign policy, transatlantic affairs, and German foreign and security policy, is director of Carnegie Europe, the European Center of the Carnegie Endowment for International Peace. Prior to this, he served at the research division of the NATO Defense College. He was director of the Alfred von Oppenheim Center for European Policy Studies at the German Council on Foreign Relations (DGAP) between 2006 and 2010, and from 2001 to 2006 he was at the German Ministry of Defense's Press and Information Department. He is a regular contributor to German and international news media.

KURT VOLKER is senior fellow and managing director of the Center on Transatlantic Relations at the Johns Hopkins Paul H. Nitze School of Advanced International Studies. He is also a senior adviser at the Atlantic Council of the United States and a member of its Strategic Advisory Group. Prior to joining SAIS, Volker was a career member of the United States Senior Foreign Service, with over twenty-three years of experience working on European political and security issues under five U.S. administrations. He served as ambassador and as the 19th U.S. permanent representative on the Council of the North Atlantic Treaty Organization (NATO) from July 2008 until May 2009. Prior to his service at NATO, he served as a deputy assistant secretary at the U.S. Department of State and was at the National Security Council.

Index